The Organization of Information

Library and Information Science Text Series

THE ORGANIZATION OF INFORMATION

Arlene G. Taylor

1999
LIBRARIES UNLIMITED, INC.
Englewood, Colorado

LIBRARIES UNLIMITED, INC.
P.O. Box 6633
Englewood, CO 80155-6633
1-800-237-6124
www.lu.com

Library of Congress Cataloging-in-Publication Data

Taylor, Arlene G., 1941-
    The organization of information / Arlene G. Taylor.
    xx, 280 p. 19x26 cm. -- (Library and information science text series)
    Includes bibliographical references and index.
    ISBN 1-56308-493-7 (hardbound). -- ISBN 1-56308-498-8 (softbound)
    1. Information science.   2. Information science--United States.
I. Title.   II. Series.
Z667.T39   1999
020--dc21   98-53625
                                                             CIP

*Dedicated to the memory of Farol Edith Haynes Taylor
1905-1998
Mother, Friend, Inspiration*

CONTENTS

LIST OF FIGURES

PREFACE

As I began work on the ninth edition of *Introduction to Cataloging and Classification* I became more and more aware that another work was needed that would precede the cataloging text. Core courses in many schools of library and information science now include a course in organizing information. These courses typically cover much more than cataloging and classification. They discuss the concept of organization and its role in human endeavors; many kinds of retrieval tools, such as bibliographies, indexes, finding aids, catalogs, and other kinds of databases; encoding standards, such as MARC, SGML, various SGML DTDs, and XML; creation of metadata; all kinds of controlled vocabularies, including thesauri and ontologies, as well as subject heading lists; classification theory and methodology; arrangement and display of metadata records and physical information-bearing packages; and system design. *The Organization of Information* addresses this need, leaving *Introduction to Cataloging and Classification* as a textbook for courses devoted to the specifics of cataloging and classification.

This work addresses the history, theory, and practice of the organization of *recorded* information. Other means are required to organize information that has been only spoken, heard, or thought about. A certain amount of disagreement exists among those in the information professions as to whether we organize, retrieve, and make use of *information* or *knowledge*. According to several dictionaries I have consulted, *knowledge* exists in the mind of an individual who has studied a matter, understands it, and perhaps has added to it through research or other means. The same dictionaries indicate that *information* is the communication or reception of knowledge. That communication occurs in great part through the recording of the knowledge in some fashion. People write, speak, compose, paint, sculpt, and in many other ways attempt to communicate their knowledge to others.

This book, for example, is a representation of my knowledge; but it is not a complete representation of my knowledge of this subject. It is, no doubt, an imperfect representation, in the sense that some concepts may not be explained as clearly as I truly understand them. (Correcting such imperfections will be one objective of a second edition.) However, it is not a representation of the reader's knowledge until the reader has read and understood it. That is, it is information that can be placed into a scheme of organization from which it can be retrieved for study by those interested in increasing their knowledge of the subject.

Thus, I have chosen to use the term *information* rather than *knowledge* as my expression of what I believe we organize when we organize for the benefit of other people. This is not a rejection of "organization of knowledge," however. The knowledge existing in the brains of people is being harnessed in many situations. I work on organizing my own knowledge every time I write. The knowledge of reference librarians is used in an organized way when they assist patrons in answering questions. This kind of organizing, however, is not covered in this text.

The goal of this book is to enable students, practicing librarians, and others interested in organizing information to understand the theory, principles, standards, and tools behind the organization of information in all types of environments. Chapter 1 looks at our basic human need to organize and how it is approached in various environments. Chapter 2 is concerned with the formats and functions of basic retrieval tools that have been developed. In chapter 3 we ask "How did we arrive at this state of organization?" and discuss the history of basic principles that have developed over the centuries. Chapters 4, 5, and 6 deal with creation of metadata, covering, respectively, encoding, description, and access. Subject approaches to organizing information are covered in chapter 7, while theory of categorization and how this translates into classification is the topic of chapter 8. Because arrangement and display of information is so important to users' retrieval of information, chapter 9 is devoted to theory and practice in this area. Finally, system design, as the ultimate arbiter of whether users will be able to make their way through metadata in retrieval tools to find what they need, is covered in chapter 10.

ACKNOWLEDGMENTS

Many people have contributed to the existence of this book. I would like to acknowledge at least some of them. First, I acknowledge my mentor and cataloging professor, Katherine Luther Henderson, Professor, University of Illinois at Urbana/Champaign, who inspired me to understand the "why" behind all the practices involved in cataloging. This approach has assisted me greatly in making all the transitions that have been necessitated by the move from a paper environment to an electronic environment during the course of my career.

Three people were particularly helpful in advising me about organization of information in particular environments. Bernadette Callery, Museum Librarian, Carnegie Museum of Natural History, assisted with discussions of the museum environment. Patrice Clemson, Data Administrator, University of Pittsburgh, gave me assistance with office environments. Elizabeth Yakel, Assistant Professor, School of Information Sciences, University of Pittsburgh, was an immense help with my understanding of organization in archives. Any errors that might be found in the discussion of these areas are, of course, my responsibility, not theirs.

A number of students in the Department of Library and Information Science at the University of Pittsburgh have given direct assistance. Cynthia Porter, doctoral student and teaching fellow, offered ideas during our discussions as the book progressed. She also read parts of the manuscript and made comments. Katherine Ryner, master's student, and now cataloger at Dowling College, served as a research assistant. In this capacity she searched for examples to illustrate certain points in the text, and she did bibliographic research. Bonnie Chojnacki, master's student, read the manuscript and commented from the viewpoint of a beginning student of library and information science. Tina Lippman, master's student, has assisted with the copy-edited stage, researching many of the editor's questions and completing flagged citations. Finally, a few years ago, Jane Greenberg, doctoral student, introduced me to the organization of information in archives. I am immensely grateful for the work of all of these students.

Some other people have made less direct contributions, but are noteworthy nonetheless. The staff of the Information Sciences Library of the University of Pittsburgh has been most helpful and patient with my needs and questions. All the students I have ever taught can take credit for contributing, because they have been my "guinea pigs" in the process of explaining theory and mixing it with practice. I would like especially to thank two former doctoral students who have encouraged me greatly in this project, as well as in life: Susan Hayes, Assistant Curator, Elmer Holmes Bobst Library, New York University; and, Sherry Vellucci, Associate Professor, Division of Library & Information Science, St. John's University.

Over the years many colleagues in the profession, too numerous to mention individually, have contributed to my understanding, first, of cataloging, and then, of broader organizing issues. I wish them to know how much I appreciate their input.

I truly appreciate the staff of Libraries Unlimited for their work in producing the book: especially Carmel A. Huestis, Managing Editor; Pamela J. Getchell, typesetter; Kay Minnis, proofreader; and, of course, Bohdan S. Wynar, President. I wish also to thank Ron Maas, with whom I worked during the writing of most of the text. His caring and flexibility contributed greatly to the successful completion of the work.

And last, but absolutely not least, I thank my husband, A. Wayne Benson, whose love, understanding, and culinary skills have sustained me through many deadlines. This book would not be here now if not for Wayne.

Arlene G. Taylor
Pittsburgh, PA

CHAPTER 1

ORGANIZATION IN HUMAN ENDEAVORS

This chapter gives an overview of the field of the organization of recorded information. Terms used here that might not be readily familiar to the person new to the field of organizing information will be explained in later chapters. In the meantime the reader will find definitions of most unfamiliar terms in the glossary of this book.

IS THERE A BASIC HUMAN NEED TO ORGANIZE?

There seems to be a basic drive in humans to organize. Psychologists tell us that babies' brains organize images into categories such as "faces" or "foods." Small children do a lot of organizing during play. With some individuals the need is much stronger than with others. Those who operate on the maxim that states, "A place for everything and everything in its place," cannot begin to work until the work surface is cleared and every stray object has been put in its place. That is, such a person has to be "organized" before beginning a new project. But even those whose work spaces appear to be cluttered or chaotic have some organization in their heads. Such persons usually have some idea, or perhaps certain knowledge, of what is in the various piles or collections of "stuff." Regardless of one's personal style, however, human learning is based upon the ability to analyze and organize data, information, and knowledge.

WHY DO WE NEED TO ORGANIZE?

We need to organize because we need to retrieve. Kitchens are organized so that cooking equipment is easily accessible and foodstuffs and spices can be used as needed. Workplaces are organized so that appropriate records are retrievable and work can be done. Learning processes are organized so that relationships among ideas can be used to assist the learner in recalling the learned material.

WHY DO WE NEED TO ORGANIZE INFORMATION?

Retrieval of information is dependent upon its having been organized. Information is needed in all aspects of life—for example, for health reasons, to understand each other, to learn about one's relationships, to fix things that are broken, or simply to expand our knowledge. Some of this information has already been assimilated and is in one's knowledge store, while other information has to be sought. If it is not organized, it is difficult, if not impossible, to find. So we have all kinds of tools that are organized to aid in the process of finding information that we need: telephone books, directories, dictionaries, encyclopedias, bibliographies, indexes, catalogs, museum registers, archival finding aids, and databases, among others.

Organization of information also allows us to keep a usable record of human endeavors for posterity. Libraries, archives, museums, and other types of institutions have been doing this for many years. (This book does not deal with organization in commercial enterprises that have put together collections for the purpose of sale, rather than collecting for posterity.)

WHAT IS ORGANIZATION OF RECORDED INFORMATION?

As mentioned in the preface, this book addresses the organization of recorded information, as other means are necessary to "organize" information that has only been spoken, heard, or thought about. Recorded information, however, includes much more than text. Therefore, instead of using words such as *book* or *item* to refer to the organizable unit of information, terms such as *information-bearing entity* and *information package* are used.

Hagler has identified six functions of bibliographic control.[1] His listing reflects the purpose of his book, that is, the emphasis is upon the work of librarians. However, the list, with altered wording, reflects the major activities involved in all of organization of information.

1. *Identifying the existence of all types of information-bearing entities as they are made available—*

    A book may be published or a web site may be established, but if no one knows of its existence except the person(s) involved in its creation, it will be of no informational use to anyone. Existence and identity can be made known in many ways: publishers' announcements, e-mail announcements, reviews, subject-related listings, to name a few. Most publishers create catalogs listing their products along with abstracts for them. Reference tools such as *Books in Print* are products of this activity.

2. *Identifying the works contained within those information-bearing entities or as parts of them—*

    A collection of short stories or a grouping of artistic works may be considered to be an information-bearing entity as a whole; alternatively, each individual story or artistic work may be considered to be an information-bearing entity. A web site that is all about a famous person may have individual digitized works of the person, biographical material, accounts of the person written by contemporaries, accounts of events contemporary to the person's life span, and other parts. The writings about the person and the events may be important works in their own right and may need to be identified separately.

3. *Systematically pulling together these information-bearing entities into collections in libraries, archives, museums, Internet communication files, and other such depositories—*

    The activity of creating collections traditionally has been thought of as the province of institutions such as libraries, archives, and museums. But collections have always been created in many other situations: personal collections made up because of an intense interest in a particular kind of information, office collections of internal information and information needed to carry out the work of the office, university departmental collections of materials needed for teaching in a particular discipline, etc. Now that it is easy to make these collections known publicly, lists are being provided at web sites.

Collections often include electronic resources not held locally. Many institutions purchase the right to allow the users of their collections to search a resource online. Some resources are accessible only online. Others are also available in print. Part of the organizing process is determining whether such resources need to be added to one's collection in some permanent way.

4. *Producing lists of these information-bearing entities prepared according to standard rules for citation—*

   Lists created in this activity include bibliographies, indexes, library catalogs, archival finding aids, and museum registers. These are important to the retrieval of individual information packages, because if one is looking for a known item, especially a tangible one that needs a physical location, it is necessary to find it listed somewhere. Such lists may be in print or electronic form.

5. *Providing name, title, subject, and other useful access to these information-bearing entities—*

   This is the activity that adds the most value to the usefulness and retrieval potential of a collection. Keyword access can be provided more or less automatically and "on-the-fly," that is, any information in electronic form can be found by searching for a word that appears in the electronic information package. However, results of keyword searches become less and less satisfactory the larger the collection being searched. More satisfactory retrieval comes from being able to search for names, titles, and controlled vocabulary that have been created under authority control, usually by humans. If a person has been identified by different forms of name, and if that name is brought under authority control, then a search for one form of the name will retrieve information packages related to the person regardless of which form of name appears in a particular package. If a work has been given different titles in its different manifestations, a search for one of the titles will retrieve all. If a system uses controlled vocabulary, a search for a word with more than one meaning (which encompasses most English words) will allow differentiation among the various meanings and will direct one to broader, narrower, and related terms. It will also bring together under one term all the synonymous terms that may be used to express a concept.

Authority controlled access is of little use unless systems are designed to take advantage of it. Therefore, a major part of organizing information is designing systems for searching and display that will allow information-seekers to find easily what they need and want.

6. *Providing the means of locating each information-bearing entity or a copy of it—*

This has, for at least a century, been a value added by institutions with collections. The catalogs or other lists created in these institutions give information on the physical location of the entity, if it has not been taken out by a patron or is not being used by someone on the premises. In many library online catalogs, circulation information is available so that if an item has been taken out of the library, that information is available with the location information. Bibliographic utilities (e.g., OCLC, RLIN, WLN) allow one to find out which locations physically own a particular item. Many library, museum, and archival catalogs are available on the Internet. One can learn from these which locations own an item, whether it is on loan at a particular location (usually a library, as archives and museums generally do not circulate items from their collections), and often whether an item is on order and when it is expected to arrive.

Traditionally, bibliographies and indexes have not given location information. Bibliographies list what exists somewhere, but seldom tell where. Indexes give the larger work in which the smaller work being listed can be found (e.g., in which journal an article can be found), but do not give the physical location of the larger work. All of this is still true for tangible resources, but for electronic resources found on the Internet, it is becoming more common to give the location (e.g., URL) in any listing that includes the electronic resource. However, the instability of URLs makes it very difficult to keep them current.

HOW IS THE ORGANIZATION OF INFORMATION APPROACHED IN DIFFERENT ENVIRONMENTS?

There are many environments in which there is a desire to organize information so that it will be retrievable for various purposes and so that at least some of it will be kept for posterity. The ones to be discussed here are libraries of all types, archives, museums and art galleries, the Internet, and data administration environments (including offices).

Libraries

We consider libraries first because they have the longest tradition of organizing information for the purpose of retrieval and for posterity. As mentioned earlier the process begins with collections. Collections in libraries are created through the process called collection development. Collections are developed most often in three ways: 1) librarians learn about existence of new works through reviews, publishers' announcements, requests from users of the library, etc., and then order appropriate materials; 2) gifts are given to the library; and/or 3) approval plans, worked out with one or more vendors, bring in new items according to preselected profiles. In addition journal collections keep growing unless subscriptions are dropped.

When new materials arrive for addition to the collections, physical entities have to be arranged in some fashion. They may be placed on shelves in the order in which they come in, or they may be placed in some more meaningful order. They could be placed in alphabetical order, and this is the way that many fiction and biography sections are arranged. Most, however, are arranged by classification.

Classification of materials is part of the process of cataloging, which is usually the first activity following receipt of the materials. Cataloging of individual items involves creating a description of the physical item; choosing certain names and titles to serve as access points for getting to the description in the catalog; doing authority work on those names and titles; doing subject analysis of the content of the work in the item; choosing subject headings and classification numbers to represent the subject analysis; and creating call numbers (location devices), usually by adding a Cutter number to the classification number to make a unique set of letters and numbers to identify the particular physical item. Virtually all records thus created are coded with the MAchine Readable Cataloging (MARC) format so that they can be displayed in online systems.

Physical items then, finally, have to be "processed" so that they can be housed with the collections. This involves removing or adding book jackets, placing security strips in or on items, placing call number labels and barcodes on the items, sending an item to the conservation/preservation department if it is an older item that is not in good shape, etc.

The two major results of the cataloging process are arrangements of collections and the creation and maintenance of the catalog that provides the major access to the collections. The catalog is able to show what exists in the collection written by certain authors, having certain titles, or on certain subjects. It also brings together (i.e., collocates) all of the works of an author and all the editions of a work, even though they might not be brought together in the collections.[2]

Before online catalogs existed, the library's main card, book, or Computer Output Microform (COM) catalog typically was supplemented by other catalogs. Catalogs for departmental libraries, serial record holdings, and shelflists containing location information for specific copies of an item were the most common. All of these have been incorporated into one database in most online catalogs. In addition most online catalogs are part of integrated systems, which means that circulation information can accompany each catalog record. This adds to the power of the location information because one can be told if an item is temporarily unavailable due to its being charged out.

Until recently the online catalog continued to contain records only for items physically held by the library system. As libraries have entered into cooperative relationships, this principle of telling "what the library has" has eroded. In union catalogs that contain records from libraries of more than one institution, the concept was expanded to "what at least one of the cooperating libraries has." More recently, the addition of Internet records has meant that a number of catalogs now contain records for "what the library can give access to," including "what the library has."

Online catalogs also can be gateways to outside systems such as bibliographic utilities (e.g., OCLC, RLIN, WLN) that can tell where an item may be found if it is not in the local catalog. The item can then be requested through Interlibrary Loan (ILL). In addition bibliographic and text databases can be accessed from a catalog gateway. Many of these have become document delivery systems. A major addition to online catalogs has been access to the World Wide Web (WWW). Many libraries are cataloging Internet resources that seem to be important for the users of that catalog, and a URL in a catalog record can be hyperlinked to the WWW for immediate access to the information package represented by the catalog record. As mentioned earlier, a major difficulty has been keeping the URLs up-to-date.

Another major part of the organization process in libraries is found in the reference process. Libraries are organized so that information can be retrieved. In the reference process the success of the organization is tested. If it is found to be difficult to use, some of the organization process must be redone.

Administrative services in libraries are also affected by organization of information. Administrators are responsible for technological decisions that are directly affected by the organization of the recorded information in that setting. Conversely, administrators' decisions affect the future, in which electronic chaos will result if organization of information is not supported.

Archives

Although libraries have become more and more standardized throughout the twentieth century, and although many information resources in a library are duplicates of resources in another, neither of these is true in archives. Archives usually consist of unique items. Therefore, it once was thought that standardization was unnecessary. Archives could not take advantage of copy cataloging (i.e., using catalog records created by other agencies) because they were not cataloging materials that were also owned elsewhere. Although not nearly as standardized as libraries, archives have seen significant standardization movements.

Archives preserve records of enduring value that document organizational or personal activities accumulated in the course of daily life and work. Organizational records consist of such things as annual reports, correspondence, personnel records, etc. Personal records may consist of such things as correspondence, manuscripts, personal papers, etc., or could be a collection of memorabilia or a scrapbook. Even though materials in archives often are thought to be "old," this is not necessarily so. Further, archival materials can be in many different formats: paper, graphic images, sound recordings, moving image recordings, and recently, in digital formats.

Archival materials have been organized for centuries. Unlike library materials, archival materials are arranged and described in groups. Until the last few decades, each archives chose its own way to organize the information, particularly regarding level of control and depth of description. There have been several major schools of thought through the years as to how organization of archival information should be done. The one that seems to have prevailed states that the basic principles of organization are provenance and original order. *Provenance* is the originator (i.e., the corporate body or individual) that created, gathered, and maintained the collection before it was sent to the archives. The term *provenance* is also used to show the ownership history of a particular artifact or collection of archival information. *Original order* is the order in which the originator of an archival collection kept or created the collection. Most archives now keep the contents of individual collections within the archives as a whole in original order, and the collections are maintained according to provenance.

Standardization and cooperation have come to the archival world in part because of the increased interest in research involving documents and archival collections housed all over the world. In addition interest has grown, especially in the academic community, in entering descriptions of archival collections into the same databases with library catalog records. It has now become possible to easily share knowledge of the existence of these collections on the Internet.

Descriptions of archival materials can take one or more different forms. An accession record summarizes information about the source of the collection, gives the circumstances of its acquisition (which are more fully treated in the donor file), and briefly describes the physical data and contents for a collection. A finding aid gives a detailed contents note of the historical and organizational context of the collection and continues by describing its context, perhaps providing an inventory outlining what is in each box. It may also contain physical details such as the presence of brittle or fragile materials. A catalog record is a much shortened version of a finding aid.

Archival materials generally are in closed stacks, accessible only to staff. There is no public browsing and so the arrangement does not need to be classified as is usually true in an open stacks library. Any classification given, in any case, would be so broad as to be almost useless, due to the varied nature of each collection.

When the archival world became interested in placing their catalog records into bibliographic databases in the 1980s, a MARC format was developed (MARC-AMC). (AMC stands for Archival and Manuscript Collections.) Despite some lingering problems, the format continues to be used to code archival catalog records (now with the name "Mixed materials" instead of AMC). In the last few years an SGML standard has been developed for the purpose of encoding finding aids so that they can be displayed on the WWW.

The organization of archival information is necessary for use, whether that use is for administrative, historical, or personal reasons. It is also useful for archives that wish to mount exhibits either in something like an academic setting or perhaps on the WWW. If collections are well organized and documented, an exhibitor can use this to find appropriate additions to the exhibit.

Museums and Art Galleries

Museums and art galleries are combined here, because the kinds of art galleries that are being discussed (e.g., National Gallery of Art) operate in ways similar to museums. The kind of art galleries that display art for the purpose of sale are not covered in this book.

Although libraries and archives both contain some visual material, the vast majority of the collections of museums and art galleries consists of visual material in two- or three-dimensional form. These collections traditionally have been organized for internal use only, but recently research needs have been given attention. Even when the needs of distant researchers are taken into account, curators may be reluctant to contribute some data because it may represent data created by individuals in the course of their research and may not yet be published.

Museum/art gallery art works or artifacts are acquired through the institution's acquisitions department. As is done in archives, accession records are created, although the practice in natural history museums differs somewhat. In natural history museums, artifacts are acquired largely from field work, and a preliminary field record is made. If it is decided to keep the objects in the collection, accession records are created. In some cases groups of similar objects are described as a single lot that is given a single accession number. Curation of individual objects, which may not happen for some time, results in departmental level catalog records with their own numerical sequences.

In museums other than natural history, items are registered after being accessioned. Registration is a process much like cataloging in libraries and archives. The register serves as a catalog in that it establishes the organizational control over the art works and artifacts. A fairly recent development is the use of bibliographic utilities for the organizational control of art and artifacts, although records thus created are still not necessarily accepted in the museum community.

In museums, as in archives, provenance is important information and is essential in determining the name of the object. Both provenance and condition must appear with all other information about the object in the catalog or registration record. An aspect of creating records for museum objects and art that is very different from creating records for text is that the objects are often imperfectly known at the time of accessioning and registering. There will be an accumulation of conflicting information over time.

Description of visual material is often more difficult than description of textual material. There is more reliance on the perceptions of the person doing the describing. Often there are no words associated with items at all; it is necessary for the describers of such items to use their own words. A single record has many more fields than does the usual library catalog record. Some fields that might be needed for art objects that are not used in libraries are: Material content, Technique(s), Studio of origin, Type of equipment used, Color(s), Texture, Design symbolism, Provenance, Exhibition history, Installation considerations, Appraised value, etc. Even with additional fields, it is not possible to anticipate all the uses a researcher might find in art or artifacts. A street scene from a century ago may be useful to historians, architects, urban planners, cultural historians, medical researchers, sociologists, students of photography, or others. Systems are being developed that start with queries that use the text of the description; then query results allow the searcher to browse surrogate images.

Subject analysis is also more difficult for visual materials—an image does not tell in words what it is about. Additionally, the line between description and subject analysis is harder to draw. One might describe a work of art as being a painting of a woman in a blue dress holding and looking at a baby—this is a description. But if one gives the subject of the work as "Mary and Jesus," one has crossed the line into interpretation (unless this is in the title of the work given by the artist). And if one uses a description like "love of a mother," one is definitely interpreting.

A barrier to cooperative cataloging has been the firmly held notion that museums hold unique objects. This is perhaps less true of natural history collections than other museum and art collections. Although each specimen of a bug or bird is unique, each represents a class of organisms that can be identified to the genus and species level. There would have to be copy-specific notes, but this does not preclude the idea of cooperative cataloging for cooperative access. However, as was true of libraries when cooperative cataloging was first introduced, museum curators fear a loss of individual control and level of detail. They are unwilling to give up their local terminology and organization in order to participate in a bibliographic utility.

Besides its major collections the museum or art gallery can also have an archives, a records management program, and a library. The library may contain published materials that document or relate to the museum or art gallery collections.

As with archival materials the museum/art gallery collections are accessible only to staff. Much of the collection is stored behind the scenes while only some of it is on display at any one time. Behind the scenes, the items are numbered in a way so that they can be retrieved as needed. Persons responsible for the exhibits must make heavy use of the system of organizational control. In addition these collections are increasingly being used for research by persons with diverse research needs.

The Internet

The Internet has been likened to a library where all the books have been dumped on the floor and there is no catalog. For several years efforts have been made to find a way to gain some control over the Internet; however, one cannot yet say that it is organized. There is so much change so fast that efforts begun are sadly out of date in a few months. It has been estimated by a number of Internet specialists that a web year is six to nine weeks. In other words the amount of change that happens in society in a year happens on the WWW in six to nine weeks. With change occurring at such a rate, getting a handle on organization is quite a challenge.

Several different approaches are being taken in the attempt to organize the Internet. Libraries have attempted to use traditional means for the organization. One project collected Internet resources in particular subjects and made them available at gopher sites. Other librarians are compiling bibliographies of web sites. Librarians have been part of the team of people who have been working on a metadata standard called the Dublin Core. Digital libraries are also being developed. These vary greatly in content and methods of organization, but all have some kind of organization, although usually not traditional library organization. Only a few of the people working on digital libraries are librarians.

In fact, much work on organizing the Internet has been done by persons other than librarians. Search engines, for example, have been developed by computer and programming specialists. Most people appreciate search engines, even though they are frustrated that the search engines are not more selective and precise. Most programs (e.g., robots, spiders, etc.) sent out to find sites to add to the indexes of search engines recognize text only; in addition to that, those programs cannot analyze a site's purpose, history, policies, etc. In order to improve the situation, work on various kinds of metadata (i.e., information about information) is ongoing and important; appropriate information is being gleaned by robots from metadata that has been added to a site by its author or by someone trained in describing and analyzing information packages. Metadata can include information about nontextual parts of a site, information about the site's purpose and history, information about the contents of the site, etc.

There is software that automatically classifies and indexes electronic documents, but automated tools categorize information differently than people do. The search site called *Yahoo!* classifies by broad subject areas using human indexers. This approach has been popular, although not completely successful as a classification. Also a research project at OCLC is improving an approach to automatic classification using the Dewey Decimal Classification.

Although some believe that organizing the Internet will be impossible, the parts of it that are important for retrieval and for posterity will be brought under organizational control. It is human nature, and the principles learned over centuries of organizing print information can be used to speed the process of organizing electronic resources.

Data Administration and Office Environments

Data administration is the terminology applied to the control of the explosion of electronic information in offices and other administrative settings. It has its roots in the office filing systems that developed throughout the twentieth century. These systems have been highly affected by developments in technology: typewriters, photocopiers, and computers (starting with sorters and collators).

As was true in other parts of our society, data administration once involved the keeping, filing, and maintaining of paper records. It was a simpler time, but also a frustrating time, because, usually, only one copy of a record was filed in only one place. The file labels of one records manager were not necessarily logical to the next. As information began being entered and stored in electronic files, access points (the file labels) became invisible. This was not an immediate problem as long as the people who developed the electronic files documented what was contained in them. The situation became more complicated when powerful personal computers began to allow persons to store and file their own information on their desktops. A problem of continuity developed when these personal files were abandoned.

For many years various operations have been automated, each with its own system. For example, payroll, general ledger, accounts payable, inventories, and other such systems have been automated separately. Within the last decade integration of these systems has been taking place with the result that the systems have many redundant data fields with little documentation of their content. These fields seem to be meant to contain the same information, but what is actually there is often different (e.g., name given in full in the payroll file, but middle name shortened to an initial in the faculty file).

Data administrators are dealing with their information explosion by using principles of organization of information. The units that need to be organized in the administrative electronic environment are such things as directories, files, programs, and, at another level, such things as field values. Organization can be by system (e.g., payroll, budget) or by type of record (e.g., person names, registration records). Data administrators must keep track of information that crosses system boundaries (e.g., person names cross boundaries when the same names are entered into several different files). There must be methods for handling concepts that have the same names but different purposes (e.g., the concept of "part-time" in a university can have different definitions depending upon whether one is talking about payroll, faculty, graduate students, or undergraduate students).

Keeping all these things straight is often done through a process called "data modeling." It can either be used as a precursor to database design or as a way to integrate the myriad systems developed over time by persons who are no longer with the corporate body. Data modeling designs a system using a series of related models. The process is to develop a conceptual model of the records management activity in the particular setting; then a logical model is developed that includes more detail; and finally, the logical model is translated into a physical data model that can be implemented as a database management system. If the data model is updated and adjusted to fit changes in the conceptual model, it can serve for a long time as the basis for the organization of information in an organizational setting.

A person's individual office organization is another matter. A major factor in one's personal office organization seems to be the use to which particular information-bearing packages will be put or have been put. For example, if an item is to be referred to in order to write a letter in the immediate future, it will be located at hand; items that have just been finished with will be filed. Also, the form of the package can be a determining factor: books may be shelved, while papers relating to the books may be placed in file folders. In one's electronic information store, it is necessary to develop electronic folders, subfolders, etc., if one is to be able to find a particular file again in the future. An importance of office organization is that some such office collections will be deposited in archives for posterity.

CONCLUSION

In this chapter we have discussed basic needs to organize, have defined organization of information, and have looked at an overview of the organizing environments that are covered in this book. The following chapters discuss in more detail the processes that have been developed for the organization of information, those that are being worked on, and the issues that affect their implementation.

NOTES

1.   Ronald Hagler. *The Bibliographic Record and Information Technology*, 3rd ed. (Chicago: American Library Association, 1997), p. 13.

2.   Charles A. Cutter. *Rules for a Dictionary Catalog*, 4th ed. (Washington, D.C.: Government Printing Office, 1904; reprint, London: The Library Association, 1962), p. 12.

SUGGESTED READINGS

Organization of Information in Libraries

Hagler, Ronald. *The Bibliographic Record and Information Technology*. 3rd ed. Chicago: American Library Association, 1997, pp. 1–41.

Stoll, Clifford. "Wherein the Author Considers the Future of the Library, the Myth of Free Information, and a Novel Way to Heat Bathwater." Chap. 11 in *Silicon Snake Oil: Second Thoughts on the Information Highway*. New York: Doubleday, 1995.

Taylor, Arlene G. "The Information Universe: Will We Have Chaos or Control?" *American Libraries* 25, no. 7 (July/August 1994): 629–32.

Organization of Information in Archives/Manuscripts

Ellis, Judith, ed. *Keeping Archives*. 2nd ed. Port Melbourne, Australia: Thorpe, in association with the Australian Society of Archivists, 1993.

Miller, Fredric. "Archival Description." In *Reference Services for Archives and Manuscripts*, edited by Laura B. Cohen, pp. 55–66. Binghamton, N.Y.: Haworth Press, 1997.

Organization of Information in Museums/Art Galleries

Bearman, David. "Functional Requirements for Collections Management Systems." *Archival Informatics Technical Report* 1, no. 3 (Fall 1987): 1–87.

Bierbaum, Esther Green. "Records and Access: Museum Registration and Library Cataloging." *Cataloging & Classification Quarterly* 9, no. 1 (1988): 97–111.

Suzor, Mary. "Art and the Information Highway." *CMA* (March 1997): 8–9.

Organization of Information in the Internet

"The Internet: Bringing Order from Chaos." *Scientific American* 276, no. 3 (March 1997): 50–51.

Lynch, Clifford. "Searching the Internet." *Scientific American* 276, no. 3 (March 1997): 52–56.

"Map to Navigating the Web." Available: http://www.zdnet.com/pccomp/webmap/ spmaps/map0896/ (Accessed October 1998).

Organization of Information in Data Administration

Ince, A. Nejat, Cem Evrendilek, Dag Wilhelmsen, and Fadil Gezer. *Planning and Architectural Design of Modern Command Control Communications and Information Systems: Military and Civilian Applications*. Boston: Kluwer Academic, 1997, pp. 90–98.

Offices

Kwasnik, Barbara H. "How a Personal Document's Intended Use or Purpose Affects Its Classification in an Office." In *Proceedings of the 12th Annual International ACM SIGIR Conference on Research and Development in Information Retrieval*. New York: ACM, 1989, pp. 207–10.

Data Modeling

Weldon, J. L. "A Career in Data Modeling." *Byte* 22, no. 6 (June 1997): 103–6.

CHAPTER 2

RETRIEVAL TOOLS

This chapter addresses retrieval tools, which are basic building blocks in the organization of recorded information. We address the following questions: Why do we need retrieval tools? What are the basic retrieval tools, what are their formats, and what are their functions?

WHY DO WE NEED RETRIEVAL TOOLS?

Retrieval tools are systems created for retrieval of information. They contain records that are surrogates for information packages. That is, each surrogate record (also called a *description* or *metadata*) gives enough information, such as author, title, and date of creation, so that it can serve as a short representation of an information package. Surrogate records are arranged or retrieved by *access points*. An access point can be a name, title, or subject term chosen by an *indexer* (also called a *cataloger* in some settings). In online systems an access point can be almost any word in a record if keyword searching of every word that is not a stopword is allowed.

Retrieval tools are essential as basic building blocks for a system that will organize as much of the world's recorded information as possible. A dream of being able to provide access to all recorded information has existed since 1892, when Paul Otlet and Henri LaFontaine organized a conference to create Universal Bibliographic Control (UBC). The magnitude of the undertaking meant that new techniques different from conventional library practice had to be developed. The tools that have been developed as a result of that dream have brought us closer to UBC.

WHAT ARE THE BASIC RETRIEVAL TOOLS, THEIR FORMATS, AND THEIR FUNCTIONS?

The basic retrieval tools discussed in this chapter are:

- bibliographies
- catalogs
- indexes
- finding aids
- registers

Databases and bibliographic utilities are also discussed because of their roles in housing retrieval tools.

Bibliographies

Bibliographies basically are lists of information packages. Bibliographies are essential to scholars and to those involved professionally with books and other sources of information (e.g., collectors, dealers, librarians), and are also useful sources of information for all serious readers. They bring together lists of sources based on subject matter, on authors, by time periods, and the like (see the more detailed list of these below). Some bibliographies include *annotations*, that is, brief notes indicating the subject matter or commenting on the usefulness of the information.

Bibliographies can be attached to a scholarly work and consist of the information packages that were consulted by the author of the work, or they can be completely separate entities—works in their own right. Each information package represented in the list has a short *description* (not to be confused with *annotation*). A typical description includes author, title, edition, publisher, place, and date of publication for a book or other such whole entity. For a part of a work, such as a journal article or a poem, one typically includes author, title, name of the larger work, volume (if applicable), date, page numbers or other part designation. Some descriptions also include physical characteristics in the description.

In a bibliography each description usually appears in only one place, usually under the author of the work. The descriptions may be constructed according to various styles, one of which is chosen by the creator of the bibliography. Examples of some of the styles are:

- APA (American Psychological Association)[1]
  Mitchell, T. R., & Larson, J. R., Jr. (1987). *People in organizations: An introduction to organizational behavior* (3rd ed.). New York: McGraw-Hill.

- Chicago Manual of Style[2]

  Mitchell, Terence R., and James R. Larson, Jr. *People in Organizations: An Introduction to Organizational Behavior.* 3d ed. New York: McGraw-Hill, 1987.

- MLA (Modern Language Association)[3]

  Mitchell, Terence R., and James R. Larson, Jr. *People in Organizations: An Introduction to Organizational Behavior.* 3rd ed. New York: McGraw-Hill, 1987.

- Science (Scientific Style and Format)[4]

  Mitchell TR, Larson JR, Jr. 1987. *People in Organizations: An Introduction to Organizational Behavior.* 3d ed. New York: McGraw-Hill.

- Turabian[5]

  Mitchell, Terence R., and James R. Larson, Jr. *People in Organizations: An Introduction to Organizational Behavior.* 3d ed. New York: McGraw-Hill, 1987.

- Style Manual (U.S. Government Style Manual)[6]

  Mitchell, Terence R., and James R. Laron, Jr. *People in Organizations: An Introduction to Organizational Behavior.* 3rd ed. (New York: McGraw-Hill, 1987).

Each bibliography has a particular focus or arrangement. The most common ones are:

- subject—bibliographies gathering together publications or other information packages that are all about a particular subject (e.g., *The New Press Guide to Multicultural Resources for Young Readers*[7])

- author—bibliographies of all or some of the works of a particular author and sometimes including sources about the author (e.g., *A Bibliography of Jane Austen*[8])

- language—bibliographies of textual entities in which the text is a certain language (e.g., *An Extensive Bibliography of Studies in English, German, and French on Turkish Foreign Policy, 1923–1997*[9])

- time period—bibliographies listing all works that came to light in a particular time period (e.g., *British Women Writers, 1700–1850: An Annotated Bibliography of Their Works and Works About Them*[10])

- locale—bibliographies listing all information packages created in a particular location. This could be a large locale such as a whole continent, or a smaller locale such as a country, region, state, city, or community (e.g., *Area Bibliography of Japan*[11]). It could also be an institution, such as a bibliography of all the works of the faculty in a particular university.

- publisher—bibliographies listing all of the products of a particular publisher (e.g., *The Stinehour Press: A Bibliographical Checklist of the First Thirty Years*[12])

- form—bibliographies listing information packages that appear in a certain form, format, or genre (e.g., videocassettes, electronic resources, poetry, biographies, etc.). These are virtually always combined with one of the other foci (e.g., *Maps and Mapping of Africa: A Resource Guide*[13]).

Two or more of these foci are often combined in bibliographies. For example, the title above that illustrates "language" is a combination of language, subject, and time period; the one illustrating "time period" is a combination of subject, locale, and time period; and the one illustrating "form" is a combination of form and locale.

Catalogs

Catalogs provide access to individual items within collections of information packages (e.g., physical entities such as books, videocassettes, and CDs in a library; artists' works in an art museum; web pages on the Internet; etc.). Each information package is represented by a description of the package that is somewhat longer than a bibliography description. The descriptions are assigned one or more *access points*. Literally, an access point can be almost any word in a record when keyword searching is used. However, the term *access point* is usually applied to a particular name, title, or subject that is listed on the record separately from the description. An access point is constructed in a certain order (e.g., surname followed by forename or forenames), and it is maintained under authority control. *Authority control* is the process of pulling together into a single authority record all the forms of name that apply to a single name; all the variant titles that apply to a single work; and all the synonyms, related terms, broader terms, and narrower terms that apply to a particular subject heading.

The descriptions are constructed according to a standard style selected by a particular community (e.g., *AACR2* for libraries, some archives, and some museums; GILS for some government information; the Dublin Core for Internet information packages; etc.). Several different standards for description are discussed in more detail in chapter 5.

Purposes of Catalogs

Catalogs have traditionally served two main groups. One group is employees of the institution who need to retrieve information packages or visual images or objects, or who need to retrieve information about those packages. For example, the catalog is used by collection development librarians in their process of discovering what the library already owns or does not own before ordering new acquisitions; another such use is by the employee of a museum who is looking for objects to place in an exhibit.

The most commonly thought of use for a catalog, though, is use by patrons of the institution who wish to borrow material or make use of it on the premises. If such users have a known work in mind, they may search for it in the catalog by author or title (called *known-item searching*). If the catalog is on-line, users might also search by keyword if they only remember certain words of the title, for example. If users know they want works of a particular author, they may search under the author's name. If users do not know of a particular work but are searching for something on a particular topic, they may use a subject search or a keyword search of subject headings and/or titles.

In online catalogs keyword searches are useful for helping a person find a record that looks like it might be on the user's topic, and then identifying from that record an authority-controlled subject heading for the topic or a classification notation for the topic. One may then do a subject search for the subject heading or may go to the location of the classification notation in the stacks to determine if there are pertinent works shelved with the one that has been identified. Some catalogs also allow a call number search of a classification notation so that one can see all the works that have been given that classification notation.

Charles Cutter gave his "objects" of a catalog in 1904, speaking only of library catalogs in which books were represented. These "objects," if broadened to archives, museums, etc., still seem to represent what catalogs are supposed to do. Cutter said that a catalog should be able:

1. To enable a person to find a book of which either

    (A) the author
    (B) the title   } is known.
    (C) the subject

2. To show what the library has

    (D) by a given author
    (E) on a given subject
    (F) in a given kind of literature.

3. To assist in the choice of a book
    (G) as to the edition (bibliographically).
    (H) as to its character (literary or topical).[14]

Another important purpose served by catalogs has traditionally been to act as an inventory of the collection—that is, to provide a record of what is owned. Often a shelflist has been used to accomplish this purpose. A shelflist includes one copy of every record in a catalog arranged in the order in which the information packages, objects, etc., are arranged on the shelf. Originally, shelflists were literally in the order of items on the shelf, starting a new sequence with each change in format, or change in collection location, or change in size. Later, shelflists often were arranged by classification notation regardless of format, etc. This is the way the concept works in online catalogs. The purpose of serving as an inventory is still there, but the mental image of a "shelflist" with arrangement as it is on the shelf is lost.

The shelflist function is very fuzzy when Internet resources are added to a catalog. When Internet resources are added, the institution may have purchased the right to make them accessible to the users, but they are not owned by the institution. With paper serials in a library, the library has always had control of how many years of back issues were kept. With Internet resources, whether right to access has been purchased or not, there is no control over how long the information will be available on the Internet, or whether it will remain at the same URL.

A *union catalog* is a variation of the concept that a catalog represents just the holdings of one institution. A union catalog represents the holdings of more than one institution or collection. A union catalog of a main library and its branches, for example, shows items that may be held in one or more branches in addition to those held in the main library. The location information indicates where an item is held. A union catalog of a consortium of institutions works the same way; location information shows which items are housed in which of the cooperating institutions. The ultimate union catalog is one maintained by a bibliographic utility (see description below). The largest of these is OCLC (Online Computer Library Center), where each information package has one master record, and associated with the record is a holdings record that shows the holding symbol of each member of the utility that has cataloged the package through OCLC or has asked that its symbol be added to the record.

Ultimately, the Internet may serve as a giant union catalog for the world. With the use of the Z39.50 protocol that allows users to search many online catalogs using the commands with which they are familiar, great progress has been made in searching for information not found locally. (Z39.50 is a national standard that defines a protocol that allows one computer to query another computer and transfer search results without the user having to know the search commands of the remote computer. It is described in more detail in chapter 10.) However, a user usually has to search one catalog after another. As more sophistication develops in adding catalogs to the Internet, there may eventually be a seamless interface among catalogs, so that one can concentrate on the search instead of having first to decide which catalogs to search.

Forms of Catalogs

Catalogs can have different formats from catalog to catalog. The formats discussed here are:

- book
- card
- COM (Computer Output Microform)
- OPAC (Online Public Access Catalog)

Book Catalogs. Book catalogs originally were just handwritten lists. After the invention of printing with moveable type, book catalogs were printed, but not always in a discernible order. Eventually, entries were printed in alphabetical or classified order, but they were very expensive and could not be reproduced and updated often. In the early 1900s book catalogs were almost completely replaced with cards that updated the catalog as soon as they were filed and were relatively inexpensive. They had a brief renaissance in the 1960s and 1970s when 1) computers again made it easy and less expensive to make book catalogs; 2) large card catalogs became unwieldy; and 3) rapid growth of new libraries and new branches made it desirable to have multiple copies of catalogs. But in order to keep a book catalog up-to-date, supplements were usually produced, resulting in multiple look-ups for one search. In addition it was usually three to six months before supplements were produced, meaning that new materials were not represented in the catalog during that time.

Online catalogs have replaced both book and card catalogs in most situations, but book catalogs are still used for catalogs of exhibits, artist's works, subject archives, etc. Book catalogs provide a way to make the contents of special collections known to users in many locations. For example, book catalogs of historical societies are popular acquisitions by collectors of genealogical materials. This use, though, may be replaced by availability of such catalogs on the WWW. Book catalogs also still exist in some libraries and archives as the only access to older materials.

An advantage of book catalogs over online catalogs and Internet versions of online catalogs is that book catalogs are compact and portable and can be consulted anywhere they can be carried. In addition scanning a page of book catalog entries is relatively fast, and many people prefer this to scrolling through screen after screen of online responses.

Card Catalogs. Card catalogs were popularized in the United States by Library of Congress (LC) cards, first made available for sale in 1901, and by H. W. Wilson cards, which began production in 1938 in response to the needs of small libraries. (Both have now ceased card production.) Technological advances encouraged further use of the card catalog. First, typewriters made handwritten cards unnecessary. Offset printing was used by LC for its cards. Then photocopying allowed the local creation of whole card sets from one master card. Finally the advent of computer printing made it possible to have customized cards made either locally or at a distant facility. When created at a distance, the cards were sent in boxes already alphabetized and ready to file.

Because of the influence of LC cards, card catalogs and the order of information on cards in libraries have been standardized for several decades. Users of card catalogs could go from library to library, using catalogs with confidence that they would be able to use distant catalogs with as much ease as their local ones. Online catalogs have not yet been standardized, and without Z39.50, searching an unfamiliar online catalog can be daunting. Museums, archives, etc., also are not yet standardized.

Online catalogs have replaced most card catalogs in the United States, but some libraries, archives, museums, and art galleries still have card catalogs, especially small institutions or those where there has been only minimal conversion of data to machine-readable form. In other countries there are many more card catalogs.

COM Catalogs. The creation of Computer Output Microform (COM) catalogs became possible in the 1960s. They are produced on either microfiche or microfilm and require a microform reader in order to be able to use them. They are produced like book catalogs, to some extent. However, because they do not have to be reproduced on paper and be bound, they can be completely reproduced with new additions every three months or so without having to go through the supplement stage.

COM catalogs have been replaced rather quickly by online catalogs. It has been found that users will use microfilm if that is the only way to get the information they need, but most people find the readers hard to use and difficult to read.

OPACs. Online Public Access Catalogs (OPACs) are the predominant form of catalog in the United States and in a number of other countries today. In these catalogs records are stored in computer memory or on CD-ROM disks. The records are displayed only as needed. There is much flexibility in the "look" of the displays. That is, there is as yet no standardization from system to system, although in two or more institutions that have purchased the same system, the displays look quite similar. Writers in the field have called for standardization, so that patrons can move from catalog to catalog and find records displayed in the same manner.

Standardization is also lacking in the way in which OPACs are searched. Commands and/or menus are quite different from system to system. However, the Z39.50 protocol has done much to allow one to search several catalogs from the same location using the local commands. In order for this to work, each catalog has to have Z39.50 installed. The protocol at the site from which the search commands are sent translates the commands to the Z39.50 standard. At the remote site being searched the Z39.50 server translates the standard to the commands of that system so that the search can be completed and results sent.

So far there have been three major "generations" of OPACs. The first generation, created in the 1980s, emulated either the card catalog or information retrieval (IR) systems, such as DIALOG or MEDLINE, which were themselves more "primitive" than they are today. The second generation, spreading from about 1992 into 1996, merged the card and IR design models, and improved access points, search capabilities, and display options. The third generation, beginning in 1996, has web interfaces, hypertext browsing, graphical user interfaces (GUIs), and Z39.50-compliant communication protocols. At this writing there are still more second- than third-generation OPACs, but this is changing rapidly.

Arrangements Within Catalogs

The records within catalogs must be arranged in some fashion or they are unusable. In card catalogs records are arranged by being filed in a certain order. In book and COM catalogs records are arranged by being printed one after another in a certain order. Records in OPACs are arranged internally within the database either in sequence of order of entry into the system or in random order. So the "arrangement" discussed here applies to the arrangement of the displayed responses to search queries in the case of OPACs.

In general there are two basic arrangements that will make sense to users, although there are many variations. A catalog can be in classified order or in alphabetical order. Within the basic order, display of records can be further subarranged in alphabetical order or in other ways such as by date of the intellectual contents.

Classified. Classified catalogs usually have more than one section. In what is considered to be the main section of the catalog, the arrangement or display is in the order of the classification scheme used in that institution. That is, this part is arranged in subject order, where the subject is represented by a classification notation. There can be as many classification notations assigned to a single record as there are subject concepts in the information package. Classified catalogs have the advantage that users can look at records for broader and narrower concepts at the same place they are looking for records on a specific concept. In a way it is similar to browsing in the stacks with a classification notation, except that in the case of the classified catalog, each information package is represented by several notations representing all of its concepts, not just one as is true of items in the stacks.

As it is nearly impossible for anyone to know all the notations relating to a subject, there should be a section of the catalog that lists verbal representations of all topics and gives the notation that represents a topic. In some situations this function is provided by placing a copy of the classification schedule at the catalog. And, of course, there are users who want to search for authors and/or titles, so there should be another section of the catalog for these. In book, card, or COM catalogs, these subject, author, and title sections are arranged in alphabetical order. In OPACs they are word-searchable and do not have to be arranged separately.

Classified catalogs have traditionally been used in European and other countries where several languages are spoken and represented in the setting. The sections of the catalog that give access to subject headings, authors, and titles can be in the language(s) appropriate to the clientele. The United States has not traditionally felt the need for this approach. Among the reasons the concept is being reconsidered today is that access to catalogs on the Internet is global, and a classified catalog can hold and display records in any language with classification notations that are universal. If indexes to a classified catalog are made in many languages, access can be gained through one of many languages. In addition it makes browsing and broadening and narrowing of searches easy, which is especially helpful for inexperienced online users.

Alphabetical. Early American catalogs were arranged by broad subject categories in alphabetical order. With a collection consisting of a few books there was little need for elaborate classification or arrangement. As catalogs grew the broad categories needed to be subdivided, so somewhat narrower categories were created and placed alphabetically within each broad category. For example, if the broad category were domestic animals, the subcategories under it might be cats, cows, dogs, horses, mules, etc. These were called "alphabetico-classed" catalogs. As subject categories multiplied, it became more difficult to predict the subject category and where it would be found. It began to make sense to place all subcategories in alphabetical order regardless of class. Charles Cutter was instrumental in the development of what he called the "dictionary" catalog. He recommended alphabetical arrangement with authors, titles, and subjects all interfiled in the same file.

The dictionary card catalog was the standard for the first half of the twentieth century. Later, catalogs in large libraries became complicated to file because of size. Attempts to break up the large files resulted in "divided" catalogs. They were sometimes divided into two files and sometimes into three files. If there were two files, they were divided so that authors and titles were in one and subjects were in the other. In three files, the division was authors in one, titles in one, and subjects in one. In the author/title/subject arrangement, records for works about a person were often filed in the subject file, while records for works the person wrote were filed in the author file. However, it was considered useful to keep records for works by and about a person together, so sometimes all *names* were placed in one file rather than just authors being placed in that file. The divided catalog was easier and less expensive for the keepers of the catalog, but assumed that users knew the difference among author, title, and subject entries, which was not always the case.

With the development of OPACs in the 1980s the divided catalog was moved online. One usually had to search either by author or by title or by subject. In this case, though, it was seldom possible to retrieve works both by and about a person in the same search. In some ways the sophistication that had been achieved in card catalogs was abandoned. For example, one could not have criticisms of a work displayed with editions of that work, and at first there were no references from unused forms of names and topics to the used forms. Many catalogs still do not allow searches for works both by and about a person or other more sophisticated searching, although efforts are being made to improve this situation. Displays are not now always in alphabetical order, although searches for *specific* authors, titles, or subjects generally bring up alphabetical displays. However, keyword search display results are often in chronological order. Some systems are beginning to allow users a choice of the order in which the results are to be displayed. Improvements of this sort will gradually be added to twenty-first-century catalogs.

Indexes

Indexes provide access to the analyzed contents of "bibliographic entities" (e.g., articles in a journal, short stories in a collection, papers in a conference proceeding, etc.). Although back-of-the-book indexes also provide access to analyzed contents of one work, they are not retrieval tools in the sense defined here; they are prepared at the time of publication, not later in an effort to provide bibliographic control. They do, however, aid with retrieval of the information found in the text at hand. Indexes that are retrieval tools give access to smaller works that are included in information packages that consist of collections of small works. Such indexes often do not have authority control of names, although most publishers of indexes use a thesaurus for selection of terms to stand for subject concepts.

Indexes are not limited to what is available in a local setting, and they do not usually give location information as such. They do give, as part of the surrogate record, the larger work in which the smaller work can be found. It is then necessary for a user of the index to search a catalog for the location of the larger work. If the larger work is not found in the local catalog, the user may search a union catalog or take a request to Interlibrary Loan (ILL).

Indexes can be found in print form or in machine-readable form—either CD-ROM or online. Some print versions are arranged in alphabetical dictionary fashion, with entries for authors, titles, and subjects. (See fig. 2.1.) Others are "divided," having an author/title part separate from the subject index. Both CD-ROM and online indexes have interfaces that dictate how these will be searched and how displays will appear. (See figs. 2.2 and 2.3.) As with OPACs there is no standardization from index to index. Although OPACs at least often have the standardization that comes from using the *Anglo-American Cataloguing Rules*, 2nd ed. *(AACR2)*, there is no standard commonly used by the various indexes.

Indexes tend to be created by for-profit organizations. Often there is a charge for using the online versions directly. The print versions are sold, usually to libraries, or libraries pay for the right to allow their patrons to use the indexes online without the charge. Some libraries have both print and online access, although there seems to be a trend to continue only with the online versions. In any case the index often is cataloged so that the whole index can be found through the catalog.

Automation

See also

Online catalogs

Retrospective conversion

Barry, R. K. The role of character sets in library automation: the development of 8-bit sets and Unicode [paper presented at the 3rd international conference Crimea 96, Foros, Ukraine, June 1996] *Int Cat Bibliogr Control* v26 p14-17 Ja/Mr '97

Dennis, N. K. The Windows95 of change [University of New Mexico Library moves to Windows 95] *Against Grain* v9 p83 Ap '97

Stielow, F. J. and others. From managerial theory and worksheets to practical MARC AMC; or, Dancing with the dinosaur at the Amistad. il *Am Archivist* v58 p464-74 Fall '95

Backlog

See Cataloging--Administration

Fig. 2.1. Sample section from the printed version of the index *Library Literature*. (Source: *Library Literature*. Bronx, N.Y.: H. W. Wilson, October 1997, p. 32.)

```
Record 1 of 1 - Library Literature 12/84-1/98

TI: From managerial theory and worksheets to practical MARC AMC; or, Dancing
      with the dinosaur at the Amistad
AU: Stielow,-Frederick-J., 1946-; Hankins,-Rebecca; Jones,-Venola
SO: The American Archivist. v. 58 (Fall '95) p. 464-74
PY: 1995
AN: 97009487
```

Fig. 2.2. Short view of Stielow entry from fig. 2.1 as it appears in the online index for *Library Literature*.

```
Record 1 of 1 - Library Literature 12/84-1/98

TI: From managerial theory and worksheets to practical MARC AMC; or, Dancing
      with the dinosaur at the Amistad
AU: Stielow,-Frederick-J., 1946-; Hankins,-Rebecca; Jones,-Venola
SO: The American Archivist. v. 58 (Fall '95) p. 464-74
PY: 1995
PD: il
IS: 0360-9081
LA: English
DE: Amistad-Research-Center; Black-archives-Cataloging; MARC-System; Special-
      collections-Special-subjects-Civil-rights; Cataloging-Automation
DT: Feature-Article
AN: 97009487
```

Fig. 2.3. Long view of Stielow entry as it appears in the online index for *Library Literature*.

Finding Aids

Finding aids are long descriptions of archival collections. A finding aid may also be called an inventory. Archives usually maintain control over collections of archival materials from personal or corporate sources, not over individual pieces. Thus, a finding aid describes a collection. Some finding aids are published, and this is increasingly true as archives add finding aids to the WWW. (See fig. 2.4 on page 30.) The finding aid itself is often cataloged; that is, a surrogate record to be available in the institution's catalog is created describing the finding aid and providing name, title, and subject access points for it.

Heinz House Papers

Finding Aid

- Scope and Contents Note

- Arrangement of the Heinz House Papers

- Description of the Heinz House Papers

  - Subgroup I. Legislative Records -- 16.7 lin. ft.

  - Subgroup II. Personal/Political Records -- 7.3 lin. ft.

  - Subgroup III. Press Relations/Media Activity Records -- 4.7 lin. ft.

  - Subgroup IV. Constituent Service Records -- 25.6 lin. ft.

  - Subgroup V. Office Administration Records -- 0.3 lin. ft.

- Appraisal and Sampling Note

- Appendices

Updated February 1997 / http://www.library.cmu.edu/Guide/Heinz/
Edward A. Galloway, Heinz Archivist, eg2d@andrew.cmu.edu

H. John Heinz III Archives

Carnegie Mellon University Libraries

**Fig. 2.4. Introductory page for a finding aid found at:
http://www.library.cmu.edu/Guide/Heinz/House/**

Registers

Registers constitute the primary control tools for museums. A register may also be called an accession log. It functions like a catalog, although it has additional kinds of access points. The process of registration in a museum is much like the process of cataloging in a library. During the process, the registrar will identify the object, the donor, any associations (e.g., having belonged to a particular person), any information needed for insurance purposes, etc. An identification number is assigned. The accession record becomes the basis for one or more files that help provide organization of the museum's content.

Databases

Databases are included here, not because they are themselves retrieval tools, but because they comprise the structure that retrieval tools take. A database is a set of records that are all constructed in the same way and are connected by relationship links. In *relational* databases the records may be divided into parts with the parts linked to each other to form individual records, but with the parts also having other links such as author-to-author or subject-to-subject.

A database can be in paper format, but is usually thought of these days as being machine-readable. Some databases contain actual facts, or text on various subjects. The ones created as retrieval tools, however, contain surrogate records. The retrieval tools discussed above can all be held in computer databases, although bibliographies and finding aids are more likely simply to be displayed as text. A computer database can be held in computer memory or stored elsewhere, such as on CD-ROM.

Bibliographic Utilities

Bibliographic utilities have as their main resource a huge database of catalog-type records. Access to the database is available for a price, and members of the utility can contribute new records and download existing ones.

Databases maintained by bibliographic utilities are essentially online union catalogs. Bibliographic utilities acquire many machine-readable cataloging records from the Library of Congress and other subscription sources. The databases also include cataloging records contributed by participating libraries. In either case, the records contain two kinds of information: 1) descriptive cataloging and classification data, typically in the USMARC format; and 2) holdings information for libraries that have added specific items to their collections.

Bibliographic utilities were organized in the 1970s to support library technical services operations through cooperative cataloging and computer-assisted card production. Although they have steadily expanded their activities, their continued emphasis on cooperative cataloging most clearly distinguishes them from other online information services that provide access to similar surrogate records. The Library of Congress MARC records, for example, are available online through the DIALOG and WILSONLINE search services, but neither of those vendors offers online entry of original cataloging data, record editing, or other services that specifically support cataloging services.

The four major bibliographic utilities discussed here are:

- OCLC—Online Computer Library Center—largest and most comprehensive

- RLIN—Research Libraries Information Network—especially important for special collections

- WLN—Western Library Network—serves western North America, and its software is used in Australia, Canada, and other places

- ISM/LIS—Information Systems Management/Library Information Services—serves Canada and a few customers in the northeastern United States

Bibliographic utilities differ in their administrative structures and customer bases. OCLC, RLIN, and WLN operate as not-for-profit membership organizations. ISM/LIS (formerly UTLAS) operates as a for-profit company. OCLC, WLN, and ISM/LIS are general-purpose bibliographic utilities that are available to libraries of all types and sizes. Although RLIN was specifically created to meet the special needs of research institutions, participation is open to other types of libraries. OCLC and RLIN offer services to all libraries all over the world. WLN's customer base is restricted to western North America. ISM/LIS is found mostly in Canada, with a few customers in northeastern United States. OCLC encourages participation through regional networks that act as its authorized agents.

More than three-fourths of the customers of bibliographic utilities are OCLC participants. Customers are libraries and other organizations that may access bibliographic utilities through one or more terminals installed at their own facilities. More and more customers gain access through the Internet. Although it is typical for organizations to subscribe to a single bibliographic utility, some libraries employ one utility for current cataloging and another for retrospective conversion, resource sharing, or other activities. Many large libraries are full members of RLIN or OCLC and at the same time are "tape loading" members of the other. (A tape loading member sends a magnetic tape containing all records cataloged through the primary utility to the other utility.)

Bibliographic utilities are specifically designed to automate cataloging. If existing cataloging copy is available, it is displayed in the full MARC format. The terminal operator can move, change, delete, or otherwise edit individual field values to meet local cataloging requirements (called *copy* cataloging). If no cataloging copy is available, the cataloger may create a record (called *original* cataloging). To facilitate cataloging decisions and promote consistency, bibliographic utilities provide online access to the Library of Congress Name Authority and Subject Authority files. OCLC and RLIN offer online access to these on a search-only basis. WLN and ISM/LIS create linkages between a library's cataloging records and their associated authority records so that unauthorized forms are automatically changed to authorized forms or are called to the attention of the cataloger before they can be added to the database.

Products still include the production of cards as well as records entered into online catalogs. All have Interlibrary Loan (ILL) subsystems, which are an obvious use of a union catalog. A variety of retrospective conversion products are offered as well.

CONCLUSION

This chapter has discussed the major retrieval tools used in the organization of recorded information. The surrogate records that make up a retrieval tool must be created and encoded. Chapters 4 through 8 address creating records for retrieval tools. But first, in the next chapter, a historical look at the development of organizing processes through a number of centuries serves to give us a perspective on where we are and how far we've come.

NOTES

1. *Publication Manual of the American Psychological Association*, 4th ed. (Washington, D.C.: APA, 1994).

2. *Chicago Manual of Style*, 14th ed. (Chicago: University of Chicago Press, 1993).

3. Walter S. Achtert and Joseph Gibaldi, *The MLA Style Manual* (New York: Modern Language Association of America, 1985).

4. *Scientific Style and Format: The CBE Manual for Authors, Editors, and Publishers*, 6th ed. (Cambridge, England; New York: Cambridge University Press, 1994).

5.   Kate L. Turabian, *A Manual for Writers of Term Papers, Theses, and Dissertations*, 6th ed. (Chicago: University of Chicago Press, 1996).

6.   U.S. Government Printing Office, *Style Manual* (Washington, D.C.: GPO, 1984).

7.   Daphne Muse, ed., *The New Press Guide to Multicultural Resources for Young Readers* (New York: New Press; distributed by W. W. Norton, 1997).

8.   David Gilson, *A Bibliography of Jane Austen* (Winchester, England: St. Paul's Bibliographies, 1997).

9.   Mustafa Aydn and M. Nail Aikan, *An Extensive Bibliography of Studies in English, German, and French on Turkish Foreign Policy, 1923–1997* (Ankara, Turkey: Ministry of Foreign Affairs, Center for Strategic Research, 1997).

10.   Barbara J. Horwitz, *British Women Writers, 1700–1850: An Annotated Bibliography of Their Works and Works About Them* (Lanham, Md.: Scarecrow Press, 1997).

11.   Ria Koopmans-de Bruijn, *Area Bibliography of Japan* (Lanham, Md.: Scarecrow Press, 1998).

12.   David Farrell, *The Stinehour Press: A Bibliographical Checklist of the First Thirty Years* (Lunenburg, Vt.: Meriden-Stinehour Press, 1988).

13.   John McIlwaine, *Maps and Mapping of Africa: A Resource Guide* (New Providence, N.J.: Zell, 1997).

14.   Charles A. Cutter, *Rules for a Dictionary Catalog*, 4th ed. (Washington, D.C.: Government Printing Office, 1904; reprint, London: The Library Association, 1962), p. 12.

SUGGESTED READINGS

Cleveland, Donald B., and Ana D. Cleveland. "The Nature and Types of Indexes." Chap. 3 in *Introduction to Indexing and Abstracting*. 2nd ed. Englewood, Colo.: Libraries Unlimited, 1990.

Inventories and Registers: A Handbook of Techniques and Examples. Chicago: Society of American Archivists, 1976.

Levy, David M. *Cataloging the Digital Order*. Available: http://www.csdl.tamu.edu/DL95/papers/levy/levy.html (Accessed October 1998).

Library of Congress Web Site. *Manuscript Finding Aids*. Available: gopher://
    marvel.loc.gov/11/research/reading.rooms/manuscripts

"Report of the Working Group on Standards for Archival Description." *American Archivist* 52 (Fall 1989): 440–61.

Wynar, Bohdan S. *Introduction to Cataloging and Classification*. 8th ed. by Arlene G.
    Taylor. "Cataloging in Context." Chap. 1. "Processing Centers, Networking,
    and Online Systems." Chap. 26. Englewood, Colo.: Libraries Unlimited,
    1992.

CHAPTER 3

DEVELOPMENT OF THE ORGANIZATION OF RECORDED INFORMATION IN WESTERN CIVILIZATION[1]

I t is often said that you can't tell where you're going until you know where you've been. This chapter looks at where we've been and addresses these questions: How did we arrive at this state of organization? What basic principles of organization have been developed over the last several centuries? Practices and ways of organizing that we now take for granted were once thought of for the first time by intelligent and serious scholars, just as we are coming up with innovative ideas for today's organization that will be taken for granted in the next century.

INVENTORIES, BIBLIOGRAPHIES, CATALOGS, AND CODIFICATION

Antiquity

One of the oldest lists of books we know about appears on a Sumerian tablet found at Nippur from about 2000 B.C.E. Sixty-two titles are recorded on this tablet of which twenty-four are titles of currently known literary works. We don't know what purpose the list served. Its use may or may not have resembled that of a catalog. However, the fact that the Sumerians were indefatigable writers makes it hard to believe that they had no catalogs. They seem to have kept everything: history books, medical prescriptions, love poems, business invoices, school children's homework assignments, and the first-known letter home from a student who threatens to drop out of school unless his parents fork over more money for a suitable wardrobe.

Through the archaeological discoveries of excavations of ancient civilizations, we know that tablets and other resources were used to inscribe titles of books, but we don't know for what purpose. They might have been ownership tags (e.g., the ones that had the names of the king and queen and a title on each small plaque), or they might have been relics of something like a bibliography or a catalog. There are more remnants of early records from Babylonia than from Egypt, probably due to the fact that Babylonians wrote on clay tablets, while Egyptians wrote on papyrus.

Around 1500 B.C.E. the Hittites evidently saw the need to convey bibliographic information as part of a written work. Their tablets bore colophons that identified the number of the tablet in a series, its title, and often the name of the scribe. (A *colophon* is a set of data at the end of a "document" that gives varying kinds of bibliographic data. It might give information usually found on a title page, and, in items after the invention of printing with moveable type, it gives such information as date of printing, printer, typeface used, etc.)

Around 650 B.C.E. people in the city of Nineveh had developed a library in which they seem to have taken great care to preserve order and authenticity. The "documents" bore elaborate colophons, but there is no evidence of anything like a catalog.

Two of the great libraries of antiquity were in Pergamum and Alexandria—two active centers of Greek civilization. Later writings have referred to *Pinakes* from both libraries. Pinakes is the plural of *pinax*, meaning a tablet with wax in the middle. If this was indeed the medium, it is no wonder that no remnants have survived. Writers have quoted from the Pinakes of Alexandria, which was created by Callimachus. The work may have been a catalog, or it may have been a bibliography of Greek literature. Callimachus has been given credit as being the first cataloger of whom we have knowledge. For more information about Callimachus's work, see: Rudolf Blum, *Kallimachos: The Alexandrian Library and the Origins of Bibliography* (Madison, Wis.: University of Wisconsin Press, 1991).

There are a few generalizations about bibliographic practices of the time that can be drawn from quotations of scholars who quoted from Callimachus's work. For example, a few general categories were considered to be a sufficient subject approach. Callimachus's subjects were epic and other nondramatic poetry, drama, law, philosophy, history, oratory, medicine, mathematical science, natural science, and miscellanea. A scholar would go to the general subject and then look for the author being sought. The arrangement of entries under the general subject was sometimes classified, sometimes chronological, and sometimes alphabetical, although the Greeks never arrived at a strictly alphabetical arrangement. They sometimes grouped entries by initial letter, but there are no examples of arrangement by any letter past the first one. This probably indicates that their lists were not nearly as long as ours.

Greek civilization seems to have given us the basis for our Western idea that "main entry" ought to be "the author." This kind of entry has not appeared in any work that has survived from early Eastern civilizations. Even today in Asian countries the traditional entry for a book is its title. One Japanese librarian of my acquaintance once observed that the principle of author entry goes along with democracy, since it rests upon belief in the importance of the individual.

Little information is available about Roman libraries. From sources that mention Roman libraries, there is evidence that there was some way of finding a designated book when it was requested. This was probably through "fixed location." One story goes that if a nobleman got into an intellectual argument, he would send a servant to the library to retrieve a certain book that would prove his point.

Middle Ages

We know that during the Middle Ages in Europe there were church and monastery libraries. There was no demand for books, and knowledge was not sought in any way that would require the use of catalogs. Through copying by monks, a system was set up by which the monastery became the sole keeper, manufacturer, and finally, lister of books through many centuries.

One of the earliest listings of the holdings of a medieval library was dated in the eighth century. It was written on the final flyleaf of a book and consisted of a list of brief titles with authors added to some of them. It probably served as an inventory record and may have represented the shelf arrangement, although there were no location symbols accompanying the titles. This list was typical of most of the so-called catalogs of the following centuries—the briefest sort of inventories recorded in the most casual places.

From the ninth through the thirteenth centuries the libraries continued to produce lists that seemed to be inventories. One list, which specified that its purpose was for inventory, stated that the library contained 246 volumes. It would be quite unrealistic to expect libraries of this size to feel any need for catalogs. Even after libraries grew to the size of 600 or 700 volumes, lists were still inventories. Occasionally such a list would use author entries, but in no discernible order. A few listed works contained in each volume, and the number of volumes to a work. (Books into which works were copied were often bound blank pages. Works were copied into them in the order in which the scribe picked them up. Several works could be copied into one bound blank volume, but it might take several bound volumes to copy a very long work.) In a few lists there was a subject arrangement, but it was very broad, often using only two categories: Biblical and Humanistic. At least one list from the thirteenth century added some unusual descriptions in designating books variously as "useless," "legible," "old," and "good," but we do not know whether they were used as an aid in identification for inventory or to help the reader by pointing out which books could be easily read.

Toward the end of the thirteenth century, someone whose identity is not known started a project that might be considered a milestone in the history of catalogs. This was the compilation of the *Registrum Librorum Angliae*, a union list of holdings of English monastery libraries in which, in a quite modern way, each library was assigned a number for coding purposes. The *Registrum* was never finished. There are evidences of later attempts to compile continuations of it, although no finished version has survived.

European Renaissance

The fourteenth century brought some improvements, and a few lists of this period might be called shelflists. The outstanding list of the fourteenth century is from St. Martin's Priory at Dover, dated 1389. In fact, it may be the first of the lists that could be justly designated a catalog. It is divided into three sections. The first is a listing by call number, a number representing fixed location even to the placing of the individual volume. The second section of the catalog, likewise arranged by call number, gives the contents of each volume, with the paging and opening words for each work included. The third part is a landmark in the development of cataloging: a catalog of analytical entries and an alphabetical listing, but with entries of the usual medieval type—some under author, others under title followed by author, with still other entries beginning with such words as *book*, *part*, or *codex*, obviously with no importance attached to the entry word. (An analytical entry is an entry made for each of the works in a volume, as opposed to making only one entry for the entire volume.)

College libraries began in the fourteenth century but did not bring any innovations to the development of bibliographic control. The earliest lists from college libraries revert to the primitive inventories of the preceding centuries. This is possibly explained by the fact that college library book collections were small; it was not unusual for a college library at that time to have only one hundred books.

The main new practice from the fifteenth century was the use of cross references. In one catalog, the cross references were not separate entries but were appended to a sort of contents note pointing out in what other place in the library a certain item might be found (e.g., "which seek in the 96th volume of theology"). In the catalog of St. Augustine's Abbey, Canterbury, though, cross references reached the status of separate entries. A typical example is "The Meditations of Bernard, not here because it is above in the Bible which was given by W. Wylmynton."

In the middle of the fifteenth century came an event that challenged everything about bibliographic control—the invention of printing. Suddenly, instead of unique manuscript copies of works, there were identical duplicates of many works. A new breed of people came into being for the task of listing the works available—people we might now call "bibliographers."

Toward the close of the fifteenth century, the German bibliographer and librarian Johann Tritheim stands out as having taken an important step in the development of bibliographic control. He not only compiled a bibliography in chronological order, which was unusual enough for his time, but he also appended to this an alphabetical author index. It is difficult to understand why such a simple and useful device had not always been used; yet it took centuries of compiling book lists to reach this degree of accomplishment.

From Inventories to Collocating Devices

Following the precedent set by Tritheim, bibliographers in the sixteenth century continued to take the lead in making improvements. One of these, Konrad Gesner, published an author bibliography in 1545 and a subject index in 1548, and in the process set a new standard of excellence. He continued to use forenames of authors for entry words, according to the tradition of the time, but he recognized the possible inconvenience of this practice and so he prefixed to his bibliography an alphabetical list of authors in which the names were inverted. In addition his main listing included cross references from variant spellings of names to the accepted entry form (e.g., Thobias, see Tobias). Gesner included in his work (titled the *Pandectarum*) the suggestion that libraries use copies of his bibliographies as their catalogs by inserting call numbers beside entries that represented their holdings, thus providing themselves with both an author and a subject catalog. This proposal, remember, was made in 1548.

In 1595, Andrew Maunsell, an English bookseller, compiled his *Catalog of English Printed Books* and in the preface stated his rules for entry. He advocated the entry of personal names under surnames rather than forenames. He set up the principle of uniform entry for the Bible, which, prior to Maunsell's collocating them, had been entered under whatever the title page said (e.g., Holy Bible, The Word of God, Bible, etc.). He insisted that one should be able to find a book under all three—the author's surname, the subject, and the translator. These were radical and sudden advances in the development of bibliographic control.

By the beginning of the seventeenth century, catalogs were begin-ning to be looked upon as finding lists rather than inventories. Early in the cen-tury Sir Thomas Bodley offered to build up the Oxford University Library, which had been destroyed by fire some fifty years before. Bodley took a great interest in the catalog because he expected that it would be useful in his acquisi-tions program; he wanted the catalog to tell him if the library already owned a work. He insisted upon a classified catalog with an alphabetical author index arranged by surname, and he also wanted analytical entries.

In 1697 Frederic Rostgaard published a discourse on cataloging in which he called for subject arrangement subdivided at once chronologically and by size of volume. For the preceding century, size of volume had been a traditional way of dividing catalogs. He proposed a printed catalog, with the spread of two facing pages divided into four parallel columns, each column to contain books of a certain size, arranged so that books of various sizes that had been published on a certain subject within the same year would come directly opposite each other in parallel columns. He recommended an alphabetical in-dex of subjects and authors to be placed at the end of the catalog, with authors entered by surname. The word order of titles as found on the title page was to be preserved. His final suggestion was that his rules not be followed when it seemed best to arrange things differently.

As the eighteenth century began, bibliographic control seemed to have hit a plateau that did not change for most of the century. Catalogs were sometimes classified and sometimes alphabetical; indexes were considered use-ful, though by no means necessary; some catalogs were still divided according to the size of books; authors were now always entered under surname and were often arranged chronologically; the wording of the title page had assumed a certain degree of prestige and was now being transcribed literally and without being paraphrased; imprints were included; bound-with notes were used; cross references were quite common; and some analytical entries were used in most catalogs.

In 1791, though, following the French Revolution, the new French government sent out instructions for cataloging the collections of the libraries that had been confiscated throughout the country. Here we have the first instance of a national code. Libraries were directed to make card catalogs—apparently the first appearance in history of the card catalog. It was introduced, not because someone thought it would be a convenient form, but because, with wartime shortages, it was a practical way of getting available materials. Confis-cated playing cards were to be used for the purpose—aces and deuces were to be reserved for the longest titles. (Playing cards of the time were blank on the back, rather than having pictures. They were also larger than today's cards.) There was no theory or philosophizing in this code. The title page was to be transcribed on the card and the author's surname underlined for the filing word. If there was no author, the keyword in the title was to be underlined. A collation was added that was to include number of volumes, size, a statement of illustration, the material of which the book was made, the kind of type, any missing pages, and a description of the binding if it was outstanding in any way. (This elaborate collation was partly for the purpose of identifying valuable books that the government might offer for sale in order to increase government revenue.) After the cards were filled in and put in order by underlined filing word, they were to be strung together by running a needle and thread through the lower left corners to keep them in order.[2] Here we have a number of procedures that have continued to the present. This code, coming at the end of the eighteenth century, makes a good stepping-stone to the extensive cataloging developments of the nineteenth century.

Period of Codification

The nineteenth century brought a period of much argument over the relative virtues of classified and dictionary catalogs, not only among librarians, but also among readers and scholars in general and even in reports to the House of Commons of Great Britain. Feelings ran very high on the subject, and rather emotional arguments were made: "from the statement that classified catalogs and indexes were not needed because living librarians were better than subject catalogs, to the opinion that any intelligent man who was sufficiently interested in a subject to want to consult material on it could just as well use author entries as subject, for he would, of course, know the names of all the authors who had written in his field."[3]

What was needed was a person who could persuade others of the value of cataloging and subject analysis. Anthony Panizzi, a lawyer and a political refugee from Italy, was appointed assistant librarian at the British Museum in 1831. When he was appointed Keeper of the Printed Books in 1837, there was much objection. One history book states that it was because "firstly, Panizzi was an Italian by birth, and it was felt that only an Englishman should be in charge of one of our national institutions; secondly, it was said that Panizzi had been seen in the streets of London selling white mice."[4] No further explanation is given. Another writer, though, gives this account: "Meetings were held against the 'Foreigner' and one of the speakers made an open statement that Panizzi had been seen in the streets of London selling white mice: had it been a few years later, possibly the distinctive title of organ-grinder would have been added."[5]

In 1836 a committee of the House of Commons was charged with inquiry into the management and affairs of the British Museum. One of the "affairs" was the state of catalogs and cataloging. During hearings on the topic, witnesses came to testify for and against the catalogs. Many of the witnesses became quite vehement about this or that sort of entry. Panizzi was able again and again to persuade the committee members to accept his views.

Panizzi wrote his views into a cataloging code known as the "91 Rules" and gained official approval for it in 1839, although he had to give up his concept of "corporate main entry" in order to get approval. Panizzi's code shows that we had at last arrived at "modern" cataloging, because he tried to deal with many of the same problems we are still arguing about today.

Halfway through the nineteenth century, cataloging in the United States began to warrant attention. Until this time American cataloging had been generally a century behind European cataloging. For example, of the three catalogs printed at Harvard, one had been divided into three alphabets according to the size of books; all three contained only very brief records; and none provided a subject approach.

In 1850 Charles C. Jewett published a code for the catalog of the Smithsonian Institution. With this code Americans began to have influence in cataloging. Jewett acknowledged his debt to Panizzi and varied in only a few instances from the instructions in the "91 Rules." Jewett is given credit for extending the principle of the corporate author further than Panizzi had. Research now shows that Jewett copied these rules word-for-word from Panizzi's original draft, which had had *more* than 91 rules.[6] Panizzi had been forced to drop his rules for entry under corporate author. So what Jewett actually did was to bring the concept of corporate authorship to public attention.

Jewett's philosophy of the purpose of a code was this: "*Uniformity* is, then, imperative; but, among many laborers, can only be secured by the adherence of all to rules embracing, as far as possible, the minutest details of the work."[7] In light of this philosophy, it is interesting to observe that the second edition of Jewett's rulebook contains only thirty-nine rules in fifty-eight pages.

When Charles Cutter published his *Rules for a Printed Dictionary Catalogue* in 1876, he strengthened the concept that catalogs not only should point the way to an individual publication, but should also assemble and organize literary units. That is, they should be collocating devices. This was not an entirely new principle: Maunsell had used the heading "Bible"; Panizzi had strengthened it by introducing corporate and government entries; and Jewett had given further support by use of real names rather than pseudonyms. But it was Cutter who actually stated it as a formal principle.

Cutter was also the first to make rules for subject headings as a way to gain subject access to materials through the catalog. And he was the last to incorporate into one set of rules instructions for the description of items, guidelines for subject headings, and rules for filing entries. At the end of the nineteenth century, each of these areas (i.e., description, subject headings, and filing) took on lives of their own and followed separate paths of development.

We will now follow the first two paths separately. (Filing arrangement is discussed in chapter 9.)

TWENTIETH CENTURY

Description

In the area of description the twentieth century has been an era of codes. The British and the Americans collaborated on a code in 1908. Its importance lies in its being the first international cataloging code, and in the extent of its rapid and widespread adoption and use by all types and sizes of libraries in the two countries.

In the 1920s four prominent American librarians helped with writing the Vatican Code, which was published in Italian in 1931. It was quickly accepted by catalogers in many countries as the best and most complete code in existence, but because it was in Italian, most Americans could not use it.

The British and Americans cooperated on a new edition of the 1908 code in the 1930s, but the outbreak of war ended this cooperation. The American Library Association (ALA) proceeded independently in producing its preliminary second edition in 1941. This code was published in two parts: one for entry and heading, and one for description of books. It was widely attacked on the grounds of complexity and too extensive enumeration of cases. The most famous attack was that of Andrew Osborn in his article entitled "The Crisis in Cataloging."[8] It is one of the classic statements in cataloging theory, and certainly, one of the historical turning points in code development.

In response to all the criticism, the ALA Division of Cataloging and Classification undertook revision of the first part (entry and heading) of the 1941 code. In 1949 the revision was published as the *A.L.A. Cataloging Rules for Author and Title Entries*. The Library of Congress (LC) *Rules for Descriptive Cataloging* was substituted for the second part (description of books) of the 1941 rules. The ALA portion of the 1949 rules again was criticized as being a continuation of Osborn's "legalistic" characterism. In 1951 ALA commissioned Seymour Lubetzky to do a critical study of cataloging rules. Lubetzky said cataloging should be done according to principles, and he drafted a code based on principles. It was welcomed by progressives, but conservatives began worrying about probable costs of changes.

An International Conference on Cataloging Principles was held in Paris in 1961, at which a draft statement of principles, based on Lubetzky's code, was submitted. The international participants agreed to adopt these principles and to work in their various countries for revised rules that would be in agreement with the accepted principles. These principles, often referred to as the *Paris Principles* (or *IFLA Principles*) are important because we had, for the first time, multinational agreement upon which to base future international developments.

The Americans and the British again cooperated on a new set of cataloging rules, and in 1967 published the *Anglo-American Cataloging Rules* (although it had to be published in separate North American and British versions because of inability to come to agreement on a few points).

In 1974 the International Federation of Library Associations (IFLA) issued the *International Standard Bibliographic Description* (*ISBD*), produced as a means for the international communication of bibliographic information. *ISBD*'s objectives were to make records from different sources interchangeable, to facilitate their interpretation against language barriers, and to facilitate the conversion of such records to machine-readable form.

AACR2, the second edition of the *Anglo-American Cataloguing Rules*, was published in 1978 to incorporate *ISBD*, to bring nonbook materials into the mainstream, to take into account machine processing of bibliographic records, and to reconcile the British and American texts. Four major national libraries (United States, Canada, Great Britain, and Australia) agreed to standard interpretation and implementation of *AACR2*, and many other countries have now adopted it for national use. A revised edition of *AACR2* was published in 1988 (*AACR2r*).

Subject Access

Verbal Subject Access

For centuries philosophers worked on classifying knowledge; Callimachus, Plato, Aristotle, and Bacon are among the most famous. Librarians tried to adapt these classifications for books by assigning letters and/or numbers to the concepts classified by the philosophers. Other than this, there was not much interest in subject access in libraries until Cutter. As already mentioned, Cutter included a section of guidelines for subject headings in his *Rules for a Dictionary Catalog*.

The *A.L.A. List of Subject Headings* was first published in 1885, and the preface stated that it was to be considered an appendix to Cutter's *Rules for a Dictionary Catalog*. It was based on headings found in five major catalogs of the time, including the Boston Athenaeum and the Harvard subject index. A second revised edition was published in 1905 with the statement that "further changes are not to be expected for many years."[9] However, new terminology became necessary rapidly, and interleaved and annotated editions became unwieldy. Many librarians asked for the list of subject headings that were appearing on

LC cards, and so in 1914 the first edition of *Subject Headings Used in the Dictionary Catalogues of the Library of Congress* was published. The title was changed to *Library of Congress Subject Headings (LCSH)* in 1975. *LCSH* has appeared in twenty editions in its printed version, with a new edition every year beginning in 1988, but it is changed daily in its online version.

The *Sears List of Subject Headings (Sears)* was first published in 1923 as *List of Subject Headings for Small Libraries*. It was prepared by Minnie Earl Sears in response to demands for a list of subject headings that was more suitable to the needs of the small library than the ALA or the LC lists. Recognizing the need for uniformity, Ms. Sears followed the form of the LC subject headings—she eliminated the more detailed ones and simplified some terminology. *Sears* continues to be published for small libraries and is now in its sixteenth edition in print. A CD-ROM version is updated quarterly.

Classification

Meanwhile, classification had developed at LC from arrangement by size in the early 1800s to arrangement by the eighteen broad categories of the Bacon-d'Alembert system in 1814 when the Library burned. To reestablish it, Jefferson sold Congress his library, which was classified using forty-four main classes based on his interpretation of the Bacon-d'Alembert system. By the end of the century it was clear that the rapidly growing collection needed more detail in classification.

Melvil Dewey, in 1876, issued anonymously the first edition of his classification. He divided all knowledge into ten main classes, with each of those divided again into ten divisions, and each of those divided into ten sections—giving one thousand categories into which books could be classified. Like its predecessors, it was enumerative in that it listed specific categories one by one. In later editions he added decimals so that the one thousand categories could be divided into ten thousand, then one hundred thousand and so on. He also introduced the first hints of "number building," or "faceting," when he made tables for geographic areas and for forms of material. (*Faceting* comprises small notations that stand for subparts of the whole topic and are strung together to create a complete classification notation. This is discussed further in chapter 8.) Notations from these tables could then be added in numerous places to show a certain subject category as being relevant to a particular geographic area.

When LC decided it must improve over Jefferson's classification, Dewey Decimal Classification was in its fifth edition, and Cutter had begun his own enumerative classification scheme, called the *Expansive Classification*. This scheme began with letters of the alphabet, expanded with second letters, and then expanded further with numbers. LC representatives talked with Dewey to convince him to allow them to adapt his scheme, but ran afoul of his intransigence. They did not adopt Cutter's classification directly, but created their own based upon his model.

The Universal Decimal Classification (UDC) was developed in 1885 by two Belgian lawyers, Paul Otlet and Henri LaFontaine. UDC was based on the DDC (then in its fifth edition), but was, with Dewey's permission, expanded by the addition of detailed subdivisions and the use of signs to indicate complex subjects. Why Otlet and LaFontaine were able to get Dewey's permission when LC was not is unclear; but it may have been because UDC was not at the outset intended as a library classification, but as a means to organize documents (see more about this below). UDC expanded Dewey's "standard subdivisions" to about a dozen generally applicable "auxiliaries," which could be joined together as needed in the form we now call "faceting."

During the twentieth century faceted classification has become of interest because it allows the classifier to express all aspects of an interdisciplinary subject in the same classification notation. The term was first used with this meaning by S. R. Ranganathan in his Colon Classification (called "Colon" because of its use of the punctuation mark "colon" as a major facet indicator) in the early 1930s. As mentioned earlier, Dewey had already provided for some "number building," and Library of Congress Classification (LCC) even included a few such facets (although developed only class by class and not applicable through the entire scheme). Ranganathan introduced the fully faceted approach by means of classification notations constructed entirely from individual facets in a prescribed sequence from the most specific to the most general.

Special Materials

Archives

U.S. developments in bibliographic control of special materials (i.e., archives, museums) have nearly all come in the twentieth century. European archival practice stemmed from working with public archives (e.g., land grants, laws, etc.). Archival materials were kept because of legal and other administrative value. The concept of *provenance* emerged in France about 1840, and the concept of *original order* came from the Prussians shortly thereafter.[10] As in libraries, the first archival catalogs were lists and then inventories. In early archival practice in the United States, material was collected for its artifactual value. It was often cataloged at the item level without any concern for provenance or original order. Thus, the context in which the archival record was originally created was lost. This practice lasted in the United States through the mid-1930s, when European ideas began to influence U.S. practice and when the National Archives and the Society of American Archivists were formed. Early cataloging codes in the United States (e.g., Cutter, *AACR*) dealt with cataloging manuscripts, but at the item level. In 1983 publication of *Archives, Personal Papers, and Manuscripts (APPM)* brought the library and archival traditions together. *APPM* is based on *ISBD* and *AACR2*, but also includes archival principles. A special MARC format was developed (called MARC-AMC). It has now been incorporated with the other special MARC formats in the process of "format integration."

Museums and Art Galleries

As in libraries and archives, museums began first with lists and later expanded to include inventories. Museum documentation is the idea that guides cataloging of art and artifacts. It is a system that provides an indispensable record of information associated with objects for research. Museums are just beginning to join the library and archives communities in codification of descriptive practice. The Internet has spurred this action because of the sudden demand from researchers for access to pictures and textual descriptions of artifacts and art. Although museums and art galleries still do not have standard means for creating surrogate records, libraries with these kinds of collections use *AACR2*'s chapter for cataloging realia and then enter these descriptions into a MARC format.

Subject Access to Special Materials

Subject access to special materials follows the needs of the user communities. For verbal subject access, archivists use *LCSH* and the *Art & Architecture Thesaurus (AAT)*. The museum community has developed specialized lists and thesauri (often called *lexicons*). Museums also use the *AAT*. Archives do not lend themselves to classification. Some collections of art and artifacts are classified, however. Some natural history museums classify specimens of organisms that can be identified to the genus and species level. Two other examples include the American Museum of Natural History, which uses Romer's classification of vertebrae, and art collections with Christian iconographic themes that use ICONCLASS, developed in the Netherlands.

Mechanization of Bibliography

Automation first entered the organization of information picture in the 1870s when the typewriter was introduced into libraries. Typewriters were highly controversial at first because they were so noisy. Many libraries were one-room affairs with the cataloger sitting at a table in the back. Patrons, who had been used to the quiet of the cataloger creating handwritten cards, found the clacking of the typewriter annoying. Some librarians objected, too, because typed cards were not esthetically pleasing compared to cards written in "library hand," a method of writing in which the letters were carefully formed to be completely readable.

The Documentation Movement

The trend to mechanize bibliography began with the Documentation Movement in Europe in the 1890s. The nineteenth century brought the development of professional organizations and the growth of scientific research, both of which created a dramatic increase in the number of published journals. Paul Otlet and Henri LaFontaine spearheaded a movement for bibliographic control in libraries to go beyond books to provide access to parts of books, articles in journals, research documents, brochures, catalogs, patents, government records, archives, photographs, and newspapers. The goal of the Documentation Movement was to capture, record, and provide access to all information in all formats for the improvement of science.

A conference organized by Otlet and LaFontaine was held in Brussels in 1892, with its focus on the creation of Universal Bibliographic Control (UBC). The magnitude of the undertaking necessitated an entirely new body of techniques different from conventional library practice for organization, subject analysis, bibliographic description, and annotation. This quest for new techniques of bibliographic control naturally led to a search for new technology. The concept of Documentation was transported to the United States in the 1930s, and in 1937 the American Documentation Institute was formed. In 1938 the International Federation for Documentation was established and was devoted almost exclusively to the promotion of Universal Decimal Classification (UDC). From its inception, UDC was not intended as a library classification, but rather as a means to organize and analyze *documents*.

An important technological advance for the Documentation field was the development of microphotography by Eastman Kodak in 1928. This was seen as a means of collecting, storing, and accessing vast quantities of information, and it was predicted that microfilm would supplant the conventional book.

World War II had an impact on the mechanization of bibliographic control in two ways. First, it created an immediate scientific information explosion, since the U.S. government's imperative was to "get the bomb first." Scientific research was conducted rapidly and in secrecy, with a critical need for immediate dissemination of research results from lab to lab. This heightened the government's awareness of the need for bibliographic control and brought with it government funding to develop a mechanized process. Second, as the outcome of the war shifted in favor of the Allies, huge quantities of German scientific literature were confiscated. This material needed immediate bibliographic control in order to be useful. Microfilms were made and distributed through a committee attached to the Office of Strategic Service. The distribution was under the direction of Frederick Kilgour. At the same time the Central Information Division of the Office of Strategic Service was working on the subject analysis of documents using IBM punched card equipment. The war itself was the impetus for many technological advances; some of these advances could now be applied to organizing and accessing the hoards of scientific and technical literature that also were an outgrowth of the war.

In 1945 Vannevar Bush opened the way for a new era in documentation and information science with his article "As We May Think." Bush developed the idea of *memex*, a "device in which an individual stores all . . . books, records and communications, and which is mechanized so that it may be consulted with exceeding speed and flexibility."[11] Using the medium of microfilm (in 1945, remember), Bush described in detail the hypertext-based scholar's workstation of today. Memex was based on the concept of *associative indexing*, similar to human thought process, where items are linked together and any item can immediately lead to the access of other related information. Bush even predicted new forms of encyclopedias where information could be coded and connected to pertinent articles. A man of vision, Bush believed that science should implement the ways in which we produce, store, and consult the record of the human race.

The 1950s and 1960s saw many and varied attempts at mechanization using the current technology. Calvin Mooers coined the phrase "information retrieval" in 1950. He and other information scientists of the day, such as Ralph Shaw and Mortimer Taube, worked on developments such as the "Rapid Selector," designed to provide subject access to microfilm by a method that used holes punched in the sides of the film. Another technique used a knitting-type needle to access subjects on punched cards. Taube was especially concerned with the linguistic problems of documentary analysis and retrieval.

In 1957 *Sputnik*, the first artificial satellite launched into space from Earth, pushed information needs to the forefront of the scientific community once again. There was increased interest in improving access to recorded knowledge in both the government (National Science Foundation, National

Library of Medicine, Library of Congress, etc.) and the private sector (IBM, General Electric, Kodak, RAND Corp., etc.). The field of Documentation became the field of Information Science with a great deal of money made available for research and development. The 1960s saw a period of tremendous technological advances in communication and information processing. The computer became established as the means of storing massive amounts of data and providing high-speed access. In 1968 the American Documentation Institute changed its name to the American Society for Information Science (ASIS). By this time the use of machines for the retrieval of information was solidly entrenched in the Information Science community, a community that had developed quite separately from libraries until this point.

Library Automation

In the late 1960s two developments changed the face of bibliographic control forever. At the Library of Congress, Henriette Avram engineered the creation of the MARC format, enabling the machine readability of bibliographic records. And Fred Kilgour began OCLC as its first director. To the astonishment of all who knew him, he left his position as Associate Director of the Yale University Library to create and run the Ohio College Library Center. He had a vision and the ambition to carry it out. With the development of the MARC format, OCLC was able to provide cataloging information via cable and terminal to all its member libraries, who in turn were able to put their original cataloging online for the use of all other members. In 1977 another major network came into being particularly to serve research libraries—the Research Libraries Information Network (RLIN).

CONCLUSION

We see here the coming together of the information science track and the library science track that had previously developed separately. There seems often to be a very wide gulf between information science and library science (e.g., jokes are cracked about information science being library science for men), but both are interested in and working on the organization of information, as we see in the chapters that follow.

NOTES

1. Much of the material in the first half of this chapter is based on Ruth French Strout, "The Development of the Catalog and Cataloging Codes," *Library Quarterly* 26, no. 4 (October 1956): 254–75.

2. Joseph Smalley, "The French Cataloging Code of 1791: A Translation," *Library Quarterly* 61, no. 1 (January 1991): 1–14.

3. Strout, "The Development of the Catalog. . .," p. 268.

4. Dorothy May Norris, *A History of Cataloging and Cataloging Methods* (London: Grafton, 1939), p. 206.

5. Louis Fagan, *The Life of Sir Anthony Panizzi*, 2nd ed., reprint (New York: Burt Franklin, 1970), p. 134. (Originally published 1880.)

6. Personal communication with Michael Carpenter.

7. Charles Coffin Jewett, *On the Construction of Catalogues of Libraries, and Their Publication by Means of Separate, Stereotyped Titles*, 2nd ed. (Washington, D.C.: Smithsonian Institution, 1853), p. 18.

8. Andrew Osborn, "The Crisis in Cataloging," in *Foundations of Cataloging: A Sourcebook*, ed. Michael Carpenter and Elaine Svenonius (Littleton, Colo.: Libraries Unlimited, 1985), pp. 90–103. Also available in *Library Quarterly* 11, no. 4 (October 1941): 393–411.

9. *A.L.A. List of Subject Headings*, 2nd ed., rev. (Boston: American Library Association Publishing Board, 1905), vi.

10. Ernst Posner, "Some Aspects of Archival Development Since the French Revolution," *American Archivist* 3, no. 2 (April 1940): 159–72, especially pp. 167–68.

11. Vannevar Bush, "As We May Think," available: http://www.ps.uni-sb.de/~duchier/pub/vbush/ Section 6, paragraph 4. (Accessed October 13, 1998). Also available in *Atlantic Monthly* 176 (July 1945): 101–8.

SUGGESTED READINGS

Baker, Nicholson. "Discards." *New Yorker* 70, no. 7 (April 4, 1994): 64–86.

Berner, Richard C. "Historical Development of Archival Theory and Practices in the United States." *Midwestern Archivist* 7, no. 2 (1982): 103–17.

Burke, Frank G. "Archives: Organization and Description." In *World Encyclopedia of Library and Information Services*, pp. 63–68. 3rd ed. Chicago: American Library Association, 1993.

Bush, Vannevar. "As We May Think." Available: http://www.ps.uni-sb.de/ ~duchier/pub/vbush/ (Accessed October 13, 1998). Also available in *Atlantic Monthly* 176 (July 1945): 101–8.

Dunkin, Paul S. "Mr. Cutter's Catalog." Chap. 1 and "The Prophet and the Law: Codes After Cutter." Chap. 2 in *Cataloging U.S.A.* Chicago: American Library Association, 1969.

Fishbein, Meyer H. "Archives: Records Management and Records Appraisal." In *World Encyclopedia of Library and Information Services*, pp. 60–63. 3rd ed. Chicago: American Library Association, 1993.

Harris, Michael H. *History of Libraries in the Western World*. 4th ed. Metuchen, N.J.: Scarecrow Press, 1995.

Humbert, de Romans. *Regulations for the Operation of a Medieval Library*. St. Paul, Minn.: Associates of the James Ford Bell Library, University of Minnesota, 1980.

Jackson, Sidney L. *Libraries and Librarianship in the West: A Brief History*. New York: McGraw Hill, 1974.

Lancaster, F. W. "Whither Libraries? or Wither Libraries." *College & Research Libraries* 39, no. 5 (September 1978): 345–57; reprinted in *College & Research Libraries* 50, no. 4 (July 1989): 406–19.

Osborn, Andrew D. "The Crisis in Cataloging." In *Foundations of Cataloging: A Sourcebook*, edited by Michael Carpenter and Elaine Svenonius, pp. 90–103. Littleton, Colo.: Libraries Unlimited, 1985.

Reynolds, Dennis. "History: The Public Catalog." Chap. 4 in *Library Automation: Issues and Applications*. New York: Bowker, 1985.

Strout, Ruth French. "The Development of the Catalog and Cataloging Codes." *Library Quarterly* 26 (October 1956): 254–75.

Taylor, Arlene G. "Cataloguing." In *World Encyclopedia of Library and Information Services*, pp. 117–81. 3rd ed. Chicago: American Library Association, 1993.

Wynar, Bohdan S. *Introduction to Cataloging and Classification.* 8th ed. by Arlene G. Taylor. "Development of Cataloging Codes." Chap. 2. Englewood, Colo.: Libraries Unlimited, 1992.

CHAPTER 4

ENCODING STANDARDS

The problems addressed in this chapter are: How and why do we encode surrogate records (metadata) for machine manipulation? As mentioned at the end of chapter 2, surrogate records in a bibliographic tool must be coded for machine manipulability if they are to be placed into an online database. This chapter addresses several ways to encode records: MARC (MAchine-Readable Cataloging) is one standard that has been used for coding library catalog records for three decades. SGML (Standard Generalized Markup Language) has come into use in the last decade for encoding text and has been adapted for encoding surrogate records. HTML (HyperText Markup Language) and other SGML applications are widely used on the WWW.

In the minds of many in the profession, metadata content and encoding for the content are inextricably entwined. Metadata records can be created by first determining descriptive content and then encoding the content, or one can start with a "shell" comprising the codes and then fill in the contents of each field. In this text encoding standards are discussed before covering creation of content. The same content can be encoded with any one of several different encoding standards and some metadata standards include both encoding and content specification. Creation of metadata content is covered in chapter 5.

HOW DO WE ENCODE RECORDS?

Surrogate records are encoded by assigning tags, numbers, letters, or words (i.e., codes) to discrete pieces of information. For example, a personal author name is given the tag "100" in MARC coding, or in HTML, it is preceded with "<author>" and is followed with "</author>."

WHY DO WE ENCODE RECORDS?

Surrogate records have to be coded in order to be able, first, to provide for display. Encoding allows for the setting off of each part of the record (called a *field*). Computer programs can then be written so that each field will display in a certain position according to the wishes of those creating the display. For example, when the MARC code 100 is used to identify a name of a person who is the author of an information package, that author's name can be displayed at the top of the record or after the title, and can have a label or not.

A second use for encoding is to provide for access to the surrogate record. In a similar manner to the manipulation of the display, encoding enables the creation of searching programs that will allow the searching of certain fields. If a user wishes to search only for personal authors, the MARC code 100 and the code 700 identify those fields as personal author fields, and the system will not have to search the rest of the record during the search for a personal author.

A third use for encoding is to allow integration of many languages and scripts to be displayed and searched in the same file. Institutions that participate in organizing recorded information collect information in many languages and many scripts. Languages that are in the roman script have always been able to be interfiled, although filing them alphabetically was sometimes a problem. Languages in other scripts had to be "romanized" in order to interfile them in the paper world. Online, however, if the display of other than roman scripts is provided for, the coding allows for identification of the fields of the surrogate record regardless of the knowledge of the human doing the organizing.

WHAT ARE EXAMPLES OF STANDARDS FOR CODING RECORDS THAT ARE CURRENTLY IN USE?

Recently a proliferation of encoding standards has erupted. The examples discussed here are:

- MARC (MAchine Readable Cataloging)
  - USMARC (United States MARC)
  - UNIMARC (UNIversal MARC)
- SGML (Standard Generalized Markup Language)
  - DTD (Document Type Definition)
    - → TEI (Text Encoding Initiative)

> ➜ HTML (HyperText Markup Language)
>
> ➜ EAD (Encoded Archival Description) DTD
>
> ➜ MARC DTD

- XML (Extensible Markup Language)

MARC (MAchine Readable Cataloging)

The MARC communications format (see fig. 4.1 on page 60) is used for transmitting data from one system to another. It has a leader, directory, control fields, and variable fields. The leader is somewhat like the leader on a roll of film. It identifies the beginning of a new record and contains a few codes that identify, among other things, the kind of information package that is being described. The record directory contains a series of fixed length (twelve characters) segments that identify the field tag, length, and starting position of each field in the record. The MARC directory was a major contribution to the information science world. Instead of fixed length fields only, which was common in databases in the 1960s, the directory allowed variable length fields, now common in most databases.

Control fields carry alphanumeric data elements, whose field tags begin with the digit 0. Several of the control fields have subfields that are fixed in length. Control fields are used for such data as classification numbers, LC control numbers, and codes for time and place covered in the information package being described. Some control fields are called fixed fields; one of these (field 008) is often called *the* "fixed field" and is displayed quite differently from other fields. Variable fields carry alphanumeric data of variable length. These fields contain traditional cataloging data.

When records are received in the MARC communications format, each system displays records according to its own programming. OCLC and RLIN put the "fixed field" at the top and use abbreviations to interpret the codes; but they do not use the same abbreviations as each other. LC puts the "fixed field" in the 008 field position, and uses no abbreviations or separations. Local systems have a "technical services" display that is quite different from utilities' displays, and public catalog displays do not include the "fixed field" at all. System displays also vary in such things as spacing before and after subfield codes, placement of indicators, etc. (see figs. 4.2, 4.3, and 4.4, on pages 61 and 62).

00723cam 22002418a 45000010013000000080041000130050017000540100018000710200027260005200284300003640033650040064001220050002600135082001700161100002000178245007400198250001200272600012002843000036504006400370650004100434| 97002718 |970417s1997   ilua   b   001 0 eng |1997112813465.1| $a 97002718 | $a0838907075 (acid-free paper)| $aDLC$cDLC|00$aZ699.35.M28$bH34 1997|00$a02 5.3/16$221|1 $aHagler, Ronald.|14$aThe bibliographic record and information technology /$cRon ald Hagler.| $a3rd ed.| $aChicago :$bAmerican Library Association,$c1997.| $axvi, 394 p. : $bill. ;$c24 cm.| $aIncludes bibliographical references (p. 375-380) and index.| 0$aMachine- readable bibliographic data.#

Fig. 4.1. Record in the MARC communications format.

```
001    97002718
003 DLC
005 19971128134653.1
008 970417s1997    ilua       b    001 0 eng
010    $a    97002718
020    $a0838907075 (acid-free paper)
040    $aDLC$cDLC$dDLC
050 00$aZ699.35.M28$bH34 1997
082 00$a025.3/16$221
100 1 $aHagler, Ronald.
245 14$aThe bibliographic record and information technology /$cRonald Hagler.
250    $a3rd ed.
260    $aChicago :$bAmerican Library Association,$c1997.
300    $axvi, 394 p. :$bill. ;$c24 cm.
504    $aIncludes bibliographical references (p. 375-380) and index.
650    0$aMachine-readable bibliographic data.
```

Fig. 4.2. Formatted display of the record in fig. 4.1, as displayed by the Library of Congress.

```
   OCLC:   36909449             Rec stat:     p
   Entered:      19970417       Replaced:     19980225     Used:      19980421
 > Type:   a    ELvl:           Srce:         Audn:        Ctrl:        Lang:  eng
   BLvl:   m    Form:           Conf:  0      Biog:        MRec:        Ctry:  ilu
                Cont:   b       GPub:         Fict:  0     Indx:  1
   Desc:   a    Ills:   a       Fest:  0      DtSt:  s     Dates: 1997,      <
 >  1   010      97-2718 <
 >  2   040      DLC $c DLC <
 >  3   020      0838907075 (acid-free paper) <
 >  4   050  00  Z699.35.M28 $b H34 1997 <
 >  5   082  00  025.3/16 $2 21 <
 >  6   090      $b  <
 >  7   049      DD0A <
 >  8   100  1   Hagler, Ronald. <
 >  9   245  14  The bibliographic record and information technology / $c Ronald
Hagler. <
 > 10   250      3rd ed. <
 > 11   260      Chicago : $b American Library Association, $c 1997. <
 > 12   300      xvi, 394 p. : $b ill. ; $c 24 cm. <
 > 13   504      Includes bibliographical references (p. 375-380) and index. <
 > 14   650   0  Machine-readable bibliographic data. <
```

Fig. 4.3. Formatted display of the record in fig. 4.1, as displayed by OCLC.

```
LTCI DONE                                                   ASB9899
                                            NOTIS CATALOGING
L15C
C1 FMT B RT a BL m T/C   DT 09/08/97 R/DT none    STAT cc E/L 8 DCF a D/S D
SRC    PLACE ilu LANG eng MOD    T/AUD    REPRO    D/CODE s DT/1 1997 DT/2
CONT b    ILLUS        GOVT    BIOG    FEST 0 CONF 0 FICT 0 INDX 1

010:   : |a    97002718
020/1:   : |a 0838907075 (acid-free paper)
035/1:   : |9 (E1)ARM8006
039:   : |a (lcb)97002718
040:   : |a DLC |c DLC
050/1:00: |a Z699.35.M28 |b H34 1997
082/1:00: |a 025.3/16 |2 21
100:1 : |a Hagler, Ronald.
245:14: |a The bibliographic record and information technology / |c Ronald
Hagler.
250:   : |a 3rd ed.
260:   : |a Chicago : |b American Library Association, |c 1997.
263:   : |a 9707
300/1:   : |a p. cm.
504/1:   : |a Includes bibliographical references and index.
650/1: 0: |a Machine-readable bibliographic data.
```

Fig. 4.4. Formatted display of the record in fig. 4.1, as displayed in the technical services version of the NOTIS cataloging subsystem at the University of Pittsburgh.

     Control and variable fields have tags, indicators, subfield codes, and field terminators. Tags are three-digit numbers (from 001 to 999) designating the kind of field. The first digit designates a broad grouping. For example the first digit "1" designates a "main heading field." A convention is followed in which all fields beginning with a certain digit, let's say 6, are identified as a group, in this case designated 6xx. 6xx fields are, in general, subject access fields (e.g., 600 is for a personal name used as subject; 610 is for a corporate name used as subject; 650 is for a topical subject, etc.). Fields with tags beginning with 7 are 7xx fields, that is, additional access points.

     Indicators consist of numbers following a tag. (In USMARC there are two indicator positions for each variable field. UNIMARC has three.) These positions contain coded information interpreting or supplementing the data in the field. They are independent of each other. An example in USMARC is the indicators for the 245 (title) field. The first indicator is supposed to tell whether a title added entry is called for. This is a holdover from card days when an additional card for title was not made when the title was the main entry. In most cases now, it really functions as an indicator of whether a title should be the main entry for the record (0=yes; 1=no). The second indicator tells how many characters (counting a blank as one character) should be skipped over to get to the first filing character. For example, for an English title beginning with "the" the second indicator is "4." Some fields do not need indicators, in which case one or more of the indicators may be identified as being "blank."

A subfield code consists of a delimiter and a letter or number that follows the delimiter. It indicates which subfield of a field is coming up. The purpose of subfield codes is to identify elements in a field that might require separate treatment. The delimiters that begin a subfield code show the "limit" of a particular subfield; that is, they are unique characters that indicate the beginning of a particular subfield (the character has a specified ASCII identification [the code "1F(16)"], but it is represented differently depending on the system: ‡ or $ or |, for example). The lowercase letter or number is a data element identifier. For example, in a title a subfield "a" identifies the title proper, and a subfield "b" identifies the subtitle or other title information. The letters and numbers have different meanings from field to field. The following are subfield codes: ‡a, ‡b, ‡2, etc.

The field terminator is a special character that follows the last data element in the field. As with the delimiter, the field terminator may be displayed in different ways or it may not be displayed at all. It is necessary that it be there, however, because the fields are variable length, and it is essential, when programming for display, to be able to tell the computer where one field ends and another begins.

USMARC

USMARC was developed at the Library of Congress (LC) in 1968. It was identified simply as MARC until other versions were developed, and then it was called LC-MARC. Finally, the name USMARC has come to distinguish it from the more than twenty other national versions (e.g., CAN/MARC, UKMARC, DenMARC, etc.).

USMARC is based on ANSI standard Z39.2, *American National Standard for Bibliographic Information Interchange* (1971, revised 1985).[1] The international version is ISO 2709: 1996, *Information and Documentation—Format for Information Exchange*.[2] The United States (USMARC) and Canada (CAN/MARC) have agreed on a "harmonized" format for the two countries. The harmonized USMARC and CAN/MARC formats will be published in a single edition in 1999 under a new name: MARC 21 (the name is meant to point both to the future and to the international character), and is to be considered a continuation of both formats in one edition. A next step will be to attempt harmonization with the British version (UKMARC).

USMARC actually has formats for five types of data. The following formats are currently defined:

- bibliographic format—for encoding bibliographic data in records that are surrogates for information packages

- authority format—for encoding authority data collected in authority records created to help control the content of those surrogate record fields that are subject to authority control

- holdings format—for encoding data elements in holdings records that show the holdings and location data for information packages described in surrogate records

- community information format—for encoding data in records that contain information about events, programs, services, etc., so that these records can be integrated with bibliographic records

- classification data format—for encoding data elements related to classification numbers, the captions associated with them, their hierarchies, and the subject headings with which they correlate.

UNIMARC

UNIMARC (UNIversal MARC) was developed in 1977 as a vehicle for interchange of MARC records between national bibliographic agencies. It conforms to ISO 2709, as does USMARC. The proliferation of national MARC formats necessitated development of UNIMARC. At first it was thought that UNIMARC would act as a conversion format. In this capacity it requires that each national agency create a translator to change records from UNIMARC to the particular national format and vice versa. When a translator is in place, records can be translated to UNIMARC to be sent to other countries, and records received from other countries can be translated from UNIMARC to the national format. In addition to this use, a few national agencies that did not already have a MARC format have adopted UNIMARC as the standard in their countries. UNIMARC has been adopted by the countries of the European Community in order to produce "unified catalogues."

Some ways that UNIMARC differs from USMARC are that UNIMARC uses the ISO character set instead of USMARC's ALA character set; UNIMARC allows for embedded fields (e.g., an authority record number may appear at the beginning of an access point field); and it deemphasizes "main entry."

SGML (Standard Generalized Markup Language)

SGML is an international standard for document markup and conforms to ISO 8879:1986, *Information Processing—Text and Office Systems—Standard Generalized Markup Language (SGML).*[3] It is a set of rules for designing markup languages that describe the structure of a document so that documents may be interchanged across computer platforms (both text and markup are in ASCII). It allows documents to be represented in such a way that text may be separated from structure without using a word processor. "Structure" means that the coding says: this is the title; this is the 1st chapter; this is a section heading; this is a paragraph; this is a quoted statement, etc. SGML is flexible enough to define an infinite number of markup languages. In the case of a surrogate record, the structure might be: this is an author; this is the title; this is the physical description; this is a subject; etc.

SGML defines data in terms of elements and attributes. An element is a particular unit from the text such as a title, a chapter title, a section heading, or a paragraph. An attribute gives particular information about an element (e.g., giving the name of the thesaurus from which a subject term has been taken). SGML prescribes markup that consists of delimiters and tags. Delimiters are defined symbols (e.g., <, >, </, "), and are used to construct tags (e.g., <author> is a tag). Tags usually appear before and after an element in the form: **<tag>element</tag>** (e.g., <author>Edward Gaynor</author>). Attribute values are delimited by "..." or '...' (e.g., <quote lang='spa'>¿Que pasa?</quote>). Tags may be nested. This is similar to MARC subfields. An example of a nested set of tags from TEI (described below) is: **<fileDesc> <titleStmt> <title>...</title> <author>...</author></titleStmt> <publicationStmt>...</publicationStmt> </fileDesc>**

DTD (Document Type Definition)

A DTD is an SGML application. It is created by following the rules for markup found in the SGML standard. A DTD defines the structure of a particular *type* of document; that is, it defines:

- all elements that might be part of that particular document type
- element names and whether they are repeatable
- in what order the elements should be placed
- the contents of elements (in a general way, not specifically)
- what kinds of markup can be omitted

- tag attributes and their default values
- names of permissible entities

A DTD may be created for only one document, in which case it may be contained at the beginning of the text, but creating a DTD is time-consuming. It makes more sense to create DTDs that can be used for many documents. Such DTDs exist separately from the texts that refer to them. It is also possible to have a customized DTD that uses a DTD that has been created for wide application; this is done by having a declaration at the beginning of a document that defines the tag sets that will be used. An SGML-conforming document must tell which external DTD is being used, or it must have an internal DTD just for that document.

Many DTDs have been created and are in general use. A few of these will be discussed below as examples. They are:

- TEI—DTD for encoding literary texts
- HTML—DTD for encoding web pages
- EAD DTD—DTD for encoding archival finding aids
- MARC DTD—DTD for encoding USMARC records

TEI (Text Encoding Initiative). The TEI DTD was created to overcome the difficulty of the multiple encoding schemes that were being used to encode old, literary, and/or scholarly texts. Once encoded, the documents could not be exchanged easily. TEI makes it possible to make features of a text explicit in a format that allows the processing of that text by different programs running on different machines. The text can be represented exactly as it appears in its original printed form (in the case of encoding text from books). Texts can be exchanged for research purposes (e.g., textual analysis).

TEI can also be used for newly created documents, especially in cases where authors have a particular vision of how the text should look. TEI was originally created for texts in the humanities but is no longer limited to humanities texts. The guidelines provide a framework that can be used to describe many kinds of texts. TEI Lite[4] is a subset of TEI in much the same way as XML is a subset of SGML (see discussion of XML below). TEI Lite may be considered to contain a "core" set of tags from TEI. The structure of the first part of a TEI Header is shown below. For an example of a completed TEI Header, see figure 4.5 on page 68.

```
<teiHeader>
  <fileDesc>
    <titleStmt>...</titleStmt>
    <editionStmt>...</editionStmt>
    <extent>...</extent>
    <publicationStmt>...</publicationStmt>
    <seriesStmt>...</seriesStmt>
    <notesStmt>...</notesStmt>
    <sourceDesc>...</sourceDesc>
  </fileDesc>
  <! -- remainder of TEI Header here -- >
</teiHeader>
```

HTML (HyperText Markup Language). The HTML DTD was developed to enable the creation of web pages. It is a basic markup language that allows almost anyone to be a web author. It provides for creation of simple structure, enables display of images, and provides for establishing links between documents. Users of an HTML-encoded document can navigate through the text itself if internal links have been made, or can move from one text to another with external links. In HTML 4.0 there are specific provisions for META elements that can be used to describe properties of a document (e.g., author, expiration date, a list of keywords, etc.), making it possible to encode Dublin Core metadata (see discussion in chapter 5). For an example of an HTML-encoded document, see figure 4.6 on page 69.

EAD (Encoded Archival Description) DTD. The EAD DTD is a scheme for archival and library finding aids—primarily inventories and registers. As with other DTDs it does not specify intellectual content but defines the encoding designations. The EAD eases the ability to interchange finding aids among institutions, and it allows users to find out about collections in distant places. For an example of an EAD-encoded document, see figure 4.7 on pages 70–71.

MARC DTD. There is more than one MARC DTD because it was not possible to include all five USMARC formats in the same DTD. The MARC DTDs treat the MARC record as a particular type of document. They define all the elements that can appear in a MARC record and specify how they will be tagged and represented with SGML coding. A goal of development of the MARC DTDs was that MARC records should be translatable to SGML automatically, and that an SGML-encoded MARC record should be easily translated back to a MARC record. One of the features that makes this possible is that each field of an SGML-encoded record contains all the tags, indicators, and subfield codes of the MARC field in addition to the contents of the field. For an example of an SGML-encoded MARC record, see figure 4.8 on page 72.

Text continues on page 73.

```
<html>
<head>
<title>Finding Aid</title>
</head><teiHeader>
```

```
<fileDesc>
<titleStmt>
<title>The Child in the House: An Electronic Edition</title>
<author>Walter Pater</author>
<sponsor><name id="CETH">Center for Electronic Texts in the Humanities (CETH)</name></sponsor>
<respStmt><resp>Digitized, proofed, edited and encoded in TEI SGML by </resp>
<name id="piez">Wendell Piez</name></respStmt>
</titleStmt>
<extent>6200 words in <gi>text</gi>; approximately 41K bytes uncompressed.</extent>
<publicationStmt>
<distributor><address><addrLine><name>Center for Electronic Texts in the
Humanities</name></addrLine><addrLine>169 College Avenue</addrLine>
<addrLine>New Brunswick NJ 08903</addrLine></address></distributor>
<availability><p id="ch0.01">Freely available for non&dash;commercial use when distributed with this header
intact.</p></availability>
<date value="1995">November 1995</date>
</publicationStmt>
<sourceDesc><bibl id="MS"><author>Walter Pater</author><title>Miscellaneous Studies</title>
<edition>Library Edition</edition>
<pubPlace>London</pubPlace>
<publisher>Macmillan and Co.</publisher><date value="1910">1910</date></bibl>
</sourceDesc>
</fileDesc>
```

```
<encodingDesc>
<projectDesc><p>This text is prepared as a dual&dash;purpose TEI pilot: to implement the TEI Lite DTD with SoftQuad
Author/Editor and WordPerfect 6.1 SGML edition SGML&dash;aware editors running on a PC platform); and to assess
application of the TEI preparatory to developing documentation for TEI markup procedures.</p></projectDesc>
<tagsDecl><rendition>The TEI tag <gi>sic</gi> appears where a doubtful reading occurs in the Library Edition and may
be rendered with its &lsquo;corr&rsquo; [correction] attribute in square brackets. The <gi>foreign</gi> tag appears for
foreign words printed in Italics in the original text, and can be so rendered.</rendition></tagsDecl>
<refsDecl><p id="ch0.05">The text of &ldquo;The Child in the House&rdquo; is designated with the unique ID
&lsquo;ch&rsquo; to distinguish it from other works of Pater in a Collected Electronic Edition. The paragraphs of this
text are designated with ID attributes, providing unique identifying codes, in the form &lsquo;chX.Y&rsquo;, where X is
0 (for paragraphs in the header) or 1 (for paragraphs in the text body), and Y is the Arabic number of the paragraph.</p><p
id="ch0.06">Empty <gi>pb</gi> [page break] elements also appear at the beginning of every page occurring in the
Library Edition. The &lsquo;ed&rsquo; attribute is specified as MS (MS designating the volume <title>Miscellaneous
Studies</title>in the Library Edition); the appropriate page number appears as the &lsquo;n&rsquo; attribute, with a code
in the form &lsquo;MS.N&rsquo; appearing as the &lsquo;id&rsquo; attribute. This information is encoded so as to
provide external references to the most commonly available complete print edition of Pater's works, and not strictly for
encoding of cross&dash;references within an electronic edition; for these, the forementioned paragraph coding, or an
extension of it, may be used.</p></refsDecl>
</encodingDesc>
```

```
<profileDesc><langUsage><language id="Eng">British English</language>
<language id="Deu">German</language>
<language id="Fra">French</language>
<language id="La">Latin</language></langUsage>
</profileDesc>
```

```
</teiHeader>
```

Fig. 4.5. TEI Lite encoded record. TEI Lite coding is in bold. (This is only the Header of a TEI-encoded document.)

```
<body bgcolor=#ffffe8 background="./yellow.jpg">
<center><h1>Heinz House Papers</h1></center>
<center><h2>Finding Aid</h2></center>
<br>
<ul>
<li> <a href="Scope.html">Scope and Contents Note</a><p>
<li> <a href="Arrangement.html">Arrangement of the Heinz House Papers</a><p>
<li> <a href="Description.html">Description of the Heinz House Papers</a><p>
<ul><li> <a href="Subgroup+I/">Subgroup I.</a>   Legislative Records -- 16.7 lin. ft.<p>
<li> <a href="Subgroup+II/">Subgroup II.</a>   Personal/Political Records -- 7.3 lin. ft.<p>
<li> <a href="Subgroup+III/">Subgroup III.</a>   Press Relations/Media Activity Records -- 4.7 lin. ft.<p>
<li> <a href="Subgroup+IV/">Subgroup IV.</a>   Constituent Service Records -- 25.6 lin. ft.<p>
<li> <a href="Subgroup+V/">Subgroup V.</a>   Office Administration Records -- 0.3 lin. ft.</ul><p>
<li> <a href="Appraisal.html">Appraisal and Sampling Note</a><p>
<li> <a href="Appendices.html">Appendices</a></ul>
<p>
<hr>

<FONT SIZE=-1>Updated February 1997 / http://www.library.cmu.edu/Guide/Heinz/<br>
Edward A. Galloway, Heinz Archivist,
<a href="mailto:eg2d@andrew.cmu.edu">eg2d@andrew.cmu.edu</a>
<p>
<b>
<a href="http://www.library.cmu.edu/Guide/Heinz/">H. John Heinz III Archives</a>
<p>
<a href="/">Carnegie Mellon University Libraries</a></font></b>
</p>
</body>
</html>
```

Fig. 4.6. HTML-encoded document. HTML encoding is in bold.

```
<!DOCTYPE EAD PUBLIC "-//Society of American Archivists//DTD ead.dtd (Encoded
Archival Description (EAD))//EN"[
<!ENTITY cutspec Public  "-//University of California, Berkeley::Library//TEXT
(CU union table specifications)//EN"  "cutspec.sgm">
<!ENTITY hdr-cu-s-spcoll PUBLIC  "-//University of California, San
Diego::Mandeville Special Collections Library//TEXT (eadheader: name and
address)//EN"  "hdrcussp.sgm">
<!ENTITY tp-cu-s-spcoll PUBLIC "-//University of California, San
Diego::Mandeville Special Collections Library//TEXT (titlepage: name and
address)//EN"  "tpcussp.sgm">
<!ENTITY ucseal PUBLIC  "-//University of California, Berkeley::Library//NONSGML
(University of California seal)//EN"  NDATA GIF>]>

<?Pub Inc>
<ead>
<?Pub Caret>

<eadheader audience="internal"  langencoding="ISO 639" findaidstatus="unverified-full-draft">
<eadid type="SGML catalog">

PUBLIC  "-//University of California, San Diego::Mandeville Special Collections
Library//TEXT (US::CU-S::MSS 0401::Arthur Conan Doyle. Sign of the four.)//EN"
"MSS 0401.sgml"
</eadid><filedesc><titlestmt>
<titleproper>Arthur Conan Doyle Sign of the four</titleproper>
</titlestmt>

<publicationstmt>
&hdr-cu-s-spcoll;<date>&copy; 1997</date>
<p>The Regents of the University of California. All rights reserved.</p>
</publicationstmt></filedesc>

<profiledesc>
<creation>Machine-readable finding aid derived from database output.</creation>
<langusage>Description is in <language>English.</language></langusage>
</profiledesc>
</eadheader>

<frontmatter>
<titlepage>
<titleproper>Arthur Conan Doyle Sign of the four, 1890</titleproper>
<num>MSS 0401</num>
<publisher>Mandeville Special Collections Library<lb>GEISEL LIBRARY<lb><extptr
displaytype="present"  entityref="ucseal"><lb>UNIVERSITY OF CALIFORNIA, SAN DIEGO
<lb>La Jolla, CA  92093-0175</publisher>
<p>&copy; 1997 The Regents of the University of California. All rights reserved.</p>
<date>This file last updated: August 1997.</date>
</titlepage>
</frontmatter>
```

```
<findaid>
<archdesc language="en" level="collection" langmaterial="en">
<did>
<head>DESCRIPTIVE SUMMARY</head>
<unittitle label="Title">Arthur Conan Doyle. Sign of the four.,
<unitdate type="inclusive">1890</unitdate></unittitle>
<unitid label="Collection number">MSS 0401</unitid>

<physdesc label="Extent">0.10 linear feet (1 item (1 leaf) in one folder.)</physdesc>

<repository label="Repository"><corpname>Mandeville Special Collections Library,
Geisel Library, UC, San Diego</corpname><address><addressline>La Jolla, CA
92093-0175</addressline></address></repository>
<unitloc label="Shelf Location">For current information on the location of these
materials, please consult the Library's online catalog.</unitloc>
</did>
<admininfo>
<head>ADMINISTRATIVE INFORMATION</head>

<prefercite>
<head>Preferred Citation</head>
<p>Arthur Conan Doyle. Sign of the four., MSS 0401.  Mandeville Special
Collections Library, UCSD.</p>
</prefercite>

</admininfo>

<bioghist>
<head>BIOGRAPHY</head>
<p>British novelist and physician.</p>
</bioghist>

<scopecontent>
<head>SCOPE AND CONTENT</head>
<p>The first leaf of the manuscript of the Sherlock Holmes novel, with
holograph corrections and printer's notations.  Glued to backing. </p>
</scopecontent>
</archdesc>
</findaid>
<ref>http://roger.ucsd.edu/search/t?ucsd MSS 401 </ref>
</ead>
```

Fig. 4.7. EAD-encoded finding aid. EAD coding is in bold.

```
<USMARC Material="BK" ID="00000008"><Leader><LRL>00825</LRL><RecStat>n</RecStat>
<RecType>a</RecType><BibLevel>m</BibLevel><UCP></UCP>
<IndCount>2</IndCount><SFCount>2</SFCount><BaseAddr>00265</BaseAddr>
<EncLevel></EncLevel><DscCatFm></DscCatFm><LinkRec></LinkRec> <EntryMap>
<FLength>4</Flength><SCharPos>5</SCharPos><IDLength>0</IDLength>
<EMUCP></EMUCP></EntryMap></Leader>
<Directry>001001400000005001700014008004100031010001400072035002000086
035001700106100003100123245005600154260003600210300003300246490004200279
500002100321504002900034265000200037165000220039183000430041395000320045 69
500032004889500032005209980007005 52</Directry>
<VarFlds><VarCFlds><Fld001>CUBGGLAD1288B</Fld001> <Fld005>19940818092701.0</Fld005>
<Fld008>830810 1982    mau            eng u</Fld008></VarCFlds> <VarDFlds><NumbCode>
<Fld010 I1="Blank" I2="Blnk"><a>81016136 </a></Fld010>
<Fld035 I1="Blank" I2="Blnk"><a>(CU)ocm07925067</a></Fld035>
<Fld035 I1="Blank" I2="Blnk"><a>(CU)GLAD1288</a></Fld035>
<Fld090 I1="Blank" I2="Blnk"><a>QA267</a><b>.S29 1982</b></Fld090></NumbCode>
<MainEnty><Fld100 NameType="Single" I2=""><a>Savitch, Walter J.,</a><d>1943-
</d></Fld100></MainEnty>
<Titles><Fld245 AddEnty="Yes" NFChars="0"><a>Abstract machines and grammars /</a><c>Walter J.
Savitch</c></Fld245></Titles>
<EdImprnt><Fld260 I1="" I2="Blnk"><a>Boston :</a><b>Little, Brown,</b>
<c>c1982</c></Fld260></EdImprnt>
<PhysDesc><Fld300 I1="Blank" I2="Blnk"><a>xiv, 215 p. :</a><b>ill. ;</b>
<c>24 cm</c></Fld300></PhysDesc>
<Series><Fld490 Traced="Differnt" I2="Blnk"><a>Little, Brown computer systems
series</a></Fld490></Series>
<Notes><Fld500 I1="Blank" I2="Blnk"><a>Includes indexes</a></Fld500><Fld504 I1="Blank"
I2="Blnk"><a>Bibliography: p. 206-207</a></Fld504></Notes>
<SubjAccs><Fld650 SubjLvl="NoInfo" SubjSys="LCSH"><a>Machine theory.</a></Fld650><Fld650
SubjLvl="NoInfo" SubjSys="LCSH"><a>Formal languages.</a></Fld650></SubjAccs>
<AddEnty></AddEnty><LinkEnty></LinkEnty>
<SAddEnty><Fld830 I1="Blank" NFChars="0"><a>Little, Brown computer systems
series.</a></Fld830></SAddEnty>
</VarDFlds></VarFlds></USMARC>
```

Fig. 4.8. SGML-encoded USMARC record. SGML coding is in bold.

XML (Extensible Markup Language)

XML is not a DTD but is instead a subset of SGML. As the web has grown, HTML has been criticized because it is too simplistic to provide for many desirable applications. Some thought for a while that full support of SGML on the web was the answer. However, SGML is fairly complex and has features that make the programming involved complicated and lengthy. Plug-ins were developed to supplement HTML, but they require the user to download the plug-in and install it. The programming language Java seemed promising for enhancement of HTML functionality, but a person has to be able to program to create a web page with it. XML has been developed as an answer to these problems. It omits many features of SGML and includes a method for reading non-ASCII text (e.g., Chinese). It implements UNICODE, of which ASCII is a subset.

One application that has been developed to use XML is RDF (Resource Description Framework). RDF is a specification or framework for creating metadata. RDF provides for more than one type of data (e.g., catalog type data; content ratings that indicate, for example, whether content is suitable for children; indication of intellectual property rights, etc.) to be included in the same metadata package. There is not yet a prescribed encoding for the Dublin Core (see discussion in chapter 5). But there is a group of people from the Dublin Core community who are working on representing the Dublin Core in RDF.

Warwick Framework

Each of the encoding standards discussed above is a kind of shell or container. The framework is there waiting for text to be inserted. The text to be inserted may be suggested in the encoding standard, or it may be controlled by another standard. For example, the text in a USMARC record is usually controlled by rules (e.g., *AACR2*) that follow the *International Standard Bibliographic Description* (*ISBD*) and the Paris Principles, and by the conventions of a thesaurus (e.g., *Library of Congress Subject Headings*) and a classification scheme (e.g., *Dewey Decimal Classification*); but there are some USMARC fields for which the rules for content appear in the USMARC standard (e.g., the USMARC field 007 gives specific codes for a "fixed field" for certain materials such as microforms or motion pictures). The combination of the encoding container and its text is called *metadata* or a *metadata record*.

The proposed Warwick Framework (named for the location of the conference where it was framed) might be considered to be a container for containers. It is described as a container architecture. As proposed it would be a mechanism for pulling together distinct packages of metadata that are related to the same information package, but that need to be separately controlled (e.g., *AACR2*/MARC record, Dublin Core record, EAD finding aid, all describing the same collection). This would help to avoid having to expand any one encoding container to include every possible piece of information needed by any specialized group of users. Each metadata package could be maintained by its respective community. In this way specific communities could focus on their specific requirements without having to generalize to the broadest scope possible.

Bringing together metadata records into the proposed Warwick Framework would allow for the interchange of data among different communities. It also would allow selective access to certain metadata records while ignoring others. Responsibility for the maintenance and updating of particular metadata records would remain with their original communities, while the information in them could be shared among all of the communities. At this writing the Framework has not been implemented, and it appears that the RDF is taking over the functions of the Warwick Framework, in which case the RDF may be implemented instead.

CONCLUSION

This chapter has discussed some of the ways of encoding surrogate record information to create metadata records. An understanding of this coding and how it is accomplished is necessary to an understanding of the systems in place today for the retrieval and display of various kinds of surrogate/metadata records. There are some separate standards for creation of the text that is to be included in surrogate/metadata records, and there are some standards that include both prescription of text and encoding in the same standard. These are discussed in the next chapter.

NOTES

1. *American National Standard for Bibliographic Information Interchange: Draft* (New York: American National Standards Institute, 1984). Revision of ANSI Z39.2-1979.

2. *Information and Documentation Format for Information Exchange*, 3rd ed. (Geneva, Switzerland: International Organization for Standardization, 1996). ISO 2709:1996(E).

3. *Information Processing: Text and Office Systems: Standard Generalized Markup Language* (SGML) (Geneva, Switzerland: International Organization for Standardization, 1988). ISO 8879:1986/A1:1988(E).

4.   Lou Burnard and C. M. Sperberg-McQueen, *TEI Lite: An Introduction to Text Encoding for Interchange* (June 1995), available: http://www-tei.uic.edu/orgs/tei/intros/teiu5.html, accessed October 1998.

SUGGESTED READINGS

Bryan, Martin. "An Introduction to the Extensible Markup Language (XML)." *Bulletin of the American Society for Information Science* 25, no. 1 (October/November 1998): 11–14.

Dougherty, Dale. "The XML Files." Available: http://www.webreview.com/97/05/16/feature/index.html (Accessed October 1998).

"Encoded Archival Description (EAD) DTD." Available: http://lcweb.loc.gov/ead/ (Accessed October 1998).

Gaynor, Edward. "From MARC to Markup: SGML and Online Library Systems." *ALCTS Newsletter* 7, no. 2 (1995): A–D.

Lagoze, Carl. "The Warwick Framework." *D-Lib Magazine* (July/August 1996). Available: http://www.dlib.org/dlib/july96/lagoze/07lagoze.html (Accessed October 1998).

Miller, Eric. "An Introduction to the Resource Description Framework." *Bulletin of the American Society for Information Science* 25, no. 1 (October/November 1998): 15–19.

National Center for Supercomputing Applications. "A Beginner's Guide to HTML." Available: http://www.ncsa.uiuc.edu/General/Internet/WWW/HTMLPrimer.html (Accessed October 1998. Last updated October 7, 1998).

"SGML." Available: http://jefferson.village.virginia.edu/iath/treport/sgml.html (Accessed October 1998. Last modified February 12, 1996).

Text Encoding Initiative. Available: http://www.uic.edu/orgs/tei/ (Accessed October 1998).

Thiele, Harold. "The Dublin Core and Warwick Framework: A Review of the Literature, March 1995–September 1997." *D-Lib Magazine* (January 1998). Available: http://www.dlib.org/dlib/january98/01thiele.html (Accessed October 1998).

"The USMARC Formats: Background and Principles." Prepared by MARBI (American Library Association's ALCTS/LITA/RUSA Machine-Readable Bibliographic Information Committee) in conjunction with Network Development and MARC Standards Office, Library of Congress. Washington, D.C.: Library of Congress, 1966. Available: http://lcweb.loc.gov/marc/96principl.html (Accessed October 1998).

Wynar, Bohdan S. *Introduction to Cataloging and Classification.* 8th ed. by Arlene G. Taylor. "Appendix A: Introduction to the MARC Formats." Englewood, Colo.: Libraries Unlimited, 1992.

CHAPTER **5**

METADATA: DESCRIPTION

As mentioned in the discussion of encoding standards, *metadata* has come to mean a complete record, including encoding, that describes and stands in place of a larger document or a collection in a bibliographic tool. Because it includes the encoding, the term is not often applied to records found in paper tools. Metadata has been defined in many places as "data about data." One computing dictionary gives a definition (April 1998) that says that **meta data** or **meta-data** "is definitional data that provides information about or documentation of other data managed within an application or environment. . . . Meta data may include descriptive information about the context, quality, and condition, or characteristics of the data."[1] The WWW community has already collapsed the two-word form and the hyphenated form into one word. The definition is accurate, though, in that it implies that metadata includes not only descriptive information such as that found in traditional retrieval tools, but also information necessary for the management and preservation of the information package being described (e.g., data about where the package is located, what its ownership relationships are, its quality and condition, etc.).

Loosely speaking, there are three parts to creating metadata for an information package: 1) encoding, 2) providing a description of the information package along with other information necessary for management and preservation of the package, and 3) providing for access to this description. Encoding was discussed in the preceding chapter. This chapter discusses description, and the next three chapters discuss access.

WHAT IS A BIBLIOGRAPHIC/SURROGATE/ METADATA RECORD?

Bibliographic record is the name that has been applied to the description of tangible information packages (e.g., books, sound recordings) for many years. Even though it has been applied to records created for motion pictures, sound recordings, computer files, etc., the word *bibliographic* has continued to have a stigma arising from *biblio-*, meaning "book." At times the term "surrogate record" has been used instead. A surrogate stands in place of someone or something else. The term can be used for records representing any kind of information package in any kind of information retrieval system. In this and following chapters, "surrogate record" is used to mean the description and access content of a metadata record.

Some definitions are in order before discussion of the creation of surrogate records. A *surrogate record* is a presentation of the characteristics of an information package. The characteristics include both descriptive data and access points. The record stands in place of (i.e., is a surrogate for) the information package in information retrieval systems such as catalogs, indexes, bibliographies, search engines, etc. An *information package* is an instance of recorded information (e.g., book, article, videocassette, Internet document or set of "pages," sound recording, electronic journal, etc.) *Descriptive data* is data derived from an information package and used to describe it, such as its title, its associated names, its edition, its date of publication, its extent, and notes identifying pertinent features. An *access point* is any term (word, heading, etc.) in a surrogate record that is used to retrieve that record. Access points are often singled out from the descriptive data and are placed under access control (also called authority control—see discussion in chapter 6).

A surrogate record serves as a filter to keep a user from having to search through myriad irrelevant full texts. Its most important function is to assist the user in evaluating the possibility that the information package that it represents will be useful. Surrogate record descriptions are most helpful when they are predictable in both form and content. Adherence to standards ensures such predictability. Some of the existing standards are discussed below.

HOW ARE SURROGATE RECORDS CREATED?

First, it is necessary to decide what the information package is that is to be described. Traditions have been established in the library world as to what constitutes a catalogable unit when dealing with tangible packages. The principle (greatly simplified) has been that one physical package is a catalogable unit with the caveat that packages that follow one another in succession and have the same title also may be a single unit. For example, this book is a single catalogable unit; each of its chapters is not. *The Works of Shakespeare in Two Volumes*, volume 1, is probably not a catalogable unit; volumes 1 and 2 together are a single unit. Packages that come in a set with the same overarching title (although each can also have its own title) also may be called a unit. For example, *Great Books of the Western World* is a set where each volume has its own (often famous) author and title. It might be cataloged as a single unit with multiple volumes, or each volume might be cataloged as a unit. Electronic resources have thrown that tradition into chaos. It can be very difficult to determine what is a "package" in the electronic environment. It could be a university's home page and everything linked to it, for example, or it could be the grading policy of one department. It is going to take time to sort this through; it may be that, given the ease of access to web pages now, a surrogate record can be created for any piece of information that someone determines needs metadata access.

Surrogate records are created by selecting important pieces of information (e.g., title, author, date, etc.) from an information package, determining certain characteristics about the package (e.g., size, terms of availability), and then placing those pieces of information in a certain order, usually dictated by a set of rules or conventions for description. These rules or conventions are created by different communities to fill the needs of those communities for descriptions of the information packages for which they are responsible. Discussed here are several examples of descriptive rules and conventions from different communities. Examples of surrogate record creation tools to be discussed are:

- *ISBD* (*International Standard Bibliographic Description*)
- *AACR2r* (*Anglo-American Cataloguing Rules, Second Edition, 1988 revision*)
- *APPM* (*Archives, Personal Papers, and Manuscripts*, 1989)
- TEI (Text Encoding Initiative) Headers
- Dublin Core
- GILS (Government Information Locator Service)
- FGDC (Federal Geographic Data Committee) Content Standard for Digital Geospatial Metadata (CSDGM)
- VRA (Visual Resources Association) Core Categories for Visual Resources
- EAD (Encoded Archival Description)

Some kinds of surrogates for which there are no nationally or internationally accepted rules or standards are also discussed:

- index records
- on-the-fly records
- museum accession records

ISBD (International Standard Bibliographic Description)[2]

The *International Standard Bibliographic Description (ISBD)* was designed in the early 1970s to facilitate the international exchange of cataloging records by standardizing the elements to be used in the description, assigning an order to these elements, and specifying a system of symbols to be used in punctuating the elements. When the *ISBD* was adopted as an international standard it was expected that national cataloging agencies would incorporate it into their national cataloging rules. It has been incorporated into several, including the *Anglo-American Cataloguing Rules, Second Edition, 1988 revision (AACR2r)*, which is discussed in more detail below.

ISBD requires that an information package be totally identified by the description, independent of any access points. It contains eight areas:

- Area 1—Title and statement of responsibility
- Area 2—Edition
- Area 3—Material (or type of publication) specific details
- Area 4—Publication, distribution, etc.
- Area 5—Physical description
- Area 6—Series
- Area 7—Notes
- Area 8—Standard number and terms of availability

Area 1 contains the title (called the title proper) assigned to the information package by persons responsible for its existence. There may be more than one title (e.g., same title in two languages, subtitle, etc.), and there may be other information necessary to the understanding of the title (e.g., information about the place and date of a conference, etc.). The statement of responsibility part of Area 1 contains the name(s) of person(s) or corporate bodies that are responsible for the intellectual content of the package (but not those responsible for its presentation and packaging).

Area 2 contains a statement about the version of the information package represented in the surrogate record being created. It might be a new edition of a work, a new version of a software package, or a version of a work that is put out for a particular geographic area (e.g., the city edition of a newspaper that serves a region). Area 2 also may contain a statement of responsibility, this one relating only to the package being described (e.g., a person who has worked on the edition in hand but did not work on earlier editions).

Area 3 contains data about an information package that is particularly important to a particular type of work (e.g., in describing serials, it is important to identify the date and the volume number of the first issue of the serial). An important point is that Area 3 is used only for some types of works, and this is determined by a specific implementation of *ISBD* in a particular national code.

Area 4 contains the name of the entity (e.g., publisher, institution, manufacturer, etc.) that is responsible for the presentation and packaging of the information package. There may be more than one such name. With the name also is given its geographic location and a date of public appearance of the package.

Area 5 contains a physical description of an information package that is in tangible form (i.e., one that can be "in-hand"). This does not include remote electronic resources. The physical description includes the extent of the item given in terms of what kind of item it is (e.g., 2 disks, 365 p., 4 videocassettes, etc.), the dimensions of the item (usually height, but also sometimes width, diameter, etc.), and other physical details such as information about illustrations or about material from which an object is made.

Area 6 contains the title of any series of which the information package is part. A series is a group of separate works that are related in subject or form and published by the same entity (e.g., Library and Information Science Text Series). There may also be information other than the series title. Series can have the same kinds of additional title information as the title proper in Area 1. Series may have statement(s) of responsibility that relate only to the series. If the series has an ISSN (International Standard Serial Number), the ISSN may appear in Area 6.

Area 7 contains notes relating to the information package being described. Notes may, to name a few, describe the nature, scope, or artistic form of the work; give the language of the text; identify the source of the title if there is no chief source of information; identify a work as a dissertation; or explain relationships of this work to others. This is the most free-form of the areas.

Area 8 contains a number that is accepted as an international standard—at the moment only the ISBN (International Standard Book Number) or the ISSN. The area also contains information about the terms of availability of the information package (e.g., it is free to members but others must pay, or it is unavailable to the public for a certain number of years, etc.).

There are two things to remember about *ISBD*. First, *ISBD* punctuation is prescribed, and it precedes and predicts the data element that comes next. For example, a space-slash-space in Area 1 says that the statement of responsibility is coming next. Second, the order of data is prescribed. For example, in Area 1 prescribed content and punctuation is: **title [GMD] : subtitle / 1st statement of responsibility ; 2nd statement of responsibility**. It can be seen that the prescribed punctuation is both preceded and followed by a space.

Finally, we should say a few words about the formats that *ISBD* records take. In the *ISBD* standard each area is to be set off from the next area by a space-dash-space. British practice in creating printed catalogs has been to have the areas follow one after another; but American practice has been to create cards and other printed catalogs by having Areas 1, 5, and 7 each begin a new "paragraph," and if there is more than one note in Area 7, each note begins a new "paragraph." (Figs. 5.1 on page 84 to 5.3 on page 85 are formatted using American practice.) In *AACR2*, both British and American formats are accepted. In most instances, at this time, format is a moot point, because the data created using rules based on *ISBD* are placed into MARC records. Displays that are based on these records seldom use the "card" format. They are much more likely to have labels (e.g., "TITLE:" for Area 1).

Anglo-American Cataloguing Rules, Second Edition, 1988 revision (AACR2r)[3]

The descriptive part of *Anglo-American Cataloguing Rules, Second Edition, 1988 revision (AACR2r)* is based on *ISBD*. (The access part of *AACR2r* is based on the Paris Principles; see discussion in chapter 6.) After a general descriptive chapter in *AACR2r*, other descriptive chapters cover different kinds of materials:

- books—chapter 2
- cartographic materials—chapter 3
- manuscripts—chapter 4
- music—chapter 5
- sound recordings—chapter 6
- motion pictures and videorecordings—chapter 7
- graphic materials—chapter 8
- computer files—chapter 9
- three-dimensional artifacts and realia—chapter 10

Rules are numbered so that the numbers of the *ISBD* areas follow the chapter number. Here is an example of *ISBD* areas as rules in chapter 5 of *AACR2r*:

- rule 5.1—Title and statement of responsibility area
- rule 5.2—Edition area
- rule 5.3—Material specific details area
- rule 5.4—Publication, distribution, etc., area, etc.

An example of the same rule in more than one chapter is:

- rule 1.1B—general title proper
- rule 2.1B—book title proper
- rule 3.1B—map title proper
- rule 4.1B—manuscript title proper

Each chapter prescribes a "chief source of information" from which much of the information is to be taken. For example the chief source of information for a book is its title page. The chief source is preferred when the elements vary on or in various parts of the same information package (e.g., if the title on the sound recording label is different from that on the container, then the one on the label is preferred). A GMD (general material designation) in Area 1 (title and statement of responsibility area) indicates the class of item being described (e.g., art original, electronic resource, motion picture, text, etc.). In the example: **American women artists [slide] : the twentieth century**, "[slide]" is the GMD. In practice there are some classes of items that are not given a GMD in accord with the practice of the Library of Congress (LC). For example, [map], [text], and [music] are in *AACR2r*'s GMD list but are not used by LC.

In *AACR2r* Area 3 [material (or type of publication) specific details] is used only for maps, printed music, computer files, and serials. Some examples of the wording that may be used in Area 3 for each of the four types of information packages are:

- map: **Scale 1:24,000; Polyconic proj.**
- printed music: **Score and parts**
- electronic resource: **Computer program**
- serial: **Vol. 1, no. 1 (Jan. 1997)-**

AACR2r itself prescribes three levels of description that are considered to conform to "standard." The first level includes the minimum elements required to meet the standard. It is most likely to be used in small libraries, but LC catalogs serials at this level "enhanced," which means that a few additional elements have been prescribed by LC. The second level is the level used by LC for most cataloging. The third level includes every possible element set out in the rules. It is used only in cataloging such things as rare items. See figures 5.1, 5.2, and 5.3.

Wireless personal communications / edited by Theodore S. Rappaport.—Kluwer Academic Publishers, 1997.

xii, 225 p. – (The Kluwer international series in engineering and computer science ; SECS 242).

"Papers in this book were originally presented at the 7th Virginia Tech/MPRG Symposium on Wireless Personal Communications held June 11-13, [10997], in Blacksburg, Virginia."

Includes bibliographical references and index.

0-7923-8017-7.

Fig. 5.1. *AACR2* first-level description.

Wireless personal communications : improving capacity, services, and reliability / edited by Theodore S. Rappaport. -- Boston : Kluwer Academic Publishers, 1997.

xii, 225 p. : ill. ; 24 cm. -- (The Kluwer international series in engineering and computer science ; SECS 424).

"Papers in this book were originally presented at the 7th Virginia Tech/MPRG Symposium on Wireless Personal Communications held June 11-13, [1997], in Blacksburg, Virginia."

Includes bibliographical references and index.

0-7923-8017-7.

Fig. 5.2. *AACR2* second-level description.

The works of the late Right Honorable Joseph Addison, Esq. : with a complete index. -- Birmingham : printed by John Baskerville, for J. and R. Tonson ... London, 1761.

4 v. : ill., port. ; 30 cm. (4to).

Vol. 1: xxv, [3], 537, [5], 415-525 (i.e. 415-537), [5] p., [4] leaves of plates; v. 2: [8], 538, [14] p.; v. 3: 579, [13] p.; v. 4: 555, [13] p. Last leaves of v. 2 and 4 blank. Page 537 of last numbered section of v. 1 misnumbered 525.

References: Gaskell, P. J. Baskerville 17.

Contents: v. 1. Preface. Poems on several occasions. Rosamond. An essay on Virgil's Georgics. Cato. The drummer, or, The haunted house. Poemata. Dialogues upon the usefulness of ancient medals -- v. 2. Remarks on several parts of Italy, &c. The Tatler. The Spectator, no. 1-89 -- v. 3. The Spectator, no. 90-505 -- v. 4. The Spectator, no. 507-600. The guardian. The Lover. The present state of the war, and the necessity of an augmentation, considered. The Whig-examiner. The Free-holder. Of the Christian religion.

LC copy: In v. 1 leaves Zzzz2-3 incorrectly bound before Zzz1. Vol. 2 lacks the blank at the end.

Fig. 5.3. *AACR2* third-level description. (Source: *Bibliographic Description of Rare Books*. Washington, D.C.: Office for Descriptive Cataloging Policy Processing Services, Library of Congress, 1981, p. 55.)

There is one additional interpretation of *AACR2r* that should be mentioned. The Program for Cooperative Cataloging (PCC), which operates out of LC but is a cooperative group of catalogers from many places, has defined a set of Core Records (slightly different for different types of materials).[4] The Core Records present the minimal standard for what to include in a nationally acceptable *AACR2r* record. The description part of the Core Record calls for complete description in Areas 1 through 6 and 8 and for some of the notes in Area 7. It is a "minimal" standard because it prescribes much less in the access points arena.

An additional source of description rules based on *ISBD* is *The Concise AACR2, 1988 Revision* by Michael Gorman.[5] It cannot be called a "standard" because it is a work of personal authorship and has not been adopted as official by any group. However, it is based strongly on *AACR2r* and provides a way of applying much of *ISBD* without complicated rules or esoteric examples.

Archival APPM (Archives, Personal Papers, and Manuscripts) Records[6]

The *APPM* is a standard for the description of archival materials that has been accepted by most of the archival community. It is based on *AACR2r*. It indicates that when cataloging archival collections, the finding aid is considered to be the chief source of information. *APPM* follows the structure of *ISBD*. Archival materials usually do not have official titles; so the cataloger must assign one. Guidelines are given for creating cataloger-supplied titles. Archival materials are not published. If a collection is published, the published version is no longer archival material. Archival materials do not have "series" as defined in the library community; archival "series" are another concept entirely. In archival collections a series is a logical group of files, books, correspondence, or other such set. The concept is discussed further in chapter 9.

TEI (Text Encoding Initiative) Headers

As discussed in the preceding chapter, TEI is an SGML DTD that was created in order to provide a way of encoding old, literary, and/or scholarly texts so that encoded versions could be exchanged easily. A part of TEI is a TEI Header, created so that there would be metadata as part of the text file. The guidelines suggest the possibility of "independent headers" and give a separate set of guidelines to govern independent TEI Headers.[7] These stand alone from the text itself and can be used as surrogate records in retrieval tools.

One strong motivation for the creation of a standard for a TEI Header was to provide a source of information for cataloging. TEI folk collaborated with library catalogers for the "file description" part of the TEI Header. They wanted the mapping from TEI to a catalog record and vice versa to be as simple as possible. The standard for a TEI Header calls for many of the same elements as does *AACR2r*; therefore the content greatly resembles *AACR2r* content.

The TEI Header has four sections, only one of which is required. The four sections are file description, encoding description, profile description, and revision description. The file description is required and contains a bibliographic description of the text. It includes, for example, the title; author(s); publication information; and the source description, which is a description of the original source from which the electronic text was derived. The encoding description explains what rules or editorial decisions were used in transcribing the text (e.g., how quotations and spelling variations were treated). The profile description contains what *AACR2r* calls added access points (e.g., name[s] other than author[s]). It also contains language information, subject access points, and classification notation(s). The revision description contains a record of every change that has been made to the text, including when each change was made and by whom.

Form of the content to go into the fields of the header is not dictated in the guidelines for TEI Headers. However, the guidelines for the independent TEI Header have mandatory and recommended elements and recommend the use of structured information rather than unstructured information. This means that one should use a standard such as *AACR2r* or *ISBD* when filling in the TEI Header elements. For some elements the recommendation is for unstructured free text, especially for those parts that are not governed by *AACR2r* or *ISBD*. For an example of a TEI Header, refer back to figure 4.5 (p. 68).

The Dublin Core

The Dublin Core (shortened form of Dublin Metadata Core Element Set) was created in order to have an internationally agreed-upon set of elements that could be "filled in" by the creator of an electronic document. Participants in the workshops and conferences that have developed the Dublin Core are experts from many different fields (e.g., publishers, computer specialists, librarians, software producers, etc.).

The Dublin Core is now being implemented through the use of HTML. It appears that with full development of RDF (see discussion in chapter 4) Dublin Core can be encoded with XML and structured with RDF. One plan is to develop a template that can be called for every time a new web page is created. The author fills in as much as possible. It might be enhanced later by a cataloger or other information organizer.

The Dublin Core Set consists of fifteen elements that can be divided into three groups:[8]

- Elements related to the content of the resource

  - Title—the name of the resource (information package)

  - Subject and Keywords—the topic(s) of the resource; use of controlled vocabularies and formal classification schemes is encouraged

  - Description—a textual description of the content of the resource; could be an abstract or a content description

  - Source—information about an original resource from which this one is derived, although it is recommended that best practice is to use one of the links for the Relation element instead; this element could be used for provenance or history information

  - Language—an indication of the language of the intellectual content (text) of the resource

  - Relation—the "identifier" of a second resource along with its relationship to the present source; relationship links include: IsVersionOf, IsBasedOn, IsPartOf, Is-FormatOf, etc.

■ Coverage—an identification of spatial characteristics (i.e., a physical region) and/or temporal characteristics (i.e., date/time of the "aboutness" coverage of the content of the resource; note that this element is for the subject and the Date element below is for the date of creation of the resource). Both spatial and temporal characteristics should be taken from a controlled list, or geographic area should be spelled out and date should be in a standard form such as YYYY-MM-DD.

● Elements related to the resource when viewed as intellectual property

■ Author or Creator—the name of the person or organization primarily responsible for creating the intellectual content of the resource (e.g., author, artist, composer, etc.)

■ Publisher—the name of the entity responsible for making the resource available (e.g., publishing house, university or one of its departments, other corporate body, etc.)

■ Other Contributor—the name of a person or organization that has made significant intellectual contributions, but ones that are secondary to the name in the Creator element (e.g., editor, illustrator, etc.)

■ Rights Management—a statement, link, or identifier that gives information about rights management (e.g., whether use is restricted until a certain time, time at which the resource will be removed from display, etc.)

● Elements related mainly to the issue of resource-as-an-instance

■ Date—the date of the creation or availability of the resource; it is recommended that ISO 8601 (Date and Time Formats) be used, especially YYYY-MM-DD as the scheme for a date

- Resource Type—a designation of the type (elsewhere called form/genre) category of the resource (e.g., home page, poem, technical report, dictionary, etc.); a standardized list is under development and is recommended for use

- Format—a designation of the software, and perhaps the hardware, required to use the resource; a standardized list is under development and is recommended for use

- Resource Identifier—a string or number that uniquely identifies the resource (e.g., URL, ISBN)

From the above elements, Subject and Keywords, Author or Creator, and Other Contributor are access point elements.

General principles for the Dublin Core, when it was established, were: 1) the core set can be extended with further elements needed by a particular community; 2) all elements are optional; 3) all elements are repeatable; and 4) any element may be modified by a qualifier or qualifiers. The form of the content of each element is not prescribed. See figure 5.4 on pages 90–91 for an abbreviated Dublin Core record.

Several groups are experimenting with applications of the Dublin Core. Among these is the Consortium for the Interchange of Museum Information (CIMI).[9] This is an important step for the museum community.

GILS (Government Information Locator Service) Records

GILS came about because in 1994 Congress passed the Paperwork Reduction Act, and the Office of Management and Budget directed all U.S. Federal agencies to create and make available to the public metadata on their information holdings. GILS was intended to require all Federal agencies to provide the records, called "locators," for all their information resources. Many agencies have created only one brief record that describes all their information as a whole. Others, though, have records for either groups of resources or individual resources. The latter is illustrated by government libraries that are able to describe their resources as a whole and then link to their catalogs, which contain individual records for most of the resources (see fig. 5.5 on page 92).

```
<HTML>
<HEAD>

<TITLE>Cataloguer's Toolbox</TITLE>

<META NAME = "DC.title"
CONTENT = "Cataloguer's Toolbox">

<META NAME = "DC.creator"
TYPE = "Name.Personal"
CONTENT = "Pennell, Charles">

<META NAME = "DC.subject"
SCHEME = "LCSH"
CONTENT = "Cataloging">

<META NAME = "DC.subject"
SCHEME = "LCSH"
CONTENT = "Unicorn (Information retrieval system)">

<META NAME = "DC.description"
CONTENT = "Gateway to tools of interest to the cataloguing community,
including local policy and procedures, national and proprietary
standards for bibliographic record creation and storage,
net-accessible remote library catalogues, vendors of
cataloguing-specific applications and products, and Web pages of other
library technical service operations.">

<META NAME = "DC.publisher"
CONTENT = "Memorial University of Newfoundland. Queen Elizabeth II
Library. Cataloguing Division">

<META NAME = "DC.date"
CONTENT = "1995">

<META NAME = "DC.type"
CONTENT = "home page">

<META NAME = "DC.type"
CONTENT = "manual">

<META NAME = "DC.format"
CONTENT = "text/html">
```

```
<META NAME = "DC.identifier"
CONTENT = "http://www.mun.ca/library/cat/">

<LINK REL = SCHEMA.dc
HREF = "http://purl.org/metadata/dublin_core_elements">

</HEAD>
<BODY>
. . .
```

Fig. 5.4. Dublin Core record. (Source: Committee on Cataloging: Description and Access, Task Force on Metadata and the Cataloging Rules. "Dublin Core and the Cataloging Rules." URL: http://www.libraries.psu.edu/iasweb/personal/jca/ dublin/ex11.htm [Example contributed by Charles Pennell].)

The GILS metadata format is complex in order to allow for any level from brief to detailed. Its elements are called "Data Elements" and include such things as Title, Author, Subject, Date of Publication, Date Last Modified, Time Period of Content, Spatial Domain, Use Constraints, Point-of-Contact, and Abstract, among many others. The format does not prescribe the content that should go into the Data Elements fields, but there are definitions of the fields, and a document called *Guidelines for the Preparation of GILS Core Entries*[10] gives examples of usage of the fields and identifies the mandatory ones. GILS was influenced by both MARC and the Z39.50 standard for sending and retrieving search results. The "GILS Profile"[11] calls for participants to have Z39.50-compliant servers. (See further discussion of Z39.50 in chapter 10.)

A GILS record presents a description that gives at least the following information:

- what information is available and why it was created
- how the information is made available for use
- whom to contact for further information
- perhaps a direct link to the information itself

Title:
Library of Congress

Originator:
U.S. Federal Government

Language-of-Resource:
ENG

Abstract:
U.S. Library of Congress is committed to make its products and search engines GILS-compliant. Also, the 1,400 Federal Depository libraries in the U.S. are required to provide GILS-aware client software for public access.

Spatial-Domain:
Place:
USA

Availability:
Available-Linkage:
Linkage-Type:
text/HTML
Linkage:
http://www.loc.gov

Point-of-Contact:
Organization:
LC Web Administrator
Country:
USA
Network-Address:
lcweb@loc.gov
Telephone:
202-707-9688

Control-Identifier:
app049

Record-Source:
USGS

Language-of-Record:
ENG

Date-of-Last-Modification:
19971215

Fig. 5.5. GILS record describing the Library of Congress as a whole. Descriptions of individual information packages in the Library of Congress collection are available through its catalogs. (Source: "GILS Demonstration Sampler, Library of Congress." URL: http://www.usgs.gov/gils/sampler/app049.htm)

As already mentioned, there is no prescribed content for what is to be described in a record. The "item" being described may include one document, an entire database, or anything in between. The GILS format may be used to describe not only paper resources and databases, but also people, events, meetings, artifacts, etc.—anyone or anything that is considered by an agency to be an information resource.

FGDC (Federal Geographic Data Committee) Content Standard for Digital Geospatial Metadata

The title of this standard is *Content Standard for Digital Geospatial Metadata*,[12] but it has become familiarly known as the FGDC metadata standard. Like GILS it was mandated in 1994 with the directive that each agency should document all new geospatial data it collects or produces. The standard aims to provide a common set of terminology and definitions for metadata about digital geospatial data.

The FGDC standard is a content standard; it does not dictate layout or an encoding scheme, although SGML is recommended. Like the standards already discussed, it provides a way for data users to know what resources are available, whether the resources will meet their specific needs, where to find the data, and how to access the data. Version 2 of the standard was published in mid-1998. It has the following sections: identification information; data quality information; spatial data organization information; spatial reference information; entity and attribute information; distribution information; metadata reference information; citation information; time period information; and contact information. Within each of the sections elements are listed. For example, within the section "Metadata Reference Information" the elements listed begin with: 1) date; 2) review date; 3) future review date; 4) contact; 5) standard name; 6) standard version, etc. The format of the content is not prescribed. Nearly all elements specify that they are "free text."

VRA (Visual Resources Association) Core Categories for Visual Resources

According to the VRA Core Categories web site[13] the core categories "are intended as a guideline for describing visual documents depicting works of art, architecture, and artifacts or structures from material, popular, and folk culture." Version 2.0 of the Core Categories was released late in 1997. This version includes guidelines for each category that give guidance for expressing the content of the categories. Format of content is not prescribed. There are twenty-three Work Description Categories and nine Visual Document Description Categories:

Work Description Categories

Work Type	Repository Name	Movement
Title	Repository Place	Nationality
Measurements	Repository Number	Culture
Material	Current Site	Subject
Technique	Original Site	Related Work
Creator	Style	Relationship
Role	Period	Type
Date	Group	Notes

Visual Document Description Categories

Visual Document Type	Visual Document Owner Number
Visual Document Format	Visual Document View Description
Visual Document Measurements	Visual Document Subject
Visual Document Date	Visual Document Type
Visual Document Owner	

EAD (Encoded Archival Description)[14]

The EAD (Encoded Archival Description) that was discussed as an SGML DTD in the preceding chapter was created specifically to encode finding aids. The guidelines for finding aids were already in existence, so the EAD does not contain prescriptions for content. However, it has a header that is based heavily on the TEI Header. The header is, in a way, metadata about the metadata in the rest of the EAD record. The content placed in the EAD Header is based on the rules in the *APPM*. In many instances archival collections have been cataloged, using *APPM*/MARC, instead of, or in addition to, finding aids being created. The EAD Header resembles such a catalog record.

Crosswalks

Crosswalks are visual instruments for showing which value in one metadata standard matches a particular value in another standard. Several crosswalks exist for relating the standards discussed above. Two examples are: "Dublin Core/MARC/GILS Crosswalk," which maps the Dublin Core to USMARC and GILS[15]; and "Monticello Electronic Library: Dublin Core Element Set Crosswalk," which maps the Dublin Core to EAD, GILS, and USMARC.[16]

Index Records

At the moment there is no official standard for the descriptive content of index records. An ANSI standard Z39.4-1984, subtitled "Basic Criteria for Indexes,"[17] has no mention of the data to be included in the description of an item. The National Information Standards Organization (NISO) tried to update this standard, but committees could not come to agreement with the American Society of Indexers, and so Z39.4 was withdrawn in 1996. NISO has issued a technical report TR-02, *Guidelines for Indexes and Related Information Retrieval Devices*, by James Anderson.[18] There is a separate standard for bibliographic references, Z39.29,[19] that guides the content to be included in entries in bibliographies.

Creators of indexes have their own standards for information to be included in an index record. Agencies like H. W. Wilson that publish several different indexes in different subject areas have some consistency from index to index. Electronic index records tend to include more information than do paper versions. As in OPACs, electronic index records tend to have labels, which are not included in paper versions. (For an example of a labeled index record, refer back to fig. 2.3, p. 29.)

On-the-Fly Records

On-the-fly records are those created electronically for immediate use; they will be changed either momentarily or within a matter of weeks. In some catalogs that now have what are called "web interfaces," the MARC records are converted to HTML encoded records on-the-fly. That is, when a user puts in a search, a listing of authors, titles, and/or dates is returned to the screen. If the user then clicks on number 4 in the list, the MARC record is quickly put through the HTML converter that has been written for that catalog so that it can be displayed on the screen. These records have much of the same descriptive content as is found in the MARC records from which they are derived. In some systems there are URLs in some records, and these may be hyperlinked so that the actual information package can be retrieved directly from the catalog record.

Another kind of on-the-fly record is that produced by search engines. Search engine surrogate records may consist of only the title of a document, or may give the first several lines of the document. All search engine surrogate records include a hyperlinked URL. (The search engine *Yahoo!* has records that are created by humans and do not qualify as on-the-fly records.) On-the-fly search engine surrogate records may or may not be helpful in the evaluation of whether or not the information package it represents will be useful to the user. If the information package has a title and the title is indicative of content, then the on-the-fly record is more useful than the record with no title. It is often necessary to look at the information package itself in order to learn what it is about and why it was retrieved in response to the search (see fig. 5.6).

1. **Elaine Svenonius**

   Elaine Svenonius. Professor Emerita Department of Library and Information Science 222 GSE&IS Bldg. -- (310) 206-9362 -- esvenoni@ucla.edu. M.L.S. and...
   http://www.gseis.ucla.edu/facpage/svenonius.html - size 2K - 14-Aug-96 - English - Translate

2. **No Title**

   FINAL PROGRAM DIGITAL LIBRARIES '96: 1st ACM INTERNATIONAL CONFERENCE ON DIGITAL LIBRARIES March 20-23, 1996 Hyatt Regency Bethesda, Maryland USA Digital..
   http://fox.cs.vt.edu/DL96/final2.txt - size 29K - 5-Mar-96 - English - Translate

3. **Professor Intner's Course Syllabus: LS 415**

   LS415: Organization of Knowledge in Libraries Sheila S. Intner, Professor Spring 1997 Section 415-01: Mondays, 6:00 - 9:00 PM Room L-308. INTRODUCTION....
   http://www.simmons.edu/gslis/intner415.html - size 30K - 7-Jul-97 - English - Translate

Fig. 5.6. Typical on-the-fly records in which it is often not possible to see why they were returned in response to the search. In this case, only four of the eighty-one "hits" had Elaine Svenonius's name anywhere in the on-the-fly records. (Source: Altavista.digital.com search on "+Elaine +Svenonius," April 21, 1998.)

Museum Accession Records

Museum objects have characteristics that differ from information packages in most other environments, and these affect the description in the surrogate record. First, museum objects are unique—each specimen is different. Even if the museum object is one of two identical pieces of furniture, let's say, it will have a different provenance, and it will have scratches in different places! Specimens in natural history museums, however, are often more alike because each one is an example of a particular species and is not very different from museum to museum, although the information about source will be different.

Another difference is that the identification of objects is often unknown at the time of acquisition. Specimens brought in from an archaeological dig, for example, may have to be researched in order to be identified. In addition information about an object often changes over time as new evidence becomes available. And there is the possibility that the object may be a forgery or otherwise be mistakenly identified. The museum community has not been able to agree, even within a discipline, on what constitutes a core record for the description of museum objects. Museums that are parts of libraries use chapter 10 of *AACR2r*, "Three-Dimensional Artefacts and Realia."

HOW DOES THE ENVIRONMENT AFFECT THE WAY A SURROGATE RECORD IS CREATED?

From the preceding descriptions one can see that the creation of surrogate records is somewhat dependent upon the community for which the records are being created. Some communities have long-standing standards. The library community's standard has the longest tradition, being based upon principles that have been developing for centuries. Other communities have recognized the library's long experience and have patterned their guidelines for creation of surrogate records after the *ISBD* standard. The creators of TEI Headers, the Dublin Core, RDF, and others have included librarians, along with other people with organizing experience, in their planning committees.

CONCLUSION

This chapter has addressed the descriptive part of metadata, which we have called surrogate records. In discussion of the value of surrogate records it was mentioned that surrogate record descriptions are most helpful when they are predictable in both form and content. The only standards that prescribe form of content are *ISBD*, *AACR2r*, and *APPM*. *ISBD* came to its prescription after years of experience with variant practices that brought an understanding of the value of predictability. *AACR2r* and, in turn, *APPM*, have followed *ISBD*. The remaining standards discussed have been developed more recently, most in the last decade. Perhaps experience with the large quantities of metadata records that have existed in the library and archival communities will soon lead the newer creators of metadata to reevaluate their need for prescribed content. The next chapter addresses access and access control, which is accepted as a necessity in the library and archival communities but has barely been considered in the other communities.

NOTES

1.   *The Free On-line Dictionary of Computing* (February 15, 1998) [accessed through the University of Pittsburgh Libraries *Digital Library*].

2.   ISBD(G): *General International Standard Bibliographic Description*. Annotated text prepared by the ISBD Review Committee Working Group, set up by the IFLA Committee on Cataloguing. New York: K. G. Saur, 1992.

3.   *Anglo-American Cataloguing Rules, Second Edition, 1988 revision* (Ottawa: Canadian Library Association; Chicago: American Library Association, 1988).

4.   Program for Cooperative Cataloging, *Introduction to the Program for Cooperative Cataloging BIBCO Core Record Standard,* available: http://lcweb.loc.gov/catdir/pcc/coreintro.html, accessed October 1998.

5.   Michael Gorman, *The Concise AACR2, 1998 Revision* (Chicago: American Library Association, 1989).

6.   Steven L. Hensen, comp., *Archives, Personal Papers, and Manuscripts: A Cataloging Manual for Archival Repositories, Historical Societies, and Manuscript Libraries,* 2nd ed. (Chicago: Society of American Archivists, 1989).

7.   *Text Encoding Initiative (TEI) Independent Headers,* available: http://www.ukoln. ac.uk/metadata/desire/overview/rev_21.htm, accessed October 1998.

8.   *Description of Dublin Core Elements,* available: http://purl.oclc.org/metadata/dublin_core_elements, accessed October 1998.

9.   *CIMI* (Consortium for the Computer Interchange of Museum Information), available: http://www.cimi.org/, accessed October 1998.

10. *The Government Information Locator Service: Guidelines for the Preparation of GILS Core Entries* (Washington, D.C.: National Archives and Records Administration, 1995). Also available: http://www.nlc-bnc.ca/ifla/documents/libraries/cataloging/metadata/naragils.txt, accessed October 1998.

11. *Application Profile for the Government Information Locator Service (GILS)*, Version 2, 1997, available: http://www.usgs.gov/gils/prof_v2.html, accessed October 1998, last updated November 24, 1997.

12. *Content Standard for Digital Geospatial Metadata,* Version 2, available: http://www.fgdc.gov/metadata/contstan/html, accessed October 1998.

13. *The Core Categories for Visual Resources—Introduction,* available: http://www.oberlin.edu/~art/vra/dscintro.html, accessed October 1998.

14. *Encoded Archival Description: Official Web Site,* available: http://www.loc.gov/ead/ead.html, accessed October 1998.

15. Library of Congress, Network Development and MARC Standards Office, "Dublin Core/MARC/GILS Crosswalk," available: http://lcweb.loc.gov/marc/dccross.html, accessed October 1998, last updated April 7, 1997.

16. Monticello Electronic Library: "Dublin Core Element Set Crosswalk," available: http://www.oclc.org:5046/~emiller/DC/crosswalk.html, accessed October 1998, last updated April 17, 1997.

17. *American National Standard for Library and Information Sciences and Related Publishing Practices—Basic Criteria for Indexes,* ANSI Z39.4–1984 (New York: American National Standards Institute, 1984).

18. James D. Anderson, *Guidelines for Indexes and Related Information Retrieval Devices* (Bethesda, Md.: NISO Press, 1997).

19. *Documentation—Bibliographic References—Content, Form and Structure,* ISO 690, 2nd ed. (Geneva, Switzerland: International Organization for Standardization, 1987).

SUGGESTED READINGS

ALA/ALCTS/CCS Committee on Cataloging: Description and Access. Task Force on Metadata and the Cataloging Rules. *Dublin Core and the Cataloging Rules.* Available: http://www.libraries.psu.edu/iasweb/personal/jca/dublin/index.htm (Accessed October 1998).

Dempsey, Lorcan, and Rachel Heery. *A Review of Metadata: A Survey of Current Resource Description Formats*. Available: http://www.ukoln.ac.uk/metadata/desire/overview (Accessed October 1998).

Dublin Core Metadata. Available: http://purl.oclc.org/metadata/dublin_core (Accessed October 1998).

FGDC Metadata. Available: http://www.fgdc.gov/metadata/metadata.html (Accessed October 1998).

GILS (Global Information Locator Service/Government Information Locator Service). Available: http://www.usgs.gov/gils/index.html (Accessed October 1998).

Gorman, Michael. *The Concise AACR2, 1988 Revision*. Chicago: American Library Association, 1989.

IFLA Digital Libraries: Metadata Resources. Available: http://www.nlc-bnc.ca/ifla/II/metadata.htm (This is essentially a bibliography with hyperlinks to the articles that are available on the Internet.) (Accessed October 1998).

Introduction to the Program for Cooperative Cataloging BIBCO Core Record Standard. Available: http://lcweb.loc.gov/catdir/pcc/coreintro.html (Accessed October 1998).

Metadata, Dublin Core and USMARC: a review of current efforts. MARBI Discussion Paper 99, January 21, 1997. Available: gopher://marvel.loc.gov/00/.listarch/usmarc/dp99.doc (Accessed October 1998).

Miller, Frederic M. *Arranging and Describing Archives and Manuscripts*. Chicago: Society of American Archivists, 1990, pp. 109–18.

Rogers, JoAnn V., and Jerry D. Saye. "Bibliographic Control of Nonprint." Chap. 1 in *Nonprint Cataloging for Multimedia Collections*. 2nd ed. Littleton, Colo.: Libraries Unlimited, 1987.

Suzor, Mary. "Art and the Information Highway." *CMA* (March 1997): 8–9.

U.S. Federal GILS. Available: http://www.usgs.gov/gils/intro.html (Accessed October 1998).

The Value of Metadata. Available: http://www.fgdc.gov/publications/documents/metadata/metabroc.html (Accessed October 1998).

Vellucci, Sherry L. "Herding Cats: Options for Organizing Electronic Resources." *Internet Reference Services Quarterly* 1, no. 4 (1996): 9–30.

Weibel, Stuart. "Metadata: The Foundations of Resource Description." *D-Lib Magazine* (July 1995). Available: http://www.cnri.reston.va.us/home/dlib/July95/07weibel.html (Accessed October 1998).

Wynar, Bohdan S. *Introduction to Cataloging and Classification*. 8th ed. by Arlene G. Taylor. "Description of Materials Using *AACR2r*," pp. 48–50. "Description— General." Chap. 3. Englewood, Colo.: Libraries Unlimited, 1992.

CHAPTER 6

METADATA: ACCESS AND ACCESS CONTROL

The problem addressed in this chapter is expressed in the question: How are surrogate records made available to users? In most online systems keyword searching is available. If a user knows exactly what words have been used in a description, then keyword searching is successful. But users who do not know exact words have to guess. This is sometimes successful and sometimes not. Most words in the English language have more than one meaning, and most meanings have more than one word (discussed further in chapter 7). Many research studies have shown that different users do not think of the same word(s) to express a concept; authors do not necessarily use the same word(s) to write about a concept; authors do not necessarily retain the same name or same form of name throughout their writing careers; corporate bodies do not necessarily use the same name in their documents nor are they known by the same form of name by everyone; and titles of works that are reproduced are not always the same in the original and the reproduction. For all of these reasons and more, the library and then the archival worlds came to the realization many years ago that bibliographic records needed access points (one of which needed to be designated as the "main" one), and these access points needed to be expressed consistently from record to record when several different records used the same access point.

The rest of the metadata world has not yet seen a need for access points with consistent form from record to record. The energy so far has been spent upon determining what descriptive information is needed for particular forms of information packages, and on how these descriptions can be encoded for display. As metadata accumulates to the massive numbers that catalogs have been dealing with, the need for access control will become more apparent. Because principles for access points currently exist only in the library and archival worlds, the principles that underlie *AACR2* are the ones discussed here. These are based upon the "Paris Principles" that were accepted internationally at the International Conference on Cataloging Principles,[1] held in Paris in 1961.

As mentioned in the preceding chapter, the creation of metadata in a broad sense requires description of the information package, attention to access points for the description, and encoding of the entire surrogate record content. The preceding chapter addressed description. The next step is the selection of access points chosen for the purpose of being able to provide controlled access to surrogate records. In sections that follow we discuss choice of access points, selection of one of them as the "main" or "primary" one, and the process of performing authority work on the access points in order to provide predictable and collocated access. The access points addressed in this chapter are the ones for names and titles. Access control for subject access points is discussed in chapter 7.

CHOICE OF ACCESS POINTS

Names, titles, and name/title combinations are the candidates for access points. *AACR2* calls for access points for persons, corporate bodies, geographic names, and titles, as well as combinations of names and titles. Some specific access points called for by *AACR2* include collaborators, editors and compilers, corporate bodies, titles (including titles of series), related works, and sometimes translators and illustrators. However, these are fairly book-oriented, reflecting the origins of *AACR2*. In fact many access points are for performers, choreographers, programmers, and cartographers, among many others.

Primary Access Point

According to the Paris Principles one of the access points that is chosen is selected to be the primary access point. The Paris Principles call this the "main entry" and say that it must be a "full entry." Full entry comes from the days of print catalogs. With print catalogs (i.e., card, book, and COM catalogs) it is necessary to place as many entries of the same surrogate record into the catalog as there are access points. Let us say that a record has the following access points: Author, Joint author, Corporate body, Subject 1, Subject 2, Title, Series title. In such a case there would need to be seven instances of the same surrogate record in the catalog—one filed alphabetically in each of the places where the Author, Joint author, etc., would appear (see also fig. 6.1). The access point is at the top or head of the copy of the surrogate record in each instance.

```
JC178   Paine, Thomas, 1737-1809.
.B7         Common sense, by Thomas Paine.
1976     Cutchogue, N.Y., Buccaneer Books, c1976.
            129 p., ill., 22 cm.

            "Epistle to Quakers": p. 117-129.


   1. United States--Politics and Government--1775-
1783.   2. Monarchy.   I. Paine, Thomas. Epistle to
Quakers.   II. Epistle to Quakers.   III. Title
```

```
        Epistle to Quakers.

JC178   Paine, Thomas, 1737-1809.
.B7         Common sense. Buccaneer Books, c1976.
1976
            129 p.
```

Fig. 6.1. The top card is the "main entry card" and is also what one might call the "full entry." The "main entry" for this record is "Paine, Thomas, 1737-1809." The bottom card is an abbreviated version of the main entry card with one of the added entries typed at the top of the card. This example would require that six cards be filed into the card catalog—one full entry at the alphabetical position for the main entry, and one brief version for each of the five added entries.

Returning to the concept of full entry, in the days of handwritten catalog entries, and later in book catalogs especially, it was often necessary to save time and space by having only one copy of the surrogate record created as a full entry (i.e., containing a complete set of all elements of the record as provided by the cataloger). The rest of the entries were abbreviated. The Paris Principles stated that the place where the full entry should be filed is the alphabetical location of the primary access point or main entry. Soon it became customary to refer to the full entry as the main entry.

Use of "main entry" to mean both "full entry" and "primary access point" causes great confusion today. Print catalogs have long since given up the practice of having one full entry and several abbreviated copies of each surrogate record. Instead, as such technology as photocopying and then computer-printed cards became commonplace, every entry became a duplicate of the full entry. The difference among the copies was that each copy had as its top line (called the "heading") one of the chosen access points.

The concept of full entry is definitely not applicable in OPACs. In OPACs there is only one copy of the complete metadata record. In response to a particular user request, that copy is displayed on the screen. In this situation "main entry" can refer only to the access point that is the "main" or primary one. In much of the literature that calls for doing away with the main entry, the argument is that we no longer have a system where one copy of a record has all the information. Others understand the current meaning of main entry as the primary access point, but some of this second group also argue against the concept. Others argue forcefully for keeping the main entry concept.

Main Entry Controversy

Controversy over main entry is more than two decades old. In 1978 Seymour Lubetzky and Michael Gorman disagreed quite publicly at a conference on the emergence of *AACR2*.[2] *AACR2*'s introduction included the observation that the concept of main entry might have outlived its time. However, there had not been enough time to research the idea, and so the concept was included in *AACR2*. It stated that a library that wished to could choose access points without designating one as the main one. Lubetzky, whose principles underlie the Paris Principles, argued that this was a step backward instead of forward. Gorman believed that the time had come to make the distinction only when necessary to cite one work on the record for another work, a situation which he guessed would happen "less than 1 percent" of the time.[3] Research, however, has shown this estimate to be quite low. Richard Smiraglia found that approximately 50 percent of a sample of works had "derivative" relationships.[4] Derivative relationships exist when one work is derived from another (e.g., editions, translations, adaptations, performances, etc.).

Controversy raged again on the listserv for the International Conference on *AACR*[5] in the fall of 1997. Martha Yee, a former student of Lubetzky, took up his cause in defense of the main entry. Some contributors suggested that system design can accomplish the same objectives (this is discussed further in chapter 10). Among the recommendations from the conference, however, none mentioned main entry.[6]

Justification for Main Entry

In chapter 2 of this text Cutter's "objects" of a catalog were quoted. As a reminder, paraphrased they are:

- to enable a person to find a book when author, title, or subject is known
- to show what the library has by a given author, on a given subject, or in a given kind of literature
- to assist in the choice of a book as to its edition or as to its character

In many ways main entry is a device for carrying out Cutter's objectives. Reasons given for a need for the main entry include the following:

- to provide a standard citation form to

  - show relationships between works and among manifestations of a work

  - identify works about other works

  - identify works contained in larger works

- to provide subarrangement under subjects (and as a corollary, to provide a way to subarrange items under classification number)

  - shows prolific authors in a field

  - brings together manifestations of a work

- to provide for collocation of all manifestations of a work, even though the work may be published with different titles (e.g., translations), or editions of a work may be published by different authors

- to assure a judgment of "most important" access point in situations where reduction of cataloging time has been mandated (especially where number of required access points has been reduced, as in the Core Record)

Let us briefly discuss each of these justifications for main entry.

Citation. First, choice of a main entry is necessary every time someone cites a work in a document or lists it in a bibliography. That is, there is only going to be one entry for the work being cited, and the citer has to put something first: the first author, the editor, the title, etc. Thus, the concept of main entry is put into practice with great frequency, but people usually do not recognize that every time they create a bibliography entry they choose a primary access point. Style manuals give suggestions for this choice, but the style manuals differ from each other, so predictability is lost.

Within a surrogate record it is often necessary to refer to another work on the record for the work that is being cataloged. This happens, for example, when one is describing a work that is based on another work (e.g., a screenplay based on a novel), when one work is a version of another work (e.g., a new edition of a work where the new edition is written by a new author), or other such cases (see fig. 6.2). In these cases it is important to refer to the related work in a note in the description of the work being described. In addition to the note an access point is constructed that places the main entry and title of the work being cited in controlled form with the main entry in the leading position.

A second kind of instance that requires reference to another work is when the intellectual content of the work for which a surrogate record is being made has as its subject another work (e.g., a criticism of a literary work). In this case one of the subject headings on the surrogate record is the work that is being discussed (see fig. 6.3 on page 110).

A third instance occurs when the work being described is part of a larger work (e.g., a volume in a series or set; a work published with one or two other works; see fig. 6.4 on page 111) or the work being described contains a smaller work within it (e.g., a critique and analysis of a musical composition contains the composition; a work contains one or more previously published works in addition to the main one being described; etc.; see fig. 6.5 on page 112).

Subarrangement. The second justification for main entry is for sorting search results. If main entries have been chosen, then the results of a subject search can be displayed in the order of the primary access point, which, in a large percentage of cases, is the name of the author or first-named author. This allows searchers to determine the authors who write most in a particular field so that those authors' names can be searched in other retrieval tools. Main entry arrangement under subject headings also serves to collocate editions of works on the same subject.

Collocation. Main entry also provides a way to collocate (i.e., bring together) all derivations of the same work. If there are several manifestations of a work—a translation, an illustrated version, a microform copy, an audio version, etc.—choosing the same main entry for them means that in most retrieval tools they will be displayed together. Of course it is helpful, when all do not have the same title, to have a "uniform title" so that the manifestations will not only be displayed under the same main entry, but will also be displayed together among all the entries under that main entry (see fig. 6.6 on page 113).

Text continues on page 114.

```
OCLC:    32544834         Rec stat:    n
Entered:    19950511        Replaced:    19950526      Used:      19970520
Type:   g     ELvl:  7     Srce:        Audn:        Ctrl:       Lang:  eng
BLvl:   m     TMat:  m     GPub:        AccM:        MRec:       Ctry:  xxu
Desc:   a     Time:  ---   Tech:  l     DtSt:  s     Dates: 1994,
   1    010      95-506926/MP
   2    040      DLC $e amim $c DLC
   3    007      m $b r $c u $d c $e b $f a $g a $h f $i s
   4    017      PA742-443 $b U.S. Copyright Office
   5    043      n-us-ny
   6    050 00   CGC 1381-1386 (ref print)
   7    090      $b
   8    049      DD0A
   9    245 00   Nobody's fool / $c a Scott Rudin/Cinehous production ; directed
and written by Robert Benton ; produced by Scott Rudin and Arlene Donovan.
  10    257      U.S.
  11    260      United States : $b Paramount Pictures : $b Capella International,
$c 1994.
  12    300      12 reels of 12 on 6 (ca. 9950 ft.) : $b sd., col. ; $c 35 mm.
ref print.
  13    500      Paramount Pictures Corporation. DCR 1994; PUB 11Oct94; REG
7Feb95; PA742-443.
  14    508      Associate producer, Scott Ferguson ; music, Howard Shore.
  15    511 1    Paul Newman, Jessica Tandy, Gene Saks, Bruce Willis, Melanie
Griffith, Dylan Walsh, Pruitt Taylor Vince, Josef Sommer, Alexander Goodwin.
  17    500      From the novel by Richard Russo.
  18    650  0   Fathers and sons $x Drama.
  19    650  0   Family $x Drama.
  20    650  0   City and town life $z New York (State) $x Drama.
  21    655  7   Features. $2 mim
  22    655  7   Adaptations. $2 mim
  23    700 1    Benton, Robert, $e direction, $e writing.
  24    700 1    Newman, Paul, $d 1925- $e cast.
  25    700 1    Tandy, Jessica, $e cast.
  26    700 1    Saks, Gene, $d 1921- $e cast.
  27    700 1    Willis, Bruce, $d 1955- $e cast.
  28    700 1    Griffith, Melanie, $d 1957- $e cast.
  29    700 1    Russo, Richard, $d 1949- $t Nobody's fool.
  30    710 2    Copyright Collection (Library of Congress) $5 DLC
```

Fig. 6.2. Metadata record for a work based on another work with an access point constructed using the main entry and the title of the original work.

```
OCLC:   33406432          Rec stat:    a
Entered:    19950601       Replaced:    19951101      Used:     19970821
Type:   a   ELvl:          Srce:        Audn:         Ctrl:         Lang:  eng
BLvl:   m   Form:          Conf:  0     Biog:         MRec:         Ctry:  nju
            Cont:   b      GPub:        Fict:  0      Indx:  0
Desc:   a   Ills:   a      Fest:  0     DtSt:  s      Dates: 1995,
       1   010         95-68761
       2   040         DLC $c DLC
       3   020         0878917527
       4   050 00      PS3537.A426 $b C3285 1995
       5   082 00      813/.54 $2 20
       6   090         $b
       7   049         DD0A
       8   100 1       Holzman, Robert S.
       9   245 10      J.D. Salinger's The catcher in the rye / $c text by Robert S.
Holzman, Gary L. Perkins ; illustrations by Karen Pica.
      10   246 18      Catcher in the rye
      11   260         Piscataway, N.J. : $b Research & Education Association, $c
c1995.
      12   300         v, 113, [1] p. : $b ill. ; $c 21 cm.
      13   440  0      MAXnotes
      14   504         Includes bibliographical references (p. [114]).
      15   600 10      Salinger, J. D. $q (Jerome David), $d 1919- $t Catcher in the
rye $x Examinations $x Study guides.
      16   700 1       Perkins, Gary L.
```

Fig. 6.3. Metadata record for a work that is about another work. The record contains a subject heading that consists of the main entry and the title of the work that is the subject of the work represented by this record.

```
    OCLC:   32683203          Rec stat:    n
    Entered:    19950605      Replaced:    19951011     Used:      19980423
>  Type:  a      ELvl:        Srce:  d   Audn:      Ctrl:        Lang:   eng
   BLvl:  m      Form:        Conf:  0   Biog:      MRec:        Ctry:   nyu
                 Cont:        GPub:      Fict:  1   Indx:  0
   Desc:  a      Ills:        Fest:  0   DtSt:  s   Dates: 1995,       <
>   1   010      95-77866 <
>   2   040      MdHyP $c DLC <
>   3   020      0679441018 : $c |$|25.00 <
>   4   042      lccopycat <
>   5   050  00  PS3568.I265 $b M46 1995 <
>   6   082  00  813/.54 $2 20 <
>   7   090      $b  <
>   8   049      DD0A <
>   9   100  1   Rice, Anne, $d 1941- <
>  10   245  10  Memnoch the Devil / $c Anne Rice. <
>  11   250      1st ed. <
>  12   260      New York : $b Knopf, $c 1995. <
>  13   300      353 p. ; $c 25 cm. <
>  14   490  1   The vampire chronicles ; $v [5th bk.] <
>  15   650   0  Vampires $x Fiction. <
>  16   650   0  Lestat (Fictitious character) $x Fiction. <
>  17   655   7  Horror tales. $2 gsafd <
>  18   800  1   Rice, Anne, $d 1941- $t Vampire chronicles ; $v [5th bk.] <
```

Fig. 6.4. Metadata record for a work that is part of a larger work. Anne Rice's *Memnoch the Devil* is the fifth book in her series called *Vampire Chronicles*. The added entry consisting of main entry and title of the series allows collocation of the series with the author's individual titles.

```
    OCLC:  36504265          Rec stat:     n
    Entered:    19970307     Replaced:    19970307     Used:     19970307
 >  Type:  a    ELvl:  I    Srce:  d    Audn:       Ctrl:        Lang:   eng
    BLvl:  m    Form:       Conf:  0    Biog:       MRec:        Ctry:   nyu
               Cont:        GPub:       Fict:  0    Indx:  0
    Desc:  a    Ills:       Fest:  0    DtSt:  s    Dates: 1835,      <
 >   1  040     NJL $c NJL <
 >   2  092     211.5 $b P14 <
 >   3  090     $b  <
 >   4  049     DD0A <
 >   5  100 1   Paine, Thomas, $d 1737-1809. <
 >   6  245 14  The theological works of Thomas Paine : $b the most complete
edition ever published. <
 >   7  260     New York : $b George H. Evans, $c 1835. <
 >   8  300     xiv, [7]-384 p. ; $c 22 cm. <
 >   9  500     "The age of reason": p. [7]-159. <
 >  10  501     With: Miscellaneous letters and essays on various subjects / by
Thomas Paine. Granville, Middletown, N.J. : G.H. Evans, 1844, and 2 other
works. <
 >  11  650  0  Deism. <
 >  12  650  0  Rationalism. <
 >  13  700 12  Paine, Thomas, 1737-1809. $t Age of reason. <
 >  14  740 02  Age of reason. <
```

Fig. 6.5. Metadata record for a work that contains a smaller work within it. The work being described contains four works of Thomas Paine. One is considered to be a major work and is given an added entry consisting of the main entry and the title (line 13).

```
OCLC:   38735799            Rec stat:      n
Entered:    19980317        Replaced:      19980317      Used:      19980320
> Type:  a    ELvl:  I    Srce:  d    Audn:         Ctrl:          Lang:  spa
BLvl:  m    Form:       Conf:  0    Biog:         MRec:          Ctry:  sp
             Cont:   b    GPub:       Fict:  0    Indx:   0
Desc:  a    Ills:       Fest:  0    DtSt:  s    Dates: 1997,      <
>  1   040    ZQP $c ZQP <
>  2   020    8440670508 : $c |$|14.95 <
>  3   041 1  spa $h eng <
>  4   049    DD0A <

>  5   100 1  Shakespeare, William, $d 1564-1616. <
>  6   240 10 Romeo and Juliet. $l Spanish <

>  7   245 10 Romeo y Julieta / $c William Shakespeare ; [traducci'on:
Jaime Navarra Farr'e] <
>  8   250    1a ed. <
>  9   260    Barcelona, Espa~na : $b Ediciones B, S.A./Grupo Zeta, $c c1997. <
> 10   300    167 p. ; $c 18 cm. <
> 11   440 0  VIB ; $v 193/8 <
> 12   500    Translation of: Romeo and Juliet. <
> 13   504    Includes bibliographical references (p. 161-167). <
> 14   600 10 Shakespeare, William, $d 1564-1616 $x Translations into
Spanish. <
> 15   650 0  English drama (Tragedy) $y Early modern and Elizabethan, 1500-
1600 $x Translations into Spanish. <
> 16   650 0  Married people $z Italy $z Verona $x Drama. <
> 17   650 0  Family $z Italy $z Verona $x Drama. <
> 18   655 7  Tragedies. $2 gsafd <
> 19   700 12 Shakespeare, William, $d 1564-1616. $t Romeo and Juliet. $l
Spanish. <
> 20   700 1  Navarra Farr'e, Jaime. <


OCLC:   33812768            Rec stat:      n
Entered:    19951128        Replaced:      19951128      Used:      19951128
> Type:  a    ELvl:  I    Srce:  d    Audn:         Ctrl:          Lang:  eng
BLvl:  m    Form:       Conf:  0    Biog:         MRec:          Ctry:  cou
             Cont:        GPub:       Fict:  0    Indx:   0
Desc:  a    Ills:       Fest:  0    DtSt:  s    Dates: 1994,      <
>  1   040    IBA $c IBA <
>  2   090    PR2831.A2 $b B4 <
>  3   049    DD0A <

>  4   100 1  Shakespeare, William, $d 1564-1616. <
>  5   240 10 Romeo and Juliet <

>  6   245 14 The tragedy of Romeo and Juliet / $c by William Shakespeare.
Edited by Richard and Joan Bell. <
>  7   260    Boulder, CO : $b Armado and Moth, $c 1994. <
>  8   300    96 p. ; $c 22 cm. + $e director's script (96 p. ; 28 cm.) <
>  9   500    Title on cover: "Mr. William Shakespeares The Tragedie of Romeo
and Ivliet. Published according to the True Originall Copies." <
> 10   500    Actor's script and director's script include preface, notes, and
glossary. <
> 11   700 1  Bell, Richard. $4 edt <
> 12   700 1  Bell, Joan. $4 edt <
```

Fig. 6.6. Two metadata records showing two derivations of a work: one that is a Spanish translation, and one with the original, but out-of-favor title. Each has a main entry and uniform title that allows them to be collocated despite the different titles.

Collocation is a most important outcome of the practice of choosing primary access points. Main entry has proved to be, so far, the only way to collocate all manifestations of a work, even when some manifestations have different titles and some editions have different authors. A number of people on the listserv for the international *AACR2* conference[7] indicated that technology could accomplish this function. It is possible this will happen, but until someone figures out how, implements it, and makes it the norm for catalog display, main entry is still the best way we have to provide collocation.

Judgment of Most Important. Finally, when times are tough and full surrogate records cannot be made, and when brief records have to be created for some information packages, choice of a main entry ensures that at least the "most important" access point will be created. The Core Record mentioned in the preceding chapter calls for the main entry and perhaps one other name or title access point to be made and brought under access control. The choice of added entries depends upon the judgment of the cataloger and/or the policy of the institution in which the cataloger works.

AACR2 Principles for Choosing Main Entry

AACR2 is made up of many rules that seem unfathomable to the uninitiated. However, they are based upon principles that can be laid out in much the same order as the rules themselves. First, most works are created by a single individual, in which case main entry is the name of the person (or a surrogate for the name, e.g., pseudonym). If the author is unknown and unidentified in any way, then main entry is the title. (*Note*: "Unidentified in any way" means that there is not even a phrase such as "Author of Little Nell" as a statement of responsibility.) Other works are works of multiple responsibility, which can be synchronous or asynchronous.[8]

Principles for Choosing Main Entry—Synchronous Responsibility. When responsibility is synchronous, it means that all persons or bodies made the *same kind* of contribution, in which case main entry is the principal responsible party, if one is identified. Under *AACR2*, if no responsible party is identified as the principal one, the first of two or three equally represented responsible parties is chosen as the main entry. If there are more than three responsible parties, and no one party is identified as having principal responsibility, the main entry is the title. The title is also chosen if the work is accepted as sacred scripture by a religious group.

The practice of making access points for only three responsible parties is a questionable one in today's information environment. More and more information packages are being created jointly by four or more persons, and research supported by large grants of money is often written up by four or more persons.

In an information environment where space is not an issue, as it was in card catalog days when the so-called "Rule of 3" was institutionalized, the practice should be rethought.

The main reason given by rule makers for not changing the practice is the perceived cost of providing authority control for so many more names. However, this cost should be weighed against the cost to users of either not being able to find a name they seek or not being able to sort through hundreds of similar names. Anyone who has tried to find a particular name on the WWW knows the difficulty that is involved in finding anything in a nonaccess-controlled environment.

Principles for Choosing Main Entry—Asynchronous Responsibility. When responsibility is asynchronous, it means that the responsible parties have made *different kinds* of contributions to the existence of the work. Basically, there are three kinds of asynchronous responsibility: 1) responsibility has varied over time, resulting in modifications of works (e.g., work of original author is revised or rewritten by a later author); 2) responsibility has varied during the creation of a completely new work (e.g., artist and writer); or 3) the work emanates from a corporate body, but is written by a person or persons.

When responsibility has varied over time, the main entry is the original author unless it is clear that a later author has greater responsibility. For example, translations are works in which the work originally written by one person is put into another language by another person. Revisions are works in which the work of an original person may have updates and additional comments written by another person. In the case of republication of a work, the original work may be intact but with a new introduction and extensive comments written by another person. In all these cases *AACR2* principle calls for entry under the original author.

On the other hand, there are situations in which a later author has greater responsibility. For example, in an adaptation the idea contained in the work is that of the original author but all the words of this particular version are those of a new author (e.g., Shakespeare's plays completely rewritten as stories for children). Also, some revisions have so much updating and change that they are really the work of the new author. In these and cases like them, main entry should be the later author.

When responsibility has varied during the creation of a new work, main entry is the party deemed to have made the most important contribution. For example, many works are the result of the work of an artist and a writer. One criterion is whether the work was a collaboration. If so, it should be entered under the one named first, unless the other is given prominence by wording or layout. On the other hand, if the work was first completed by the writer and then had illustrations added by the artist, the writer is clearly the one with primary responsibility. In a work that gathers together works of the artist, and the writer has added only short captions for the works, the artist would be the primary access point.

Another example of a situation where responsibility varies during the creation of a new work is the report of an interview or exchange. If the work is written up as a report, all in the words of the interviewer (or perhaps with a few quotations), then the principal responsibility is that of the interviewer. If the work is presented in the exact words of the interviewed person(s), however, that person (or the first-named person) is chosen as the main entry.

When responsibility involves a corporate body, both the Paris Principles and *AACR2* list situations when corporate body is to be main entry (*AACR2*'s list is longer), and in the remainder of cases the main entry is to be a person or the title. Main entry, according to the Paris Principles, should be a corporate body when the work is the expression of the corporate thought or activity of the body (e.g., official reports, rules and regulations, manifestos, etc.) or when the wording of the title and the nature of the work imply that the corporate body is collectively responsible for the content (e.g., serials whose titles consist of a generic term like *Bulletin* preceded or followed by a corporate body name, if they include some account of the activities of the body).

The concept of "corporate author" has been a matter of international controversy. Some traditions have declared that corporate bodies cannot be "authors." When the new edition of *AACR* (that resulted in *AACR2*) was being hashed out, a compromise solution was agreed upon. Its essence was that even though a corporate body is not in a real sense an author, there are times when a corporate body is so tied to a document (e.g., an annual report) that the body must be chosen as the main entry. Main entry, according to *AACR2*, should be the corporate body, if the work falls into one of six categories:

- administrative nature
- some legal, governmental, or religious works
- collective thought of the body
- collective activity of a conference
- collective activity of a performing group (that goes beyond mere performance)
- cartographic materials emanating from a corporate body[9]

Some instances when title is main entry have been mentioned in the preceding discussion, but it is useful to have all of these listed together. The main entry should be title when:

- a work is truly anonymous (*Note:* This does not include works that use a phrase for an author.)

- a work has more than three responsible parties and none is singled out as having had primary responsibility
- a work has been produced under editorial direction
- a work has a corporate body involved, but the rules for corporate body main entry require title main entry instead

Additional Access Points

In all the cases just discussed, every responsible party and title that has been considered to be a candidate for primary access point should be an access point, if not the primary one. In the cataloging world these nonprimary access points are also called "added entries." When access points are made for every responsible party, it is not necessary for a user to have to guess which one has been chosen to be the primary access point or even to understand what main entry is all about. The usefulness of choosing a primary access point is to be able to display results of searches in a logical and collocated fashion, not to require a user to understand it. The fact that our systems do not provide such displays is a criticism of system design (see discussion in chapter 10).

ACCESS (AUTHORITY) CONTROL

The process called both access control and authority control today was once only called authority control because it was thought necessary to determine an "authorized" form for every entity known by variant forms. Thus, for example, the English form of Confucius has been determined by the Library of Congress to be the authoritative form, and the names given to this person in many other languages, including his Chinese name for himself, have been relegated to positions of "unauthorized" forms.

As the world of information becomes more global, a need has been felt to recognize that multiple language forms can be "correct" forms for access purposes. Thinking in terms of access control allows the possibility for authority records (or access control records) to contain all variant forms for an entity, without designating one as the "right" one. In such a circumstance one of the variants could be designated as the default display, but a good system would allow the user to bypass the default if desired. In any case a search for any one of the variants for an entity should retrieve all metadata records associated with the entity.

All access points (whether main or added entries) need to be under access control so that:

- persons or entities with the same name can be distinguished from each other,

- all names used by a person or body, and/or all manifestations of a name of a person or body will be brought together,

- all differing titles of the same work can be brought together.

Therefore, current practice dictates the establishment of a "heading" for each name or title that is intended to be an access point. The term *heading* comes from print catalog days, as already mentioned, when each access point was printed at the top of the copy of the surrogate record and was called the heading for the record (see fig. 6.7). In the online world "heading" has come to mean the exact string of characters of the authorized form of the access point as it appears in the authority record. It no longer appears at the head of a record, although sometimes it is at the head of a list of records in a catalog display (see fig. 6.8).

```
Calorie guide to brand names and
            basic foods

641.10 Krause, Barbara.
Kra      Calorie guide to brand names and basic
         foods / by Barbara Krause. -- New York :
         Penguin Books, 1996. -- 262 p. -- ISBN
         0-451-18524-2

         1. Calories (Food).  2. Food--Caloric
      content--Tables.  I. Title.
```

Fig. 6.7. Catalog card showing the title placed at the top of the record as the "heading" for the card.

```
Search Request: T=CATALOGIN                        University of Pittsburgh
 Search Results: 125 Entries Found                             Title Index
-----------------------------------------------------------------------------
      CATALOGING AND CLASSIFICATION A WORKBOOK
   9   MANHEIMER MARTHA L <1975>  (C1)
  10   MANHEIMER MARTHA L <1980>  (C1)

      CATALOGING AND CLASSIFICATION AN INTRODUCTION
  11        CHAN LOIS MAI <1981>  (C1)
  12        CHAN LOIS MAI <1994>    (B1)
  13        CHAN LOIS MAI <1994>    (C1)




---------------------------------------------- CONTINUED on next page ----
STArt over                Type number to display record        <F8> FORward page
HELp                      GUIDE                                 <F7> BACk page
OTHer options
```

Fig. 6.8. Screen from PITTCAT, the online catalog at the University of Pitts-burgh, showing "headings" followed by lines for separate records for the editions of the work in each case.

In access control, even though there may be a desire to provide more global access by not designating one of the variants as the authorized one, it is still necessary to go through the process of creating a heading in particular locales so that one form can be designated for default display for cases where a user does not wish to designate a preference. The following section discusses the principles involved in heading creation.

Headings for Access Points

Headings are maintained in authority files, which are collections of authority records. Each authority record identifies the form of name or title that has been selected as "authoritative" according to the rules. It lists many of the variant forms of name or variant forms of title that belong with the authorized form. It identifies sources of information about the variant forms of name or title or about the person or body or work represented by the name or title (see fig. 6.9, p. 120).

In the process of creating headings for *names* one must make at least one of three choices, and often must make all three: 1) choice of which name to use, 2) choice of which form of that name to use, 3) choice of format. In the third choice there are two subchoices: a) choice of entry word; b) choice of what additions need to be made to the name to distinguish it from same or similar names.

```
                         LC/NACO - NAME
 ARN:    618798
 Rec stat: c        Entered:      19810716
 Type:     z        Upd status:   a    Enc lvl:   n    Source:
 Roman:             Ref status:   a    Mod rec:        Name use: a
 Govt agn:          Auth status:  a    Subj:      a    Subj use: a
 Series:   n        Auth/ref:     a    Geo subd:  n    Ser use:  b
 Ser num:  n        Name:         a    Subdiv tp:      Rules:    c
    1  010      n  81073496 $z n  82138607
    2  040      DLC $c DLC $d DLC
    3  005      19970917125903.8
    4  100 00   Diana, $c Princess of Wales, $d 1961-
    5  400 10   Spencer, Diana Frances, $c Lady, $d 1961-
    6  400 00   Di, $c Lady, $d 1961-
    7  670      Dunlop, J. Charles and Diana, a royal romance, c1981 (subj.) $
 p. 6, etc. (Lady Diana Frances Spencer; b. July 1, 1961)
    8  670      Leete-Hodge, L. The Country Life book of the royal wedding,
 1981: $b table of contents (Diana, Princess of Wales)
    9  670      Carretier, M.-P. Lady Di chez elle, c1987.
   10  670      The Washington post, Aug. 31, 1997 $b (Diana d. Aug. 31, 1997
 from a fatal car accident)
```

Fig. 6.9. An authority record showing the "authoritative" heading for Princess Diana (in bold) and two variant forms of her name (lines 5 and 6).

In the process of creating headings for *titles*, it is necessary to: 1) choose which title will be used, and 2) decide upon the arrangement of the title and whether it is to be followed by distinguishing factors such as language and date. Principles for making these decisions are presented in the following subsections.

Principles for Choice of Personal Name

Choice of which name to use is involved in cases where a person has used different names, not including differently shortened forms of a single name. The first principle is to use the latest name of a person if the person's name has been changed. Examples:

- Chris Wallace changed to Notorious B.I.G.—use Notorious B.I.G.

- Sarah Ferguson married and became the Duchess of York—use Duchess of York, that is, "York, Sarah Mountbatten-Windsor, Duchess of"

The second principle is to use the predominant name of a person who is known by more than one name. Examples:

- Bill Clinton is also known as William Jefferson Clinton—use Bill Clinton
- Mildred Zaharias was known in pro golf as Babe Zaharias—use Babe Zaharias

The third principle is for persons who use pseudonyms. One should use the pseudonym if only one pseudonym is always used with all works. However, if the same writer used different names for separate bibliographic identities, one should use each of the names and create a separate authority record for each bibliographic identity. Different bibliographic identities are represented if a person has used one name for one kind of work and has used another name for another kind of work. Examples:

- Carolyn Heilbrun writes literary criticism using her own name but uses the pseudonym Amanda Cross for her mystery novels—use both names
- Charles Dodgson wrote serious mathematical works using his own name but used the pseudonym Lewis Carroll for his children's stories—use both names

However, if the writer is "contemporary" and uses more than one pseudonym or a real name and one or more pseudonyms, one should use each one for the works that are created using that name. Examples:

- Molly Keane and M. J. Farrell are the same person but the names are used with separate works—use both names
- Evan Hunter, Ed McBain, Hunt Collins, and Richard Marsten are the same person—use all four names

Principles for Form of Personal Name

Once the *name* has been chosen, one then determines which *form* of that name will be used. There may be variants in fullness, language, and spelling. Any of these may be affected by country of residence or activity. The overriding principle is that the form of name used by a person in his or her country of residence or activity is the form that is to be used.

When variant fullnesses have been used by a person, one should use the form most commonly found. For example, one should choose C. S. Lewis over Clive Staples Lewis. If no form predominates, one should choose the latest form. If in doubt, one should use fullest form. However, the form used in the person's country of residence or activity takes precedence. Even though the English-speaking world produces Hans Christian Andersen's works using the full form of name, during his lifetime in his country he preferred H. C. Andersen; so that is the form that should be chosen for the heading.

When there are variants in language one should use the form used by the person in his or her own country of residence or activity. For example, the person known in English as Benjamin Netanyahu has a name that transliterates to Binyamin Netanyahu. Therefore, the form chosen for the heading should be Binyamin, not Benjamin.

Variants in spelling call for using an official change in orthography, if this applies, or otherwise, using the predominant spelling. For example, the Arabic name, Qaddafi, can also be transliterated Gadhafi, Kaddafi, Qadhafi, Kadhafi, Gadafi, etc. The predominant spelling seems to be Qaddafi.

Principles for Entry Word and Remaining Structure of Personal Name

The structure of a personal name in an access-controlled record is usually the family name (or surname), followed by forenames, and often followed by dates of birth and/or death. In cases where a person does not have a family name or surname, the entry word is the person's first forename. A good rule of thumb is to use as entry word the part of the name that would be entered first in a telephone book in the person's country of residence or activity. For example, in Brazil the entry word is the last name of a compound surname; in Argentina the entry word is the first name of a compound surname; in Iceland the entry word is the given name (forename) because the last names of persons in Iceland are patronymics, not family names (i.e., a person's last name is the given name of one's father with either "son" or "dottir" attached to it). If a person has a known preference for the entry word to be used, then the person's preference takes precedence (e.g., a person with an unhyphenated compound surname in English that would ordinarily be entered under the last part may prefer entry under the first part).

Persons with only given names include royalty, persons of religious vocations, pop stars, etc. In some cases the name consists only of one name followed by distinguishing additions; or, as in the case of royalty, there may be several names. When there is only one name (e.g., Aristotle), that name is the entry word, but there will likely be distinguishing additions.

In order to distinguish an author from others with the same name, additions may be made. The most common ones are birth and/or death dates and full forenames added in parentheses. For example, the name of H. C.

Andersen would be followed by full forenames: Andersen, H. C. (Hans Christian). LC has as its policy to add birth and/or death dates and full forenames when they are known at the time of creating the heading for the name, even if there is not yet a conflict with an identical name.

Principles for Choice of Corporate Name

Corporate names differ from personal names in that corporate name changes may signal what is really a new corporate body. And corporate bodies can merge with another body, split into two or more bodies, or absorb another body, among other changes. The rules for choice of corporate names in *AACR2* reflect practice more than they do principle. According to the rules one is to create a new heading and a separate authority record for each name change. This eliminates the necessity of determining whether a name change signals a new body with a new purpose or is simply a name change, perhaps for political or other such reasons. Then each heading is to be used as the access point on surrogate records for information packages that were created during the time the body had that name.

Each authority record contains a connection to the preceding name of the body or bodies and to the following name. For example, the American Documentation Institute once had the name "Science Service. Documentation Division," and in 1937 the American Documentation Institute changed its name to American Society for Information Science. A properly constructed catalog would have references from each of the second two names to its preceding one and also references from each of the first two names to the name following it (see fig. 6.10, p. 124). Practice once included the entire history of name changes of a corporate body in one record, but the great amount of work involved dictated an abandonment of the practice in the United States.

Publications of corporate bodies often have more than one form of the body's name on the same information packages. There can be an abbreviation, an acronym, a shortened form, or a popular name in addition to the official name. If a variant is not an official name change, one is to use the predominant name. For example, the conventional name Westminster Abbey would be chosen over the official name Collegiate Church of St. Peter in Westminster. If the name is for an international body, and the name is in more than one language, *AACR2* calls for choosing the English form if there is one. It is hoped that with the move to international access control a new principle would be to choose the name in whichever language is best for the users of the catalog, which is the principle stated in the Paris Principles.

```
Science Service. Documentation Division

        search also under later name

American Documentation Institute
        _____


American Documentation Institute

        search also under earlier name

Science Service. Documentation Division
        _____


American Documentation Institute

        search also under later name

American Society for Information Science
        _____


American Society for Information Science

        search also under earlier name

American Documentation Institute
```

Fig. 6.10. References necessary in order to connect all three names of an organization.

Principles for Entry Word and Form of Heading for Corporate Names

In creating a heading for a corporate body, the general principle is to use the most common form of the name written in direct order as it appears on publications of the body. However, if the body is a government, religious, or otherwise subordinate body, the principle is that the heading for the subordinate body is its own name, if that name is distinctive and can stand alone; otherwise, the body's name is added as a subheading to the name of the superior body (e.g., in the heading "American Library Association. Cataloging and Classification Section," the name of the section cannot stand alone; it must be identified by the body in which it is a section). For many government bodies this means that the first word of the heading is the name of the government, which is usually the geographic name of the area governed (e.g., "United States. Federal Bureau of Investigation"). Under *AACR2* government names are all in English, if there is an English form, but according to the Paris Principles geographic names for governments are to be in the language suitable to the users of the catalog.

Principles for Choice of Uniform Title

Uniform titles are created when works have more than one manifestation and need to have title resolution. For example, if a work that has one title is made available in a different form, especially if it has a different title, there needs to be a way to bring these two manifestations together in the retrieval tool (e.g., the film "Gettysburg" based on the novel *The Killer Angels* by Michael Shaara). Uniform titles have been used for many years in the creation of bibliographic records for music. It has taken much longer for them to be accepted as useful in other situations, although the Library of Congress has long used uniform titles to subarrange and collocate the large number of records that fall under a famous prolific author such as Shakespeare or Mark Twain.

Use of the principle of uniform title requires an understanding of what constitutes a work, and this really has not been dealt with by any professional group of organizers, although a number of individuals have done research in this area.[10] Therefore the rules themselves reflect some inconsistency of interpretation.

The general principle is that if manifestations of a work appear under various titles, one must be chosen, and the original title in the original language is to be preferred unless another title in the same language has become better known. In the case of simultaneous publication of different titles, the choice should be the title of the edition published in the home country of the responsible party. With publication on the WWW it remains to be seen how the issue of variant titles will play out. One likely situation that will need uniform title work will be translations of works where there is an original title and a translation title.

Uniform titles also serve to differentiate identical titles of different works, especially when title is the principal access point. For example, different serials often have identical titles (e.g., *The Times* is a popular newspaper title that needs to be differentiated by city).

Principles for Arrangement of Uniform Titles

Basically, the words of a uniform title are in direct order as they appear on at least one manifestation of a work. In the United States initial articles are omitted because USMARC has no allowance for skipping over initial articles in the process of arranging uniform titles for display. Thus, Dickens's *The Pickwick Papers* has a uniform title *Pickwick Papers* so that it will be displayed with other titles beginning with "P" rather than those beginning with "T."

There are three main cases where additions to uniform titles may be needed: 1) for conflict resolution, 2) for language identification, and 3) to show parts of a work. An example of conflict resolution is: "Scarlet letter (Choreographic work : Graham)." This is clearly not the famous novel *Scarlet Letter*. An example of language identification is: "Nome della rosa. English." This would bring the English translation, *The Name of the Rose*, together with its Italian original. An example of a uniform title showing a part of a work is: "Paradise lost. Book 4."

Music uniform titles can be made for all these reasons, but in addition, they are used to organize the works of composers. Such works often do not have distinctive titles, and the same work often has a variety of titles (e.g., Beethoven's Fifth Symphony may be titled Beethoven's Fifth, Symphony no. 5, or The Fifth Symphony, to name only a few). Uniform titles provide a way to organize collections of concertos, quartets, symphonies, etc. (e.g., Mozart, Wolfgang Amadeus, 1756–1791. Concertos, flute, harp, orchestra, K. 299, C major).

Uniform titles are also used for some types of collections in *AACR2*. The theory behind this is dubious, but it seems to be necessary for the purpose of displaying all works of a particular kind together if their titles proper are not distinctive. Thus the record for a work called "Selected works of William Shakespeare" would display with the record for the title "Some works of Shakespeare," if both had the uniform title "Selections." Some uniform titles used in this way are: "Works," "Laws, etc.," "Piano music," and "Novels" (see fig. 6.11).

International Access (Authority) Control

Work is proceeding toward international access control. If this were to be accomplished, all forms of name would be on one record, with none chosen as "the" one that must be used. Each form would be identified by language. If there were several variant forms in one language, one of them would be designated as preferred for that language. A default display could be whichever form is most appropriate for users in a particular setting. A search for any one of the forms would retrieve records related to the entity represented by the record. One first step toward this goal is the AAAF (Anglo-American Authority File) being implemented at the British Library using the USNAF (U.S. Name Authority File) and the BLNAL (British Library Name Authority List). The USNAF itself is international, containing records contributed from Australia, Canada, Great Britain, and others.

International access control requires standards, and there are several that may be used to good advantage. The Z39.50 protocol (described in more detail in chapter 10) makes it possible to retrieve and display authority records on the Internet. This will enable the contributions of headings in different languages,

```
OCLC:   36033332            Rec stat:     n
  Entered:    19961204        Replaced:    19961204      Used:     19961204
> Type:  a       ELvl:  I     Srce:  d     Audn:        Ctrl:        Lang:  eng
  BLvl:  m       Form:        Conf:  0     Biog:        MRec:        Ctry:  nyu
                 Cont:        GPub:        Fict:  1     Indx:  0
  Desc:  a       Ills:        Fest:  0     DtSt:  s     Dates: 1885,    <
>   1  040       NOC $c NOC <
>   2  090       PR4652 $b  1885 <
>   3  090       $b  <
>   4  049       DD0A <

>   5  100 1     Eliot, George, $d 1819-1880. <
>   6  240 00    Novels. $k Selections. $f 1885 <

>   7  245 10    Adam Bede ; $b Silas Marner, the weaver of Raveloe ; Impressions
of Theophrastus Such / $c by George Eliot. <
>   8  246 3     Adam Bede ; Silas Marner, the weaver of Raveloe ; Impressions of
Theophrastus Such <
>   9  250       [Library ed.] <
>  10  260       New York : $b J. B. Alden, $c 1885. <
>  11  300       484, 167, 148 p. ; $c 21 cm. <
>  12  700 12    Eliot, George, $d 1819-1880. $t Silas Marner. $f 1885. <
>  13  700 12    Eliot, George, $d 1819-1880. $t Theophrastus Such. $f 1885. <
>  14  740 02    Silas Marner. <
>  15  740 02    Impressions of Theophrastus Such. <
```

```
OCLC:   31134215            Rec stat:     p
  Entered:    19940825        Replaced:    19950407      Used:     19980225
> Type:  a       ELvl:        Srce:        Audn:        Ctrl:        Lang:  eng
  BLvl:  m       Form:        Conf:  0     Biog:        MRec:        Ctry:  nyu
                 Cont:        GPub:        Fict:  1     Indx:  0
  Desc:  a       Ills:        Fest:  0     DtSt:  s     Dates: 1995,    <
>   1  010       94-24675 <
>   2  040       DLC $c DLC <
>   3  020       0517122235 <
>   4  043       e-uk-en <
>   5  050 00    PR4652 $b  1995 <
>   6  082 00    823/.8 $2 20 <
>   7  090       $b  <
>   8  049       DD0A <

>   9  100 1     Eliot, George, $d 1819-1880. <
>  10  240 10    Novels. $k Selections <

>  11  245 10    George Eliot, selected works. <
>  12  260       New York : $b Gramercy Books ; $a Avenel, N.J. : $b Distributed
by Random House Value Pub., $c 1995. <
>  13  300       xii, 820 p. ; $c 24 cm. <
>  14  505 0     Silas Marner -- The lifted veil -- Brother Jacob --
Middlemarch. <
>  15  651 0     England $x Social life and customs $y 19th century $x Fiction. <
>  16  740 01    Selected works. <
```

Fig. 6.11. **Two metadata records for two works that pull together different groupings of George Eliot's novels. The uniform title "Novels. Selections" allows these two works to be displayed together under the main entry "Eliot, George."**

and forms of heading in any particular language can be verified by experts in that language. The Working Group on Transnational Exchange of Authority Data (a group that is part of the International Federation of Library Associations) has looked at the possibility of an International Standard Authority Data Number (ISADN). At this writing the ISADN is on hold while the group considers whether a UNIMARC authority record standard that could be interchanged via Z39.50 would eliminate the need for a standard number.

CONCLUSION

We have discussed in this chapter the creation of name and title access points for surrogate records. The only metadata standards so far that deal with choice and form of name and title access points are: 1) *AACR2*, the access points part of which is based on the Paris Principles, and 2) the *APPM*, which is based on *AACR2*. The massive amounts of data dealt with in libraries and archives have led to the development of the concepts of authority control and access control. Searchers for information need to be able to find works related to specific persons, corporate bodies, places, or other works. As the number of names and titles increases to a critical number, the ability to find specific names and titles and sort them out from similar and identical ones becomes impossible without access control. This is likely to be the next step for metadata.

Most information packages have a subject content. It is often the subject content that is sought by users of retrieval tools. The next chapter addresses the myriad ways of providing verbal access to subject content.

NOTES

1. A. H. Chaplin and Dorothy Anderson, eds. International Conference on Cataloging Principles (1961: Paris, France), *Report* (London: IFLA International Office for UBC, 1981).

2. Doris Hargrett Clack, ed., *The Making of a Code: The Issues Underlying AACR2* (Chicago: American Library Association, 1980).

3. Michael Gorman, "AACR2: Main Themes," in *The Making of a Code*, p. 46.

4. Richard Smiraglia, "Authority Control and the Extent of Derivative Bibliographic Relationships" (Ph.D. diss., University of Chicago, 1992).

5. Joint Steering Committee for Revision of Anglo-American Cataloguing Rules, *International Conference on the Principles and Future Development of AACR*, available: http://www.nlc-bnc.ca/jsc/index.htm, accessed October 1998.

6. Ibid.

7. Ibid.

8. See also Wesley Simonton and Marilyn Jones McClaskey, *AACR2 and the Catalog: Theory, Structure, Changes* (Littleton, Colo.: Libraries Unlimited, 1981).

9. *AACR2*, pp. 313–14.

10. Martha M. Yee, "The Concept of Work for Moving Image Materials," *Cataloging and Classification Quarterly* 18, no. 2 (1993): 33–40; Smiraglia, "Authority Control"; Gregory Hart Leazer, "A Conceptual Plan for the Description and Control of Bibliographic Works" (Ph.D. diss., Columbia University, 1993); Sherry L. Vellucci, *Bibliographic Relationships in Music Catalogs* (Lanham, Md.: Scarecrow Press, 1997).

SUGGESTED READINGS

Barnett, Linda. "Access Control Records: Prospects and Challenges." Paper presented at OCLC's *Authority Control in the 21st Century: An Invitational Conference*, March 31–April 1, 1996. Available: http://www.oclc.org/oclc/man/authconf/barnhart.htm (Accessed October 1998).

Chan, Lois Mai. *Cataloging and Classification: An Introduction*. New York: McGraw-Hill, 1994, pp. 107–12, 123–27.

Hagler, Ronald. *The Bibliographic Record and Information Technology*. 3rd ed. Chicago: American Library Association, 1997, pp. 95–106, 213–52.

Rogers, JoAnn V., and Jerry D. Saye. "Access Points for Nonprint Materials." Chap. 10 in *Nonprint Cataloging for Multimedia Collections*. 2nd ed. Littleton, Colo.: Libraries Unlimited, 1987.

Tillett, Barbara B. "21st Century Authority Control: What Is It and How Do We Get There?" In *The Future Is Now: Reconciling Change and Continuity in Authority Control*. Dublin, Ohio: OCLC, 1995, pp. 17–21.

Wilson, Patrick. "The Catalog As Access Mechanism: Background and Concepts." In *Foundations of Cataloging: A Sourcebook*, edited by Michael Carpenter and Elaine Svenonius, pp. 253–68. Littleton, Colo.: Libraries Unlimited, 1985.

Wynar, Bohdan S. *Introduction to Cataloging and Classification*. 8th ed. by Arlene G. Taylor. "Choice of Access Points." Chap. 9. Englewood, Colo.: Libraries Unlimited, 1992.

CHAPTER 7

VERBAL SUBJECT ANALYSIS

$\mathcal{S}$ubject approaches in the electronic age have become a major way of finding information. Search engines have tried to fill the void on the Internet, yet users become more and more frustrated with the thousands of "hits" from keyword searches. With the massive increase in availability of recorded information it becomes more and more evident that keyword searching alone will not suffice. Virtually every word in the English language has more than one meaning or sense, and many of those senses have more than one nuance; many words can be used as nouns, verbs, adjectives, or adverbs. Search systems that purport to allow the user to use "natural language" cannot yet successfully distinguish among meanings or parts of speech in very large general systems, although progress has been made in narrow subject areas.

In addition there is evidence that people writing about the same concepts often do not use the same words to express a concept, and people searching for the same concept do not think of the same words to search for it. Most of the myriad studies of "interindexer consistency" have asked participants to think up words in their heads, not to take vocabulary from a list; therefore, although these studies have been used by some authors to "prove" that subject indexing is worth very little because indexers are "inconsistent," what the studies really show is that people do not think of the same terms to express the same concept. Thomas Mann has given an excellent analysis of some interindexer consistency studies that support these observations.[1] The clear implication is that controlled vocabulary is needed to reconcile all the various possible words that can be used to express a concept and to differentiate among all the possible meanings that can be attached to certain words.

Several questions are addressed in this chapter. They include: What is the process for determining subject content? How is subject content determined for nontextual materials? How is subject content expressed verbally in surrogate/metadata records? How should an indexing vocabulary be structured? Is a controlled indexing vocabulary necessary or can Natural Language Processing (NLP) be used instead? How do ontologies assist in NLP? How is keyword searching used for finding subject content?

SUBJECT ANALYSIS PROCESS[2]

At a recent institute at OCLC there was unanimous agreement among faculty and participants that access to electronic resources requires controlled vocabulary and classification.[3] So far these cannot be assigned automatically with a satisfactory degree of accuracy. It is still necessary for humans to determine the concepts that need controlled vocabulary terms assigned to them. The need for humans to do conceptual analysis is great; yet many persons who are currently working to apply index terms from a controlled vocabulary have only had instruction in assigning terminology from a particular list, and not instruction in the process of determining "aboutness."

Subject analysis is the part of indexing or cataloging that deals with, first, the conceptual analysis of an information package. *Conceptual analysis* is the determination of what the intellectual content of an item is "about" and/or determining what an item "is." Second, subject analysis deals with translating the conceptual analysis into the conceptual framework of the classification or subject heading system being used by the cataloger, indexer, or classifier. This means that if one is using the Dewey Decimal Classification (DDC), for example, one must place the concept in a hierarchy starting with one of DDC's top ten categories. Or if one is using *Library of Congress Subject Headings* (*LCSH*), one must conceptualize a sentence concerning what the information package is "about," and then make note (physically or mentally) of terms from the sentence that need to be searched in *LCSH* to choose the controlled vocabulary terms to express the concept. Following these conceptual steps, the framework must be translated into the specific classificatory symbols or specific terminology used in the classification or controlled vocabulary system. That is, at this step, one would assign terms from a controlled vocabulary such as *LCSH* or would assign classification notation(s) from a classification schedule such as DDC.

A first step in conceptual analysis is to examine the parts of the information package that stand out. In many instances this information will be found in the information packages themselves, but in other instances it will be found in accompanying materials (e.g., user manuals, containers, inserts from

CD-ROM cases, labels, etc.). There are also outside sources such as publishers' announcements.

Somewhat different techniques have to be used for information packages that contain text versus information packages that contain nontextual information. Concentrating first on the information packages that contain text, the following parts should be considered:

- title and subtitle

  A title can be helpful in giving an immediate impression of the topic of a document, but a title can also be misleading. The title of the web page *Proceedings of the OCLC Internet Cataloging Colloquium*[4] is quite straightforward. On the other hand, the title *Alleghany Airlines Book Club Presents*[5] is not so clear, and is not even assisted much by its subtitle, *A compendium of tiddlywinks perversions*. Another example is *What the Thunder Said*,[6] which turns out to be a web site devoted to the life and works of T. S. Eliot.

- table of contents

  A list of contents can help clarify the topic and identify subtopics. A list of contents can be especially helpful for items that are collections of articles, papers, etc., by different authors. The table of contents for the *Proceedings of the OCLC Internet Cataloging Colloquium*,[7] shows the variety of specific topics covered as well as different levels of specificity (see fig. 7.1).

- introduction, or equivalent

  An introduction often is an aid in determining the author's plan or objective and may serve to indicate an author's point of view. The introduction to *Japanese Garden Database*,[8] for example, explains that this is not just descriptions of the gardens but draws upon literature, paintings, images, etc., to provide information "on the history, construction, materiality, people, language, patterns, and processes by which these gardens were constructed."

- index terms, words, or phrases that are printed in typeface different from the rest; hyperlinks; abstract if provided, etc.

  These elements provide confirmation or contradiction of impressions gained from examination of the title, table of contents, introduction, etc. A back-of-the-book index can show what topics are given the most attention by showing the number of pages devoted to each.

Proceedings of the OCLC Internet Cataloging
Colloquium

San Antonio, Texas
January 19, 1996

Introduction

Field Reports

- The "Ambivalent" Library, Mark Watson, University of Oregon
- Does It Really Matter?: The Choice of Format, Order of Note Fields, and Specifics of 856, Jackie Shieh, University of Virginia Library
- Access Information on the Internet: A Feasibility Study of MARC Formats and AACR2, Amanda Xu, MIT Libraries

Position Papers

- Using Library Classification Schemes for Internet Resources, Diane Vizine-Goetz, OCLC
- Cyberstacks, Gerry McKiernan, Iowa State University
- The Traditional Library and the National Information Infrastructure, Vianne T. Sha, Timothy B. Patrick, Thomas R. Kochtanek, University of Missouri-Columbia
- Access to Networked Documents: Catalogs? Search Engines? Both? Arlene G. Taylor and Patrice Clemson, University of Pittsburgh
- Catalogers and the Creation of Metadata Systems : A Collaborative Vision at the University of Michigan, Kevin Butterfield, University of Michigan
- Modifying Cataloging Practice and OCLC Infrastructure for Effective Organization of Internet Resources, Ingrid Hsieh-Yee, Catholic University of America

ISBN 1-55653-219-9

Fig. 7.1. Web page table of contents for the proceedings of a conference in which the papers are about many different subtopics of the main theme. (Source: http://www.oclc.org/oclc/man/colloq/toc.htm)

- illustrations, diagrams, tables, captions
  Illustrations and their captions are particularly important in assessing the subjects in fields such as art, where, in many cases, illustrations make up the vast majority of the content and therefore must be examined in order to determine "aboutness." The captions for illustrations are often quite descriptive of subject content.

For nontextual information, one has to examine the object, picture, or other representation, itself. Some such information packages are manufactured and include accompanying materials such as boxes with text, instruction sheets, labels, etc. Electronic nontangible information packages that are basically pictures or other forms of artistic work quite often have captions that explain something about them in text form. For individual works or objects with no accompanying text, however, one must examine the items themselves, and translating ideas into words can be difficult.

Exhaustivity

As one examines documents for subject content, one must have a clear idea about the level of exhaustivity that is required. Exhaustivity is the number of concepts that will be considered in the conceptual framework of the system. The number of concepts any given agency's catalogers/indexers will assign often is guided by local policy. A. G. Brown identifies two basic degrees of exhaustivity: depth indexing and summarization.[9] Depth indexing aims to extract all the main concepts dealt with in an information resource, recognizing many subtopics and subthemes. Summarization identifies only a dominant, overall subject of the item, recognizing only concepts embodied in the main theme.

In library cataloging subject analysis has traditionally been carried out at the summarization level, reserving depth indexing for other enterprises such as periodical indexes. That is, in the cataloging of books and serials in libraries, the cataloger generally has attempted to find the one overall subject concept that encompassed the whole item. Depth indexing has traditionally been reserved for parts of items (e.g., articles in journals, chapters in books) and has usually been done by commercial indexing enterprises. In the case of an electronic serial such as *Journal of Statistics Education*,[10] the subject at the summarization level can be no more in depth than "education about statistics," even though the subjects of individual articles are much more specific. There is no reason, however, that "whole items" cannot be indexed more exhaustively. At the summarization level, *Proceedings of the OCLC Internet Cataloging Colloquium* would be about cataloging of Internet resources (see again fig. 7.1). A look at the table of contents, however, shows that depth indexing at another level would allow indexing of various concepts involved in the cataloging of Internet resources, such as classification of the Internet, metadata, search engines, etc.

It should be pointed out that many books have extensive back-of-the-book indexes, and this has been one of the justifications for subject indexing at the summarization level. That is, there is a difference in degree between "document retrieval" and "information retrieval" (see fig. 7.2). Summarization allows for document retrieval, after which many users use a document's internal index (which, in electronic resource terms, may mean the word search capability) to retrieve the relevant information they need from the document. Depth indexing, however, allows retrieval at a much more specific level, even to the retrieval of sections or paragraphs in a document.

Fig. 7.2. Illustration of the concept that summarization leads to document retrieval and depth indexing leads to information retrieval. The line moves gradually from summarization to depth indexing, and it is possible to have a subject analysis system that is halfway between the two extremes.

The summarization approach is very useful in retrieving tangible resources (e.g., CD-ROMs, videocassettes, print journals, etc.). As we do more and more indexing of intangible electronic resources (e.g., web sites), we will have to think carefully about summarization versus depth indexing. Search engines do the ultimate "depth indexing." Often, the occurrence of a word anywhere in a web site means the web site will be retrieved by a search on that word, whether or not the word reflects any topic covered in the information package.

In addition to deciding the level of indexing, we face the problem of deciding what is an analyzable unit. Traditionally, as already stated, whole items have been analyzable units in libraries, collections have been analyzable units in archives, and articles in journals have been analyzable units for commercial indexing enterprises (along with individual poems, stories, or essays published in collections). On the Internet there is so far no definition for an analyzable unit. Should it be the whole electronic journal; individual issues of that journal; the whole web site (i.e., a "home" page along with all links located and controlled at that site); or individual pieces of a web site? Once we've decided that, we have to rethink whether our users need summarization-level subject headings or depth indexing vocabulary for the analyzable unit.

Identification of Concepts

Different types of concepts can be used as subjects of information packages. The types discussed in this section are:

- topics
- names

  - persons

  - corporate bodies

  - geographic areas

  - named entities (e.g., buildings, architectural sites, etc.)
- time periods
- form

Topics Used As Subject Concepts

Determining what an information package is about can be difficult. Patrick Wilson has discussed the difficulty imposed upon us starting with Cutter, whose second function of a catalog, in part, was that it should show what a library has on a given subject. Wilson has suggested that part of the problem is that we take Cutter's statement to mean that there is an obvious subject in every information package and that we should be able to identify it as "the" subject. In fact a subject can have many facets and there may not be just one thing to mention in response to the question: "What is it about?"[11]

Although some information packages seem to have an easily determined subject, it may not really be so easy. A work entitled *History of Sociology* is about the discipline of sociology; but it is more specifically about sociology from a historical perspective while not being about the discipline of history. This distinction has a certain subtlety that is learned through education in our present-day Western tradition. It is possible that in another place and time, history would be considered to be the major subject of anything historical, regardless of the specific topic.

Cultural differences. An understanding of the place of one's culture as well as one's education in determining subject matter is also important. Lakoff has written about the research of Berlin and Kay on the understanding of color depending upon one's language. They found that there are eleven basic color categories in English, but in some other languages there are fewer basic color categories. In languages that have only two basic color terms, the terms are the equivalent of *black* and *white*, or *cool* and *warm*. The effects upon subject analysis of growing up in different cultures with different languages, then, means that persons from different places cannot perceive reality in exactly the same way.[12]

Another example is provided by Langridge. He comments upon the unconscious effect that must occur in the mind of a person used to the arrangement of the library in the People's University of China, where all knowledge is divided into three groups: Theory of knowledge; Knowledge of the class struggle; and Knowledge of the productive struggle.[13] Although Western cultural differences are perhaps not so different as those between Western and non-Western, different indexers can expect to see things differently depending upon such things as educational background and cultural upbringing.

Wilson's methods. Wilson has described some of the methods that people use to come to their own understanding of what a work is about.[14] Wilson did not name these methods himself. The names used here have been supplied by the author. The first might be called the *Purposive method*. One tries to determine what the author's aim or purpose is. If the creator of the information package gives a statement of purpose, then we can presume to know what the work is "about." But some creators give no such statement, and others seem to aim at several things at once.

Wilson's second method of deciding what a work is about might be called the *Figure-ground method*. Using this method, one tries to determine a central figure that stands out from the background of the rest of the information package. However, what stands out depends on the observer of the package as well as on its creator. What catches one's interest is not necessarily the same from person to person, and may not even be the same for the same person a few weeks later.

Wilson's third method is the *Objective method*. One tries to be objective by counting references to various items to determine which one vastly outnumbers the others. Unfortunately, an item constantly referred to might be a background item (e.g., Germany in a work about World War II). It is also possible that the concept that is central to the "aboutness" might not ever be expressed concretely. Wilson gives the example of a work being about a person's political career, but those words are never used in the work. Collantes found that when people were asked to read abstracts and then write down subject words or phrases that they believed conveyed the meaning in the abstracts, 8 percent of the readers used words that did not appear anywhere in the abstract.[15]

The last of Wilson's methods is that of *Appealing to unity or to rules of selection and rejection*. When using this method one tries to determine what holds the work together, what cohesiveness there is, and what has been said (selection) and not said (rejection). Again, the observer of the information package has to be objective and also has to know quite a lot about the subject in order to know what was rejected. There may be several ways in which the work can appear to be unified; and creators do not always reach the ideal of a completely unified presentation.

As this discussion indicates, there seems to be no one correct way to determine "aboutness." One can use any or all of these methods, but the different methods will not necessarily lead to the same result. If they give the same result, as they often could, it would appear that *the* subject has been identified. However, a single person might arrive at three or four different subjects using the different methods, and several persons might arrive at different results using the same method.

Consistency. As mentioned earlier, evidence of the difficulty in determining "aboutness" consistently is found in a number of studies in which people have been asked to give terminology they would use to search for specific items. For example, in a 1954 study by Lilley, 340 students looked at six books and suggested an average of sixty-two different terms for each book.[16] In the 1992 study already mentioned, Collantes found "an average of 25.6 [topical] names per object or concept."[17] Please note that *this is not a failure of controlled vocabulary*! It is a failure of individuals to determine the same "aboutness" in a document or to come up with the same natural language in cases where the same "aboutness" has been determined. There is evidence that catalogers using the same controlled vocabulary and the same rules for it will produce consistent subject headings, as long as they have the same conceptual analysis to draw upon.[18]

Langridge does not agree that there may be a variety of possible answers to the question "What is it about?" He believes that inconsistencies are the result of confusing this question with the question "What is it for?"[19] Even if one cannot agree with his assessment that determining "What is it about?" is no problem, his "What is it for?" question provides a valuable insight. For example, Richard W. Unger's *The Art of Medieval Technology: Images of Noah the Shipbuilder* appears at first glance to be about Noah and the Ark. However, upon examination of the author's purpose, the table of contents, and the captions with the illustrations, one learns that the work is really about changes in the techniques used in shipbuilding in the Middle Ages. Artists' depictions of Noah building the Ark changed as the techniques changed through the centuries.

Another example is found in the title mentioned earlier: *History of Sociology*. In our culture we treat its aboutness as sociology, treated from the perspective of history. The topic of a resource entitled *Introduction to Sociology* is also sociology, but these two resources would look very different. A user looking for one of these treatments probably would not be happy with the other. Answering the "What is it for?" question helps to separate these two treatments.

Nontextual information. Determination of topics of nontextual information packages is even less clear-cut than for textual resources. Several levels of conceptual analysis may be attempted. Barnett has listed three levels:

1. identification of a concept or combination of concepts representing topical coverage,

2. pre-iconographic or generic identification and enumeration of objects and scenes represented,

3. identification of interpretive thematic or iconographic significance associated with objects and scenes depicted.[20]

With art works it is perhaps easiest to enumerate objects and scenes represented. It may also be possible to identify a subject concept (e.g., a depiction of a battle scene) and to determine from a work's title a specific instance of the concept (e.g., the battle of Gettysburg). With musical works it is much harder to identify concepts or enumeration of what is represented. If one wants true conceptual analysis of nontextual information packages, such analysis usually must be at the interpretive thematic level. It is fairly easy to describe how objects look, but identification of interpretive thematic or iconographic significance for any nontextual information packages requires special study and training.

Names Used As Subject Concepts

In the process of determining what a document is about, it may be found that the topic, or one aspect of the topic, is a person, a corporate body, a geographic area, or some other named entity.

Persons. An individual person is the topic of a web site or other resource that is biographical or that covers aspects of a person's career (e.g., the aforementioned site dedicated to T. S. Eliot). Such a work is also, in a sense, about one representative of a group of persons (e.g., literary writers). The Library of Congress in applying the *Library of Congress Subject Headings (LCSH)*, for example, has the policy of making a subject heading for the group, as well as for the person, on the assumption that if an information seeker wants to learn about, let's say, "literary writers," then a site about one such person may be of use.

Corporate Bodies. A corporate body may be the topic of an information package about an entity such as an oil company or a library. There are also entities whose names resemble corporate body names, but they are not the same. A corporate body is an organization or group of persons who are identified by a name and who act as an entity. Sometimes such bodies have the same name as the building they work in. This is often true of churches, for example, and one then has to be certain whether the building or the corporate group is the topic of the work.

Geographic Names. Geographic names can take different roles in the determination of subject content. In some cases a document may actually be about a specific place, as, for example, something about the history and growth of Pittsburgh, Pennsylvania. However, much of the time, the geographic area provides a context for the topical content of the work, as in a work about the projects and life of architect Julia Morgan who did virtually all of her work in California. Falling between these extremes is the case where the geographic area is the topic of the topic. An example is the exhibition catalog, *"A Sweet Foretaste of Heaven": Artists in the White Mountains, 1830–1930.*[21] The exhibition consisted of landscape paintings of the White Mountains of New Hampshire.

Named Entities. Some named entities resemble both corporate names and geographic names, but are neither. An example is the archaeological site name, Megiddo (Extinct city).

Chronological Elements As Subject Concepts

The time period can be an important aspect of the subject content of information packages. Time periods limit the coverage of the topic and therefore dictate content in subtle ways. For example, information packages about computer access to information in the 1970s will not be likely to include information about the World Wide Web or about SGML.

Time can be expressed in a number of ways. Named periods (e.g., World War II) and styles (e.g., Renaissance) often act as surrogates to chronology. These are of particular importance in the fields of art, architecture, music, and literature, but they have not been particularly well handled by controlled vocabularies or by the MARC format. Only specific dates or date ranges are usually treated separately. Named periods and styles generally have been treated as topical information.

The Concept of Form As Subject

The final step in the conceptual analysis process is the identification of the form of the information package being analyzed or of important parts of that information package. *Form* is not strictly a subject feature. According to Langridge:

> There remain a number of very important characteristics requiring identification which have always been treated as part of the process of subject analysis. I shall refer to these as formal characteristics to distinguish them from the real subject features. Though none of these formal elements alters the subject of a document, some of them can make a considerable difference to its treatment or presentation.[22]

Form is a concept that has been associated with subject analysis from the inception of the idea that books could be entered in catalogs and placed on shelves according to the category they belonged to. Early categories included such forms as encyclopedias, biographies, and histories, as well as subjects such as chemistry and religion. Later, as subject headings evolved to mean what an item is about instead of a category to which the book belonged, the idea of form remained as part of the subject heading process. Because it was often difficult to separate the ideas of "aboutness" from "form," as in the case of "history," which seems to incorporate elements of both, the concept of form has only recently begun to be treated differently in surrogate records.

In an effort to aid in the process of separating the concept of form from the concept of subject, the Subject Analysis Committee of the American Library Association (ALA) devised a definition for form. The definition was officially approved by appropriate ALA bodies in January 1993:

> Form data are those terms and phrases that designate specific kinds or genres of materials. Materials designated with these terms or phrases may be determined by an examination of:
>
> > their physical character (e.g., videocassettes, photographs, maps, broadsides)
> >
> > the particular type of data that they contain (e.g., bibliographies, questionnaires, statistics)
> >
> > the arrangement of information within them (e.g., diaries, outlines, indexes)
> >
> > the style, technique, purpose, or intended audience (e.g., drama, romances, cartoons, commercials, popular works) or a combination of the above (e.g., scores)

A single term may be modified by other terms, in which case the whole phrase is considered to be form data (e.g., aerial photographs, French dictionaries, conversation and phrase books, wind ensemble suites, telephone directories, vellum bound books, science fiction).[23]

Separating form from subject has become increasingly important as the organizing world has become more attuned to organizing information that is not in textual form. Identification of form in the area of music has always been very important and has been accommodated in the past by treating it as subject. Now more information seekers are looking for other kinds of information forms (e.g., chalk drawings, digital maps, sculpture reproductions, etc.). By separating form from subject it will be possible to take advantage of system design that allows searching for forms of information.

TRANSLATING CONCEPTS INTO INDEX TERMS

Answering a series of questions, either formally or informally, can help one go through the subject analysis process quickly. A sample set of questions and an example is found in the appendix.

Once the conceptual analysis is complete, the concepts identified must be translated into the controlled vocabulary being used (e.g., *Art & Architecture Thesaurus (AAT)*, *Library of Congress Subject Headings (LCSH)*, *Medical Subject Headings (MeSH)*, etc.). Specific rules for using these systems are found in their introductions, as well as, in some cases, manuals that accompany them. Before being able to make the best use of the specific tools, however, it is helpful to understand controlled vocabularies in general and how they work.

CONTROLLED VOCABULARY

A controlled vocabulary operates by choosing a preferred way of expressing a concept and then making certain that synonymous ways of expressing the concept will be connected to the preferred terminology. Traditionally, the non-used terminology appears in the controlled vocabulary listed under the preferred terminology and is often preceded by the abbreviation **UF** meaning "used for." For example:

Maintenance
    UF Preventive maintenance
          Upkeep

The reverse of this entry in a list is an entry at each of the unused terms that refers the user to the preferred term:

> Preventive maintenance *use* **Maintenance**
> Upkeep *use* **Maintenance**

A controlled vocabulary also keeps track of the hierarchical relationships of a concept. The preferred term is shown in relationship to its broader term(s), narrower term(s), and related term(s), if any. These are often designated by the abbreviations **BT**, **NT**, and **RT**, respectively. For example:

> **Maintenance**
> > **BT** Maintainability (Engineering)
> > **RT** Repairing
> > **NT** Grounds maintenance

(This example is not exhaustive, but only illustrative.) These relationships are reciprocal: under "Maintainability (Engineering)," Maintenance would be listed as a narrower term; under "Repairing," Maintenance would be listed as a related term; and under "Grounds maintenance," Maintenance would be listed as a broader term.

Some controlled vocabularies also give hierarchical listings of the vocabulary terms. In these lists the terms are placed in juxtaposition to each other so that one can visualize broader and narrower relationships. Such lists are helpful in seeing where a term fits within an entire hierarchy, not just its relationship to the terms above and below it.

A major national standard exists for the creation of controlled vocabularies. ANSI/NISO Standard Z39.19-1993 is entitled *Guidelines for the Construction, Format, and Management of Monolingual Thesauri.*[24]

Controlled Vocabulary Problems

In the process of creating a controlled vocabulary there are certain verbal difficulties that must be dealt with. An understanding of these problems can enhance one's ability to use a particular existing controlled vocabulary.

Specific vs. General

The level of specificity must be decided at the outset of establishing a controlled vocabulary. Various lists may have different thresholds for how specific the terminology will be. "Cats" is not as specific as "Cat breeds." "Cat breeds" is not as specific as "Siamese cats." "Siamese cats" is not as specific as "Bluepoint Siamese cats." In *Library of Congress Subject Headings* (*LCSH*), for example, the most specific term is "Siamese cats"; in *Sears List of Subject Headings* (*Sears*) the most specific term is "Cats," although an instruction is given that, if needed, a term for a specific breed of cat may be created.

To some extent the decision on this matter is a function of the type of users who are intended to use the list, and upon the nature of the information packages that are to be assigned terms from the list. If the collection has mainly general kinds of information, then "Cats" is probably sufficient, even to cover a few more specific items. If the users are children likely to be looking for general kinds of information, then again "Cats" is probably sufficient as the most specific level.

Synonymous Concepts

The English language rarely has absolutely true synonyms—i.e., situations where two words mean the same thing and have no variations in nuance. However, there are multitudes of synonymous words and phrases that mean so close to the same thing that they can be interchanged for each other. These are the terms that make keyword searching so tricky and frustrating.

In the creation of a controlled vocabulary it is necessary to identify all the synonymous terms that should be brought together under one term. Do "attire," "dress," and "clothing" mean the same thing? If not exactly the same, or if they have different nuances, are the differences important enough to warrant separate vocabulary terms for them? Determination should take into account which term is best known to the intended user; but with regional, national, and international differences in English-language usage, a decision may have to be arbitrary.

Word Form for One-Word Terms

Words in English often have more than one form that can mean the same thing (e.g., "clothing" and "clothes"). Also language evolves, and as it does so, a concept has a tendency to be expressed first as two words, then as a hyphenated word, then as one word (e.g., "on line," "on-line," "online"). Sometimes all three forms appear in use at the same time. British and American spellings give us another case of word form difference (e.g., "catalogue" and "catalog").

Prefixes to a word can create a word with a different meaning, but in some cases, where the meaning is opposite, it would not make sense to use both terms in the controlled vocabulary because one of the concepts can never be discussed without the other (e.g., "armament" and "disarmament," "equality" and "inequality").

A major word form difference is singular versus plural. There is no rule on which form to use. Most of the time the plural will have the broadest coverage (e.g., "videocassettes" rather than "videocassette"); but at times the singular is broader (e.g., "apple" can apply to both the fruit and the tree; "apples" refers only to the fruit). Sometimes the singular and the plural forms of a word have different meanings (e.g., in *LCSH* "art" refers specifically to visual art; "arts" refers to various subdisciplines including visual arts, literature, and the performing arts).

Sequence and Form for Multiword Terms and Phrases

In some controlled vocabularies there are terms and phrases made up of two or more words. Some of these are modified nouns (e.g., Environmental education); others are phrases with conjunctions or prepositions (e.g., Information theory in biology); and a third group has qualifiers added in parentheses (see discussion below). A problem in constructing such terminology in a controlled way is being consistent in the order and form of the individual words used. For example, "Energy conservation" and "Conservation of energy resources" mean the same thing. The first phrase places the concept with other headings beginning with the word "energy"; the second phrase puts the concept with other things having to do with conservation. If the list creates such phrases, it must be certain to have references from every possible construction of the phrase—referring from them to the construction that was chosen.

Some controlled vocabularies (notably *LCSH*) present some multiword terms and phrases in inverted order (e.g., Education, Bilingual; Asylum, Right of). Much of this was done in the past in order to collocate a group of headings on a broad concept with subconcepts arranged alphabetically below it. Thus, instead of "Bilingual education" being found in "B" and "Higher education" being found in "H," both were found in "E" as "Education, Bilingual" and "Education, Higher."

Research has shown that few searchers think of such phrases in inverted order, but look for them in direct order. In *LCSH* few new inverted forms are being established, but already established ones still exist. One therefore finds inconsistencies such as "Moral education" and "Medical education" juxtaposed with "Education, Humanistic" and "Education, Greek."

Homographs and Homophones

Homographs are words that look the same but have very different meanings. "Mercury" can be a liquid metal, a planet, a car, or a Roman god; "bridge" can be a game, a structure spanning a chasm, or a dental device. In a controlled vocabulary there must be some way to differentiate among the various meanings. Two common ways are either to use qualifiers (see discussion below) or to choose a synonym for the homograph to use as the preferred term.

Homographs may or may not be pronounced the same (e.g., "mare" pronounced as one syllable with a "silent e" is a mature female horse; "mare" pronounced as two syllables is a large, dark area on the moon [possibly derived from the Italian *mare*, meaning "sea"]). Traditionally, the fact of different pronunciation did not matter in controlled vocabulary, because the vocabulary was treated visually.

Homophones, which are words that are spelled differently but pronounced the same, have also been ignored in controlled vocabularies in a visual world (e.g., moat and mote, fowl and foul). Because what appears on computer screens is now quite regularly read aloud electronically to visually impaired people, we need to give attention to pronunciations of homographs and to distinguishing among homophones.

Qualification of Terms

One of the ways of dealing with homographs is to add a qualifier to one or more of the meanings. For example:

Mercury (Planet)

Mercury (Roman deity)

Qualifiers are also used to differentiate usages of a word in different settings. For example:

Adultery (Aztec law)

Adultery (Jewish law)

Adultery (Yanzi law)

Qualifiers can also be used to help in identifying the context of unfamiliar words. For example:

> Yanzi (African people)

Abbreviations and Acronyms

Traditionally, abbreviations and acronyms have either been spelled out, or not, depending upon the intended users of the controlled vocabulary and their expected knowledge. With a move to more global retrieval needs one cannot assume a certain population. Under these circumstances it would probably be best to assume that abbreviations and acronyms should be spelled out. A few, however, have global recognition. One such is AIDS, the acronym for Acquired Immune Deficiency Syndrome (although in Spanish the acronym is SIDA, so in a global index even this acronym might need to be spelled out).

Popular vs. Technical

When a concept can be represented by both technical and popular terminology, the creator of a controlled vocabulary must decide which will be used. For example, *Medical Subject Headings* (*MeSH*) uses "Neoplasms" where *LCSH* uses "Cancer." If the list is intended to be used for information packages that will be used by a specialized audience only, then specialized terminology is justified. However, in a global information world, one can no longer be certain of a particular audience. Perhaps this is another area where access control, as discussed in the preceding chapter, should be put into use. With access control technical terms and their equivalent popular terms could reside on the same access record that could be activated by a search on any of the equivalent terms.

Subdivision of Terms

Subdivisions are used in controlled vocabularies that precoordinate terms (see discussion below). Among the uses of subdivisions are:

- to separate by form/genre (e.g., Chemistry—Dictionaries)
- to show treatment of only a part of the larger subject (e.g., Merchant marine—Officers)
- to show special aspects of the larger subject (e.g., Merchant marine—Watch duty)

- to show geographical or chronological limitations (e.g., Black theater—Pennsylvania—19th century)

Precoordination vs. Postcoordination

Index terms can be assigned either in a precoordinated fashion, or in a fashion that requires the searcher of the system to coordinate the terms (i.e., postcoordination). When terms are precoordinated in the controlled vocabulary or are precoordinated by the cataloger or indexer, some concepts, subconcepts, place names, time periods, and form concepts are put together in subject strings. This does not mean that all concepts used for indexing a particular item will be placed in the same subject string. That happens only when the subject analysis system attempts to have each subject heading be coextensive with the subject of an item (see discussion of coextensivity and PRECIS below).

With the use of most controlled vocabularies, some postcoordination must still be done by the searcher, even if the cataloger or indexer has already done some precoordination. It is a matter of degree. *LCSH*, for example, has no precoordinated terminology for the concept "dancers and musicians." It is up to the user who wants a work covering this concept to look up "dancers" and "musicians" separately and then determine which records have both terms in the controlled vocabulary sections. In true postcoordinated systems, each concept is entered discretely, without any stringing together of subconcepts, place names, time periods, or form. Searchers must combine terms using Boolean techniques. Keyword searching is the ultimate in postcoordinate indexing.

Postcoordination is sometimes confused with depth indexing, but these are different concepts. Although it is often the case that the numerous terms that result from depth indexing are entered into a postcoordinate system with discrete terms, there is nothing to keep a depth indexer from stringing together concepts with subconcepts or modifiers to make more meaningful precoordinated index terms.

General Principles for Applying Controlled Vocabulary Terms

Literary Warrant

Controlled vocabulary tends to be created using the principle of *literary warrant*. This means that terminology is added to a subject heading list or thesaurus when a new concept shows up in the literature and therefore needs to have specific terminology assigned to it. Usually, no attempt is made to add new terminology to a list until it is needed for use in surrogate/metadata records.

Specific Entry

The principle of *specific entry* is that a concept should be assigned a term from the thesaurus that is the most specific term for the concept that is available in the controlled vocabulary. An information package about "musicians" should be entered under "musicians," not under "performing artists." Specific entry allows an experienced user to know when to stop searching for an appropriate controlled vocabulary term. One does not have to keep trying broader terms unless no information is found under the most specific terms.

It should be noted that the concept of specific entry is not the same as the concept of *coextensive entry*. At least one system for subject analysis, the PREserved Context Indexing System (PRECIS), attempts to make subject headings coextensive with the concepts covered in the document analyzed. That is, the subject heading will cover all, but no more than, the concepts or topics covered in the information package. In order to have coextensive coverage using *LCSH*, for example, a resource about musicians *and* dancers requires *two* specific entries: one for "musicians" and another for "dancers." There is no one specific term to cover these two types of performers. In order to have just *one* heading that is coextensive with the subject of such a resource, the heading would have to be "musicians and dancers," a phrase not available in *LCSH*.

It once was true that "specific entry" could be treated in a relative way. In a small collection there might be only one or two items about "musicians," while there might be several items about "performing artists" that included "musicians" as one type of performing artist; for that collection, there might be a decision that "performing artists" would be the most specific heading used. Now that we are all essentially contributing to a global union catalog, however, we must follow the principle of specific entry in order for searching to be effective.[25] And, if we could break out of tradition and make references from specific to general, then "too specific" would not have to be a concern.

Direct Entry

Another principle is that of *direct entry*, which is the entry of a concept under the term that names it, rather than entry as a subdivision of a broader concept. For example, in *LCSH* there is currently a preference for a modified term to express a concept (e.g., Railroad stations) over the use of a broader term subdivided by a narrower term (e.g., Railroads—Stations).

Number of Terms Assigned

There should be *no arbitrary limit on the number* of terms or descriptors assigned. If the conceptual analysis has been done at the summarization level, then the number of terms given should be the number that are needed to express that summary. Likewise, if the conceptual analysis has been depth analysis, the number of terms necessary to cover all of the concepts should be allowed.

Concept Not in Controlled Vocabulary

If a concept is not present in the controlled vocabulary, it should be represented temporarily by a more general concept, and the new concept should be proposed as a new addition to the subject list or thesaurus (e.g., Use "Artificial intelligence" until a new heading for "Machine discovery" is established).

Index Terms for Names

Although the names for many topical concepts are controlled by the controlled vocabulary list itself, proper names are generally controlled by a separate authority file. The Library of Congress (LC), of course, maintains a name authority file, called the USNAF (United States Name Authority File), for names of persons, corporate bodies, geographic names of political entities, and titles of works. Geographic names that are not political entities and other names such as names of archaeological sites are also controlled by LC, but as subject headings rather than as names.

Kinds of Controlled Vocabularies

Controlled vocabularies fall broadly into three categories: 1) subject heading lists, 2) thesauri, and 3) ontologies. The first two are discussed in this section. Ontologies are discussed below following an introduction to Natural Language Processing (NLP), which is the origin of ontologies.

Subject heading lists and thesauri are similar but also different. Subject heading lists have been created largely in library communities; thesauri have been created largely in indexing communities. Both attempt to provide subject access to information packages by providing terminology that can be consistent rather than uncontrolled and unpredictable. Both choose preferred terms and make references from non-used terms. Both provide hierarchies so that terms are presented in relation to their broader terms, narrower terms, and related terms.

There are certain differences that are worth noting:

- Thesauri are made up of single terms and bound terms representing single concepts. Bound terms occur when some concepts can only be represented by two or more words (e.g., Type A Personality: the words "type," "A," and "personality" cannot be separated as meaningful components; the entire phrase is necessary for expressing the concept). Terms in thesauri tend to be called *descriptors*. Subject heading lists have phrases and other precoordinated terms in addition to single terms.

- Thesauri are more strictly hierarchical. Because they are made up of single terms, each term usually has only one broader term. The rules in the *NISO Guidelines for the Construction, Format, and Management of Monolingual Thesauri*[26] that have to do with identifying broader, narrower, and related terms are much easier to follow when working with a single-term system than when working with a phrase system.

- Thesauri are narrow in scope. They are usually made up of terms from one specific subject area. Subject heading lists tend to be more general in scope, covering a broad subject area or, indeed, the entire scope of knowledge.

- Thesauri are more likely to be multilingual. Again, because single terms are used, equivalents in other languages are easier to find and maintain.

Subject Heading Lists

Among the best-known and most-used subject heading lists are *Library of Congress Subject Headings* (*LCSH*), *Sears List of Subject Headings* (*Sears*), and *Medical Subject Headings* (*MeSH*). A brief description of each follows, but more detailed descriptions can be found in other sources, some of which are suggested at the end of this chapter.

Library of Congress Subject Headings (LCSH). Starting in 1988 with the eleventh edition, new print versions of *LCSH* have been produced once a year. *LCSH* is updated continuously, and electronic updates are available by subscription through the *Cataloger's Desktop*, and through various bibliographic utilities such as OCLC and RLIN. *LCSH* covers the world of knowledge. It is used by all kinds of libraries in many different kinds of settings, including countries other than the United States. In the indexing process *LCSH* is used in conjunction with the *Subject Cataloging Manual: Subject Headings*.[27] The manual gives the policies and practices of the Library of Congress, which is responsible for the maintenance of the list; it is an essential tool if one wishes to apply *LCSH* correctly. A sample from *LCSH* is shown as figure 7.3.

Hair
       [GN (Physical Anthropology)]
       [QL942 (Comparative anatomy)]
       [QM488 (Human anatomy)]
   BT   Body covering (Anatomy)
       Head
   RT   Scalp
   NT   Beard
       Bristles
       Eyebrows
       Eyelashes
       Gray hair
       Guard hair
       Horsehair
       Molting
       Mustache
       Redheads
       Wigs
       Wool
       . . .
   --- Coloring
       USE Hair--Dyeing and bleaching

Hair dyes   *(May Subd Geog)*
       [TP984 (Chemical technology)]
       [TT969 (Hairdressing)]
   UF   Dyes and dyeing--Hair
       Hair tints
       Tints, Hair
   BT   Hair preparations
   --- **Law and legislation**   *(May Subd Geog)*

Fig. 7.3. Sample entries from *Library of Congress Subject Headings* (LCSH), as found in *Cataloger's Desktop*, 1998, Issue 1 (February 1998).

Sears List of Subject Headings (Sears). Sears is now in its sixteenth edition in print form but is updated continuously, and updates are periodically available in electronic form. This list is intended for small collections used by persons with general needs. Its main users are public libraries (usually small to medium-sized) and school libraries. For most of its existence *Sears* has followed the lead of *LCSH* in format and in terminology choices. However, *Sears* has used only the more general terminology and has not included the more specific terms or the ones geared for research audiences. In addition *Sears* has fewer subdivisions. A sample from *Sears* is shown as figure 7.4.

Hair   612.7; 646.7

> Use for general materials on hair as well as
> for materials on hairdressing and haircutting.
> UF   Barbering
>   Coiffure
>   Hair and hairdressing *[Former heading]*
>   Haircutting
>   Hairdressing
>   Hairstyles
>   Hairstyling
> BT   **Head**
>   **Personal Grooming**
> NT   **Wigs**

Fig. 7.4. Sample entry from *Sears List of Subject Headings* (*Sears*), 16th ed., 1997, p. 332.

Medical Subject Headings (MeSH). The National Library of Medicine calls *MeSH* a thesaurus,[28] and in the sense that it provides a strict hierarchical structure and it is subject-oriented, it is a thesaurus. But in the sense that it precoordinates phrases (e.g., "Sensitivity Training Groups"; "Life Change Events") it is a subject heading list. It also has a subdivision list from which terms are to be taken to subdivide the terms and phrases found in the list proper.

MeSH is used for providing subject access points on every bibliographic record created at the National Library of Medicine, whether it be MEDLINE, the Library's catalog, or *Index Medicus*. In print form *MeSH* has three volumes: a hierarchical listing; an alphabetical arrangement that includes scope notes; and a permuted alphabetical listing, in which every word of a phrase heading is brought into the lead position and arranged alphabetically. In machine-readable form *MeSH* is provided free to those who license MEDLINE. The hierarchical listing (or "Tree Structures") is available on the WWW.[29] A sample from *MeSH* is shown as figure 7.5.

From *MeSH*'s *Annotated Alphabetic List*:

Hair
  A1.835.288+
  includes fur of animals; abnormally pulling at one's hair =
  TRICHOTILLOMANIA; HAIR FOLLICLE is available
  LANUGO was see under HAIR 1963-78
  use HAIR to search LANUGO 1966-78
  X   Lanugo

  . . .

Hair Dyes
  D26.313.300.299   D26.408.355
  J1.516.213.450.426
  D25-26 qualif
  91(79); was see under HAIR PREPARATIONS 1980-90; was see under
  COSMETICS 1979
  X   Coloring Agents, Hair
  X   Dyes, Hair
  X   Hair Colorants

From MeSH's *Tree Structures*:

Body Regions (Non MeSH)
  Head
  . . .
  Skin   A1.835
    Hair   A1.835.288
      Eyebrows   A1.835.288.296   A1.456.505.
      Eyelashes   A1.835.288.421   A1.456.505.   A9.371.337.
      Hair Follicle   A1.835.288.710   A10.272.497.
    Nails   A1.835.472
    . . .

Miscellaneous Drugs and Agents (Non MeSH)
  . . .
  Cosmetics   D26.313   J1.516.213
  . . .
  Deodorants   D26.313.295   J1.516.329
  Hair Preparations   D26.313.300
    Hair Dyes   D26.313.300.299   D26.408.355   J1.516.213.
  Mouthwashes   D26.313.548   D25.583   J1.516.599
  . . .

Fig. 7.5. Sample entries from *Medical Subject Headings* (*MeSH*), 1996 [annotated list] p. 473; [tree structures] pp. 4, 561.

Thesauri

There are many, many thesauri for different subject areas. Representative of thesauri are *Art & Architecture Thesaurus* (*AAT*), and *Thesaurus of ERIC Descriptors*. Brief descriptions follow; suggested readings giving more detailed information are given at the end of the chapter.

Art & Architecture Thesaurus (AAT). The *AAT* is intended to assist in verbal access to all kinds of cultural heritage information.[30] Terms are provided for describing objects, textual materials, images, architecture, and material culture. *AAT* is widely used in several communities: archives, libraries, museums, visual resources collections, and conservation agencies. In structure it is arranged in seven facets (categories) that progress from the abstract to the concrete: Associated concepts, Physical attributes, Styles and periods, Agents, Activities, Materials, and Objects. The facets are divided into subfacets, each of which gives a hierarchical listing of all terms in that subfacet.

AAT is available in print in its second edition, published in 1994. It has two major sections: a hierarchical listing and an alphabetical listing, which gives full entries for each term, including a scope note and all other thesaural relationships. A CD-ROM version is available, and a web site also provides full access.[31] Electronic versions are constantly updated; some terms in the second edition in print appear differently in the online versions. A sample from *AAT* is shown as figure 7.6.

Thesaurus of ERIC Descriptors. ERIC is an acronym for the Educational Resources Information Center, which is a national information system designed to provide access to a large body of education-related literature. Among the documents that ERIC indexes besides journal articles are descriptions and evaluations of programs, research reports, curriculum and teaching guides, instructional materials, position papers, computer files, and resource materials. These materials are indexed using terms from the *Thesaurus of ERIC Descriptors*.

The thesaurus consists of four parts: the main Alphabetical Display, the Rotated Display, the Hierarchical Display, and the Descriptor Group Display. The Alphabetical Display is like the display in *LCSH*. The Rotated Display provides an alphabetical index to every word in the thesaurus, including access to unused terms as well as main terms. The Hierarchical Display shows broader and narrower terms in relationships to each other. The Descriptor Group Display offers a kind of table of contents by placing all descriptors into a set of broad categories. A sample from the alphabetical display from the ERIC thesaurus is shown as figure 7.7 on page 158.

Part III: Alphabetical Display

dye

	MT.2022	(H,L,R)

HN March 1993 scope note changed
January 2992 descriptor moved

SN A colored substance that dissolves or
is suspended in a liquid and imparts
its color by staining or being absorbed, or by serving as a pigment.

. . .

hair

MT.2558

HN March 1992 scope note changed
February 1992 descriptor moved

SN The fibrous outgrowths of the skins
of various animals, composed of the
protein keratin, used, among other
things, for making fabrics, as
stuffing, and for making brushes.

Part II: Hierarchical Displays

MT.1 materials

MT.1673 <materials by function>
MT.2010 colorant
MT.2011 <colorant for dye and pigment>
MT.2022 dye
MT.2023 <dye by composition or origin>
MT.2024 natural dye
MT.2025 oxgall
MT.2026 Tyrian purple
MT.2027 vegetable dye

MT.2513 <materials by origin>
MT.2514 animal material
MT.2555 <keratinous material>
MT.2557 <hair and hair components>
MT.2558 hair
MT.2559 <hair by composition or origin>
MT.2560 camel hair
MT.2561 goat hair
MT.2562 horsehair
MT.2563 human hair

Fig. 7.6. Sample entries from *Art & Architecture Thesaurus*, 2nd ed., 1994, vol. 4, p. 136; vol. 3, p. 533; vol. 2, p. 117; vol. 2, p. 128.

```
COLOR                                    Oct. 1969
          CIJE: 589     RIE: 242    GC: 490
UF        Color Presentation (1969 1980)
          Color Television (1969 1980)#
          Hue
RT        Art
          Color Planning
          Contrast
          Dimensional Preference
          Light
          Painting (Visual Arts)
          Visual Environment
          Visual Perception
```

Fig. 7.7. Sample entry from *Thesaurus of ERIC Descriptors*, 13th ed., 1995.

NATURAL LANGUAGE PROCESSING (NLP)

Although there has been some work in computer processing of spoken words, most work has been done on the processing of written words. Therefore, in discussing Natural Language Processing (NLP), we are concentrating on written language processing. One goal of NLP is to be able to create Information Retrieval (IR) systems that can accomplish three things: 1) interpret users' information needs as expressed in free text; 2) represent the complete range of meaning conveyed in documents; and 3) "understand" when there is a match between the user's information need and all (and no more than) the documents that meet it. In order to do this certain language problems have to be addressed:[32]

- English sentences are often incomplete descriptions of what they mean. For example, "The door opened." does not tell whether the door was opened by a person, the wind, or its own weight. If the next sentence is "Susan walked in." then the implication is that Susan opened the door.

- The same expression can mean different things in different contexts. For example, "Where's the water?" can mean that one is thirsty; or, it can mean that one wants to know which way it is to the beach.

- Natural language is constantly gaining new words, usages, expressions, and meanings. During the 1998 Olympics one could hear that "The United States has not yet medaled." Many people had not heard "medal" used as a verb before that.

- There are many ways to say the same thing. For example, "Mary registered for two summer courses." and "Mary signed up for two courses for the summer term." mean essentially the same thing.

- Sentences that are constructed identically can mean different things. In the two sentences "Jennifer took the course with Professor Jones." and "Jennifer took the course with Mary.", the first indicates that the professor taught the course Jennifer took. But the second could mean that Jennifer and Mary are both students and took a course together, or it could mean that Professor Mary Jones likes to be addressed by her first name. Such ambiguities can often be sorted out through the context of surrounding sentences.

Rich and Knight identify the following steps as necessary for NLP:[33]

- Morphological analysis—separate components of words (e.g., prefixes, suffixes, possessive endings, etc.) and separate punctuation from words.

- Syntactic analysis—analyze the linear sequences of words to show how the words relate to each other; the computer converts the flat sequence of words into a structure. For those who learned to diagram sentences in grammar classes, diagramming is essentially what is done in this step.

- Semantic analysis—map individual words into appropriate places in the knowledge base; create a structure to indicate how the meanings of the individual words combine with each other (e.g., the sentence "She wants to print a WWW page." indicates a wanting event in which "she" wants a printing event to occur wherein she must have access to a WWW browser and a printer).

- Discourse integration—determine the meaning of an individual sentence in relation to the sentences that precede and follow it. For example, the meaning of pronouns such as "it," "them," "her," can be given individual meanings only if what or who they refer to can be determined.

- Pragmatic analysis—reinterpret the structure that represents what was said to show what was actually meant. For example the question "Do you have the time?" should be interpreted as a request to be told the time. In the case of an IR system the result of this analysis should be a translation to a command to be executed by the system. If the system is asked a question such as "Do you have anything on artificial intelligence?" the response should be a list of sources on artificial intelligence, not the word "Yes."

Semantic analysis includes as its first step looking up individual words in a dictionary (often called *lexicon* in NLP) to determine which of a word's meanings or nuances is meant in the sentence at hand. Such a resource must give not only definitions, but also must give semantic markers. For example, the word "at" requires a time or a location as its object. Identification of this fact is a semantic marker. Others might be: physical object, abstract concept, animate object, etc. These dictionaries/lexicons are now often referred to as *ontologies*.

Ontologies

In the field of philosophy the term *ontology* has a long and respectable history meaning a systematic account of existence. At some point in the last decade the word was adopted by the information science community to designate the building blocks that are used to help computers and humans share knowledge.

In the information science field of Artificial Intelligence (AI) an "intelligent agent" (e.g., robot) is only able to perceive the part of the world that is allowed by its ontology. The broadest usage of ontology in AI is for formal representations of what, to a human, is common sense. Categories in this sense are such things as space, time, and structure of physical objects. Such formal representations are useful in creating intelligent agents that can perform certain tasks (e.g., vacuum a floor). Such an ontology is a nonlinguistic ontology.

There have been some attempts to formalize abstract concepts, as well. An ontology in NLP must formalize the reality of using language for communication. These are called linguistic ontologies and may include realities of grammar, semantics, syntax, etc. The parts that deal with semantics are called lexicons or lexical dictionaries, but as noted above, they are also called ontologies.

Some lexical ontologies appear to be hierarchical listings of terminology of a particularly narrow subject area (see fig. 7.8 on pages 161–62). Others, however, appear to be categorized controlled vocabularies. These include semantic analysis of words, putting them into categories such as nouns, verbs, adjectives, and adverbs (see description of *WordNet*® below). This is in contrast to subject heading lists and thesauri that tend to give only noun forms of the terminology contained within them (along with modifiers in other than noun form). The semantic analysis in ontologies also organizes terms into synonym sets, and then uses relationships to link the synonym sets.

Theory BIBLIOGRAPHIC-DATA

- Last modified: Tuesday, 27 September 1994
- Source code: bibliographic-data.lisp
- List of other known theories

Theory documentation:

The bibliographic-data ontology defines the terms used for describing bibliographic references. This theory defines the basic class for reference objects and the types (classes) for the data objects that appear in references, such as authors and titles. Specific databases will use schemata that associate references with various combinations of data objects, usually as fields in a record. This ontology is intended to provide the basic types from which a specific database schema might be defined.

Notes:

- Copyright: Copyright (c) 1992 Thomas R. Gruber

Cross Reference Report:

Theories included by Bibliographic-Data:

Frame-Ontology
Slot-Constraint-Sugar

No theories include Bibliographic-Data.

70 classes defined:

Biblio-Text
　Biblio-Name
　　Title
　　Keyword
　　City-Address
　　Agent-Name
　　Author-Name
　　Publisher-Name
　Biblio-Nl-Text
Biblio-Thing
　Agent
　　Person
　　Author
　　Organization
　　　Publisher
　　　University
　　　　•••

[clicking on <u>Author</u> yields the following:]

Class AUTHOR

- Defined in theory: Bibliographic-data
- Source code: bibliographic-data.lisp

Slots on this class:

Documentation:

An author is an agent who writes things. An author must have a name, which is its real name as an agent. The name as author may or may not be the agent's name, but usually is.

Subclass-Of: Agent

Slots on instances of this class:

Agent.Name:
Slot-Cardinality: 1

Notes

- See-also: <u>author.name</u>

Fig. 7.8. Part of a listing from a lexical ontology showing the hierarchical listing followed by the result from clicking on one of the terms in the hierarchy. (Source: http://ksl-web.stanford.edu/knowledge-sharing/ontologies/html/bibliographic-data/index.html)

Among the relationships shown in lexical ontologies are synonyms, coordinate terms, hypernyms, hyponyms, meronyms, holonyms, and antonyms.

- *Synonyms* have the same, or nearly the same, meanings and often can be substituted for each other. A synonym is like the "used for" relationship in thesauri.

- *Coordinate terms* might be called siblings; they all have the same parent term. A coordinate term is like the "related term" relationship in thesauri.

- A *hypernym* is the parent term of all the instances that are "kinds of" the hypernym (e.g., "family" is a hypernym for "nuclear family," "extended family," "foster home," etc.). A hypernym is like the "broader term" relationship in thesauri.

- A *hyponym* designates a member of a class (e.g., "nuclear family" is a hyponym of the class "family). A hyponym is like the "narrower term" relationship in thesauri.

- A *holonym* is the name of the whole of which the *meronym* is a part. With a holynym one has the name of a whole that has parts (e.g., a family has members: child, parent, sibling, etc.).

- With a meronym one has a constituent part or a member of something (e.g., "sister" is a meronym of "family"). Holonyms and meronyms are also like "broader term" and "narrower term" relationships in thesauri.

- *Antonyms* have opposite meanings (e.g., "hot" is the antonym of "cold"). Antonyms are not dealt with in thesauri.

Keywords

One of the first approaches used by NLP researchers was the manipulation of keywords. The success of keyword searching depends upon at least two assumptions: 1) that authors writing about the same concepts will use the same words in their writings, and 2) that searchers will be able to guess what words those authors used for the concept. A 1993 study of journal articles in the pure sciences and social science looked at articles that shared common references.[34] An assumption was made that if articles shared common references they dealt with the same or a related subject. It was found that few articles with common references shared common keywords. Another study the same year reported difficulty in choosing keywords for a literature search due to the use of multiple terms representing the same concepts.[35]

Among other problems discovered with keyword searching were that not all related information was retrieved, and searches often led to the extraction of irrelevant materials. A synonym list approach was tried. Synonym lists were databases consisting of groupings of synonymous terms. When a keyword search was done, the synonym list was tapped to provide synonyms without the searcher having to be the one to think of all of them. This approach also failed for several reasons. The lists were not large or general enough; they were implemented in very small and specialized domains. Also the lists did not attempt any level of word role assignment; for example, although one could substitute "aircraft" for "planes" and "big" for large," it was not possible to substitute "big aircraft" for "large planes" because the system had no "knowledge" of adjectives and nouns and which kinds of words could be used together to make a phrase.[36]

WordNet®

There has also been much work with full-text analysis. Again, though, tests have been conducted in limited specialized domains. Results have not been able to be transferred to general, multiple domain searches. Textual analysis typically is not done in real-time, especially as the amounts of data grow. Texts are analyzed and "indexed" when they are entered into the system; changes in the indexing mechanism require reindexing every document. Although full-text analysis retrieval systems are being marketed, many systems (e.g., distributed networks, WWW) cannot transmit the complete text of hundreds of documents in response to a search query. Banerjee and Mittal proposed an indexing system using keyword searching combined with a well-developed linguistic ontology. They used *WordNet*®[37] as an example of a linguistic ontology that could be used in this way.[38]

WordNet® calls itself an "on-line lexical reference system whose design is inspired by current psycholinguistic theories of human lexical memory."[39] It allows five categories of words: nouns, adjectives, adverbs, verbs, and function words. Relationships between words and their meanings are "many to many"; that is, some words have different meanings (*polysemy*), and some meanings have several different ways of being expressed (*synonyms*). A word can be placed into as many of the five categories as are appropriate, and in each category there can be as many different meanings (or senses) as are appropriate. For each sense all synonyms are grouped together in "synsets," and unlike controlled vocabularies, none of the synonyms is designated as the "used" term with all others designated as "unused." At the main screen that shows all the senses (see fig. 7.9), one can ask for screens that show coordinate terms, hyponyms, hypernyms, meronyms, holonyms, and antonyms.

WordNet 1.6 overview for "romance"

The **noun** "romance" has 5 senses in WordNet.

1. love affair, **romance** -- (a relationship between two lovers)
2. romanticism, **romance** -- (an exciting and mysterious quality (as of a heroic time or adventure))
3. Romance, Romance language, Latinian language -- (the group of languages derived from Latin)
4. love story, **romance** -- (a story dealing with love)
5. **romance** -- (a novel dealing with idealized events remote from everyday life)

Search for | Synonyms, ordered by frequency ▼ | of senses [   ]
☑ Show glosses
☐ Show contextual help
[Search]

The **verb** "romance" has 4 senses in WordNet.

1. woo, court, **romance**, solicit -- (make amorous advances towards; "john is courting Mary")
2. **romance** -- (have a love affair with)
3. chat up, flirt, dally, coquet, coquette, **romance**, philander, mash -- (talk amorously; "The guys always try to chat up the new secretaries"; "My husband never flirts with other women")
4. **romance** -- (tell romantic or exaggerated lies; "This author romanced his trip to an exotic country")

Search for | Synonyms, ordered by frequency ▼ | of senses [   ]
☑ Show glosses
☐ Show contextual help
[Search]

The **adjective** "romance" has 1 sense in WordNet.

1. Romance, Latin -- (relating to languages derived from Latin; "Romance languages")

Search for | Synonyms ▼ | of senses [   ]
☑ Show glosses
☐ Show contextual help
[Search]

Choose a different search word

Fig. 7.9. Main screen from *WordNet*® showing all the "senses" of the term *romance*. (Source: http://www.cogsci.princeton.edu/~wn/)

Banerjee and Mittal have proposed the following model[40] (enhanced by the author): For each query (e.g., "family crisis") of an IR system that uses *WordNet*®, results of an exact match would be given first. If there were insufficient matches the system would prompt the user for other options. It could first substitute adjective synonyms and present a list to the user who would choose the combinations that make sense. (The user would be involved also at each of the following stages.) Our example would yield the search terms: household crisis, house crisis, home crisis, etc. Then the system would substitute noun synonyms, resulting in a search for family emergency. The system would then drop adjectives, resulting in "crisis" being searched. Then the noun would be generalized to its hypernyms, resulting in: family situation, family state of affairs, family juncture, family occasion. Then the adjective synonyms could be combined with the noun hypernyms, resulting in: household situation, household state of affairs, home situation, home state of affairs, etc. Also the hyponyms of both noun and adjective could be searched, resulting in: family challenge, family complication, family nightmare, foster home crisis, couple crisis, marriage crisis, etc. Thus, a very large lexical ontology covering many fields of knowledge could be used to enhance keyword searching of full-text documents.

CONCLUSION

This chapter has addressed verbal approaches to provision of subject access to information packages. The process of determining what information packages are about was addressed as a crucial first step in providing subject access. In the provision of verbal subject approaches, the determination of aboutness is followed by translation of that aboutness into index terms, usually controlled vocabulary. Controlled vocabularies all have to deal with issues and problems during their construction; understanding these issues contributes to making the best use of the vocabulary, as does understanding the general principles. Subject heading lists, thesauri, and lexical ontologies make up three kinds of controlled vocabularies in use today. Subject heading lists were the first, created by libraries. Thesauri are more strictly hierarchical and, for the most part, grew up in subject-specific situations and/or commercial indexing services. Ontologies have grown out of Natural Language Processing (NLP), which holds promise for sophisticated keyword approaches. The next chapter is also concerned with subject access, but from the point of view of categorization and classification.

NOTES

1. Thomas Mann, " 'Cataloging Must Change!' and Indexer Consistency Studies: Misreading the Evidence at Our Peril," *Cataloging & Classification Quarterly* 23, nos. 3/4 (1997): 3–45.

2. Some of this section appeared in an earlier form in Arlene G. Taylor, "Books and Other Bibliographic Materials," in *Guide to Indexing and Cataloging with the Art & Architecture Thesaurus*, ed. Toni Petersen and Patricia J. Barnett (New York: Oxford University Press, 1994), pp. 101–19.

3. OCLC Institute, "Knowledge Access Management: Tools and Concepts for Next Generation Catalogers," institute held November 17–19, 1997, Dublin, Ohio. (Observations of author, who was in attendance.)

4. Available: http://www.oclc.org/oclc/man/colloq/toc.htm, accessed October 1998.

5. Available: http://www.cpcug.org/user/rwtucker/tiddlywinks/alleghany-index. html, accessed October 1998.

6. Available: http://www.deathclock.com/thunder, accessed October 1998.

7. Available: http://www.oclc.org, accessed October 1998.

8. Available: http://pobox.upenn.edu/~cheetham/jgarden/index.html, accessed October 1998.

9. A. G. Brown, in collaboration with D. W. Langridge and J. Mills, *An Introduction to Subject Indexing*, 2nd ed. (London: Bingley, 1982), frames 48, 51.

10. Available: http://www.stat.ncsu.edu/info/jse/, accessed October 1998.

11. Patrick Wilson, "Subjects and the Sense of Position," in *Two Kinds of Power: An Essay on Bibliographical Control* (Berkeley: University of California Press,1968), pp. 69–92. Also, reprinted in *Theory of Subject Analysis: A Sourcebook*, ed. Lois Mai Chan, Phyllis A. Richmond, and Elaine Svenonius (Littleton, Colo.: Libraries Unlimited, 1985), pp. 309–20.

12. George Lakoff, *Women, Fire, and Dangerous Things: What Categories Reveal About the Mind* (Chicago: University of Chicago Press, 1987), pp. 24–26.

13. D. W. Langridge, *Subject Analysis: Principles and Procedures* (London: Bowker-Saur, 1989), p. 4.

14. Wilson, "Subjects and the Sense of Position," pp. 78–88.

15.   Lourdes Y. Collantes, "Agreement in Naming Objects and Concepts for Information Retrieval" (Ph.D. diss., Rutgers University, 1992), p. 154.

16.   Oliver L. Lilley, "Evaluation of the Subject Catalog: Criticisms and a Proposal," *American Documentation* 5, no. 2 (1954): 41–60.

17.   Collantes, "Agreement in Naming Objects," p. 154.

18.   For example: Regene C. Ross, Chair, Task Force on Copy Cataloging, *Report of the Task Force on Copy Cataloging*, May 12, 1993, cited by Thomas Mann, in " 'Cataloging Must Change!'," pp. 37–38.

19.   Langridge, *Subject Analysis,* p. 9.

20.   Patricia J. Barnett, "Indexing with the *AAT*," in *Guide to Indexing and Cataloging with the Art & Architecture Thesaurus*, ed. Toni Petersen and Patricia J. Barnett (New York: Oxford University Press, 1994), pp. 33–40.

21.   *"A Sweet Foretaste of Heaven": Artists in the White Mountains, 1830–1930*, with essays by Robert L. McGrath and Barbara J. MacAdam (Hanover, N.H.: Hood Museum of Art, 1988).

22.   Langridge, *Subject Analysis*, p. 45.

23.   American Library Association, Association for Library Collections and Technical Services, Subject Analysis Committee, 1993, *Definition of Form Data*, available: http://www.pitt.edu/ ~ agtaylor/ala/form-def.htm

24.   National Information Standards Organization, *Guidelines for the Construction, Format, and Management of Monolingual Thesauri* (Bethesda, Md.: NISO Press, 1994). "ANSI/NISO Z39.19-1993."

25.   Mann, " 'Cataloging Must Change!'," pp. 9–10.

26.   Ibid.

27.   *Subject Cataloging Manual: Subject Headings*, prepared by The Cataloging Policy and Support Office, Library of Congress, 5th ed. (Washington, D.C.: Cataloging Distribution Service, Library of Congress, 1996).

28.   National Library of Medicine, *Fact Sheet, Medical Subject Headings (MeSH®)*, available: http://www.nlm.nih.gov/pubs/factsheets/mesh.htm

29.   National Library of Medicine, *Medical Subject Headings (MeSH®): 1998 MeSH Tree Structures*, available: http://www.nlm.nih.gov/mesh/mtrees.html

30.   Getty Information Institute, *About the AAT*, available: http://www.gii.getty.edu/ aat_browser/intro.htm

31.   Getty Information Institute, *The Art & Architecture Thesaurus Browser*, available: http://www.ahip.getty.edu/aat_browser/, accessed December 1998.

32.   Elaine Rich and Kevin Knight, *Artificial Intelligence*, 2nd ed. (New York: McGraw-Hill, 1991), pp. 377–79.

33.   Ibid., pp. 379–80.

34.   S. N. Ali, "Subject Relationship Between Articles Determined by Co-occurrence of Keywords in Citing and Cited Titles," *Journal of Information Science* 19, no. 3 (1993): 225–31.

35.   R. B. Bush, "A Bibliography of Monographic Works on Biomaterials and Biocompatibility," *Journal of Applied Biomaterials* 4, no. 2 (1993): 195–209.

36.   Sujata Banerjee and Vibhu O. Mittal, *On the Use of Linguistic Ontologies for Accessing and Indexing Distributed Digital Libraries*, available: ftp://violet.tele.pitt.edu/pub/Telecom_Faculty/Banerjee/Papers/DL-94.ps

37.   *WordNet*®, available: http://www.cogsci.princeton.edu/ ~ wn/

38.   Ibid.

39.   Cognitive Science Laboratory, Princeton University, *WordNet*®*—A Lexical Database for English*, available: http://www.cogsci.princeton.edu/ ~ wn

40.   Banerjee and Mittal, *On the Use of Linguistic Ontologies*, p. 3.

SUGGESTED READINGS

Bates, Marcia J. "Subject Access in Online Catalogs: A Design Model." *Journal of the American Society for Information Science* 37, no. 6 (1986): 357–76.

Dooley, Jackie M. "Subject Indexing in Context." *American Archivist* 55, no. 2 (Spring 1992): 344–54.

Lancaster, F. W. "Indexing Principles." Chap. 2 and "Abstracts: Types and Functions." Chap. 7 in *Indexing and Abstracting in Theory and Practice.* Champaign, Ill.: University of Illinois, Graduate School of Library and Information Science, 1991.

Pettee, Julia. "The Subject Approach to Books and the Development of the Dictionary Catalog." In *Theory of Subject Analysis: A Sourcebook*, edited by Lois Mai Chan, Phyllis A. Richmond, and Elaine Svenonius, pp. 94–98. Littleton, Colo.: Libraries Unlimited, 1985.

Taylor, Arlene G. "On the Subject of Subjects." *Journal of Academic Librarianship* 21, no. 6 (November 1995): 484–91.

Wellish, Hans H. "Aboutness and Selection of Topics." *Key Words* 4, no. 2 (March/April 1996): 7–9.

Wynar, Bohdan S. *Introduction to Cataloging and Classification*. 8th ed. by Arlene G. Taylor. "Subject Arrangement of Library Materials." Chap. 15. "Verbal Subject Analysis." Chap. 21. Englewood, Colo.: Libraries Unlimited, 1992.

LCSH

Berman, Sanford. *Joy of Cataloging*. Phoenix, Ariz.: Oryx Press, 1981.

Mann, Thomas. *Doing Research at the Library of Congress: A Guide to Subject Searching in a Closed Stacks Library*. Washington, D.C.: Library of Congress, Humanities and Social Sciences Division, 1994.

Pugh, Mary Jo. "The Illusion of Omniscience: Subject Access and the Reference Archivist." *American Archivist* 45, no. 1 (Winter 1982): 33–44.

Wynar, Bohdan S. *Introduction to Cataloging and Classification*. 8th ed. by Arlene G. Taylor. "Library of Congress Subject Headings." Chap. 22. Englewood, Colo.: Libraries Unlimited, 1992.

Sears

Miller, Joseph, ed. *Sears List of Subject Headings*. 15th ed. Bronx, N.Y.: H. W. Wilson, 1994, pp. vii–xxxvi.

Wynar, Bohdan S. *Introduction to Cataloging and Classification*. 8th ed. by Arlene G. Taylor. "Sears List of Subject Headings." Chap. 23. Englewood, Colo.: Libraries Unlimited, 1992.

MeSH

"*MeSH* Introduction." In *Medical Subject Headings: Annotated Alphabetic List*. Bethesda, Md.: National Library of Medicine, 1998, pp. I–3 to I–166.

Wynar, Bohdan S. *Introduction to Cataloging and Classification*. 8th ed. by Arlene G. Taylor. "Other Types of Verbal Analysis." Chap. 24. Englewood, Colo.: Libraries Unlimited, 1992.

AAT

Barnett, Patricia J., and Toni Petersen. "Extending MARC to Accommodate Faceted Thesauri: The *AAT* Model." In *Beyond the Book: Extending MARC for Subject Access*, edited by Toni Petersen and Pat Molholt, pp. 7–23. Boston: G. K. Hall, 1990.

Getty Information Institute. *The Art & Architecture Thesaurus Browser*. Available: http://www.ahip.getty.edu/aat_browser/ (Accessed December 1998).

ERIC

Barnett, Lynn, and Anita Colby. "ERIC's Indexing and Retrieval: 1995 Update." In *Thesaurus of ERIC Descriptors*, edited by James E. Houston, pp. xiv–xxiii, 13th ed. Phoenix, Ariz.: Oryx Press, 1995.

NLP and Ontologies

Banerjee, Sujata, and Vibhu O. Mittal. *On the Use of Linguistic Ontologies for Accessing and Indexing Distributed Digital Libraries*. Available: ftp://violet.tele.pitt.edu/pub/Telecom_Faculty/Banerjee/Papers/DL-94.ps (Accessed October 1998).

Harris, Mary Dee. *Introduction to Natural Language Processing*. Reston, Va.: Reston, 1985, pp. 3–12.

Heylighen, F. "Ontology, introduction." Available: http://pespmc1.vub.ac.be/ONTOLI.html

Rich, Elaine, and Kevin Knight. "Natural Language Processing." Chap. 15 in *Artificial Intelligence*. 2nd ed. New York: McGraw-Hill, 1991.

Vickery, B. C. "Ontologies." *Journal of Information Science* 23, no. 4 (1997): 277–86.

Weinstein, Peter C. "Ontology-Based Metadata: Transforming the MARC Legacy." Available from the author: peterw@eecs.umich.edu

WordNet®. Available: http://www.cogsci.princeton.edu/~wn/

CHAPTER 8
CLASSIFICATION

In the previous chapter we discussed verbal methods of providing subject access to information packages. Another kind of subject access is provided by classification. Classification has a much longer history than that of controlled vocabularies. Philosophers have tried to categorize knowledge for many centuries. Classification basically is categorizing, but during the twentieth century, classification has come to be associated with assigning some kind of notation to physical information packages, and, in the thinking of many persons, the connection to categorizing has been lost. However, the categories devised by philosophers in past centuries are the basis for the major classification schemes in use today.

Classification theory has not received as much attention in the United States as it has in other places such as European countries. There has been a tendency in the United States to see classification only as a way to arrange physical information packages. But there is great potential use for categorizing electronic resources. This chapter addresses this potential along with answering the following questions: How do humans categorize? How is subject content expressed symbolically in surrogate/metadata records? What conflicts arise in the application of classification to information packages? What is the role of automatic classification in organizing information?

CLASSIFICATION THEORY

Classical Theory of Categories

The roots of current classification systems can be traced back to Aristotle's theory of categories. He espoused the idea that things are placed into the same category on the basis of what they have in common. Aristotle's theory, the "classical theory of categories," went essentially unchallenged until the mid-1900s, because, Lakoff says, categories were thought to be well understood. A category was like an abstract container with things either inside or outside the container. The properties the things inside the container had in common were what defined the category.[1] Aristotle's categories, it should be noted, were arranged in a hierarchical fashion, the belief seeming to be that there was a perfect hierarchy for the world—all we had to do was find it.

A brief history of the research of the second half of the twentieth century will serve to illuminate the process of categorizing and its relationship to classification. This history is summarized from Lakoff.[2] Cracks began to appear in the classical theory of categories in 1953, when Ludwig Wittgenstein showed that a category like *game* does not fit the classical mold. This category has no single collection of common properties. For example, a game may be for education, amusement, or competition, and it may involve luck or skill. The game category has no fixed boundary, because new kinds of games such as video games and interactive computer games can be added to it. Wittgenstein proposed the idea that *family resemblances*, not a set of common properties, is what unites games into what we call a category. Just as members of a family have similarities, so do games.

J. L. Austin, in a paper published in 1961, extended Wittgenstein's analysis to the study of words. He wondered why we call different things by the same name (e.g., foot of a mountain, foot of a list, person's foot). Should not *mountain*, *list*, and *person* be in the same category if they all have a foot? But there are times when words do belong in the same category even though they share no common properties (e.g., *ball*, *bat*, and *umpire* can all go into the category *baseball*). Austin, like Wittgenstein, helped to show that traditional views of categories were inadequate.

Lotfi Zadeh contributed *fuzzy set theory* to the chipping away of the classical theory of categories. He noted that some categories are well defined while others are not. One either is or is not a member of a club, but whether one is tall or not depends to some extent upon the observer. The category of tall is graded—one may be neither clearly tall or clearly short; and a short person, looking at someone of medium height, would probably say that the person is tall. In 1965 Zadeh devised a form of set theory to deal with graded categories.

Floyd Lounsbury's studies of Native American kinship systems also chipped away at the classical theory. He found that among various groups, the same name is used to express the kinship relationships of several relatives. For example, in one group, uncles, great-uncles, and nephews on one's mother's side of the family are all called by the same word. (Perhaps they find it strange that in the dominant culture there is no verbal distinction between uncles who are the mother's brothers and uncles who are the father's brothers!) A challenge to classical theory here is that what seem to be definite and distinct categories in one culture and language are not the same categories in another culture and language.

Brent Berlin and Paul Kay (also mentioned in the preceding chapter) published their work on color in 1969. They found that in different languages there can be expressions for two to eleven basic colors. Although people speaking languages that have fewer than the eleven basic color names of English can conceptually differentiate all the colors, they cannot express them as different words. For example, red, orange, and yellow may all be expressed as the same word. Again it is shown that language and culture play a major role in the establishment of categories.

Paul Kay of the previous team and Chad McDaniel did follow-up work with colors and reported it in 1978. They drew on work that had been done in neurophysiology to conclude that human biology influences perception of color. They drew on fuzzy set theory to determine that in all cultures that have fewer than eleven basic colors, "cold" colors always include green, blue, and black, while "warm" colors always include red, orange, yellow, and white. Thus, color categories are not quite as arbitrary as might have been implied by the Berlin/Kay studies.

Roger Brown began the study of "basic-level categories." His work published in 1965 observed that there is a first level at which children learn categories (e.g., flower [for any variety of flower]). Yet there are many names that can be used for such categories, some more specific (e.g., rose, daffodil) and some more general (e.g., plant). Brown considered the child-level to be "natural," while the specific and general levels were viewed as "achievements of the imagination."

Brent Berlin and associates, in research on naming plants and animals, published from 1969 to 1977, showed that there seems to be a universal level at which humans name things, and for plants and animals it is more likely to be at the genus level (e.g., oak, not tree and not white oak; although this might not hold true for someone with experience only in an urban culture or for someone whose training has led to a more precisely honed level). It can be suggested that certain basic levels of categories have to do with being human and will be the same across cultures.

Prototype Theory

A major crack in classical theory of categories came when Eleanor Rosch developed "prototype theory" with her work between 1973 and 1981. She theorized that if, as classical theory states, categories are defined only by properties that all members share, then no members should be better examples of the category than any other members. She further theorized that if categories are defined only by properties that all members share, then categories should be independent of the humans doing the categorizing. She found that, contrary to classical theory, categories *do* have best examples (i.e., prototypes). For example, Rosch found that people in her research thought that *robin* was a better example of *bird* than was *ostrich*. And she found that human capacities *do* play a role in categorization (e.g., for someone 5 feet tall, there are many more "tall people" in the world than there are for someone 6 feet tall). This is the *fuzzy set theory*, mentioned earlier. *Ad hoc* categories also figure in here. Ad hoc categories are those that are made up on the spur of the moment. Different people will put different things into a category such as "things to take camping," depending upon their experience, where they are going, how they will camp, etc.

Because the most widely used classification schemes in the United States are based upon the classical theory of categories, classifiers using them are sometimes quite frustrated to find that they have a subject concept that does not fit neatly into one of the categories. They are often relieved to learn that classical theory has major cracks, so it is not unusual to run into nonprototypes and fuzzy sets.

HIERARCHICAL, ENUMERATIVE, AND FACETED CLASSIFICATIONS

Classification schemes as we know them are relatively new in the history of organization. Early depositories of recorded information usually had some arrangement: title, broad subject, chronology, author, order of acquisition, or size. Callimachus's *Pinakes* had at least ten broad categories (or main classes). Arrangement within the classes tended to be by author. This seemed to be a model for arrangement of catalogs and bibliographies into the early Middle Ages.

During the mid-Middle Ages when monastery libraries became the keepers of books through many centuries, there was little need for classification because the libraries were so small. The universities of the late Middle Ages divided their books according to the Trivium and Quadrivium, the seven subject fields taught. But within the seven classes, the books had fixed locations.

Starting in the sixteenth century, librarians devised many different classification schemes. Often these were based upon philosophers' systems of knowledge. However, none caught on, and fixed locations continued to predominate. With the rapid growth of libraries in the nineteenth century librarians felt a need for better arrangement so that the content of the collections would be more apparent to the user. Philosopher Francis Bacon in the early seventeenth century divided knowledge into three basic "faculties": history (natural, civil, literary, ecclesiastical); philosophy (including theology); and works of imagination (poetry, fables, etc.). This scheme had widespread influence, and numerous classification schemes were based upon it. The most famous was that of Thomas Jefferson, who classified his own library before he eventually gave it to the Library of Congress as the basis of a new collection in 1815.

Some history of the development of specific classification schemes in the nineteenth and twentieth centuries is discussed in chapter 3 and need not be repeated in full here. Very briefly, in 1876 Melvil Dewey devised his Dewey Decimal Classification (DDC), and shortly afterward, Charles Cutter began work on his Expansive Classification. Otlet and LaFontaine developed the Universal Decimal Classification (UDC), based on DDC in 1885. At the beginning of the twentieth century the Library of Congress created its own classification (LCC), based loosely on Cutter's Expansive Classification. S. R. Ranganathan created his Colon Classification in the early 1930s and adapted the word *facet* as a term to indicate the various subparts of the whole classification notation.

As all of these were devised before anyone challenged the classical theory of categories, these schemes were (except for Colon Classification) firmly based in *hierarchical* arrangements. Hierarchical schemes follow classical theory, creating categories from general to specific. For example, DDC starts with ten main classes, divides each of those into ten divisions (one hundred), divides each of the divisions into ten sections (one thousand), divides each of those into ten subsections (ten thousand), and so on into potential infinity (see fig. 8.1 on page 178).

The same classification schemes were also fairly *enumerative*. Enumerative schemes attempt to assign a designation for every subject concept (both single and composite) needed in the system. All schemes have elements that are enumerative, but some much more than others. LCC is much more enumerative than is DDC (see fig. 8.2 on page 179). UDC started out based on DDC, and so was hierarchical and enumerative at its base; it has now developed more into what we call a *faceted* scheme.

Text continues on page 180.

DEWEY DECIMAL CLASSIFICATION
21st edition

First Summary
The Ten Main Classes

000	Generalities
100	Philosophy & psychology
200	Religion
300	Social sciences
400	Language
500	Natural sciences & mathematics
600	Technology (Applied sciences)
700	The arts Fine and decorative arts
800	Literature & rhetoric
900	Geography & history

Second Summary
The Hundred Divisions

. . .

600	Technology (Applied sciences)
610	Medical sciences Medicine
620	Engineering & allied operations
630	Agriculture & related technologies
640	Home economics & family living
650	Management & auxiliary services
660	Chemical engineering
670	Manufacturing
680	Manufacture for specific uses
690	Buildings

. . .

Detailed hierarchy for 646.724

640	Home economics & family living
646	Sewing, clothing, management of personal and family living
646.7	Management of personal and family living Grooming
646.71-646.75	Grooming
646.72	Care of hair, face, skin
646.724	Care of hair
	Including braiding, care of beards, dyeing, hairweaving, permanent waving, relaxing, shaving

Fig. 8.1. Illustration of hierarchical arrangement in the Dewey Decimal Classification (DDC).

LIBRARY OF CONGRESS CLASSIFICATION

A		General Works
B-BJ		Philosophy. Psychology
BL-BX		Religion
BL, BM, BP, BQ		Religion: Religions, Hinduism, Judaism, Islam, Buddhism
BX		Religion: Christian Denominations
C		Auxiliary Sciences of History
D		History: General and Old World (Eastern Hemisphere)

. . .

A		General Works
AG	1-600	Dictionaries and other general reference books
	1-90	Dictionaries. Minor encyclopedias
		Including popular and juvenile encyclopedias
	103-190	General works, pocketbooks, receipts, etc.
	195-196	Questions and answers
	240-243	Wonders. Curiosities

. . .

AM	1-501	Museums (General). Collectors and collecting (General)
	10-101	Museography. Individual museums
	111-160	Museology. Museum methods, technique, etc.
	200-501	Collectors and collecting. Private collections

. . .

AM	111-160	<u>Museology, Museum methods, technique, etc.</u>
	111	General works
		Prefer AM5
	121	Organization
	122	Finance
	(123)	Architecture, <u>see</u> NA6700
	127	Equipment
	129	Furniture
	133	The collections
	135	Collecting
		Cf. QH61-63
	139	Registration. Accessioning
		Preparation and preservation
	141	General works
	145	Special methods (Not A-Z)
	148	Security measures
	151	Exhibition
	153	Classification. Arrangement
	157	Labels. Marking

Fig. 8.2. Illustration of the hierarchical and enumerative arrangement of the Library of Congress Classification (LCC).

If one thinks of each of the faces of a cut and polished diamond as a *facet* of the whole diamond, one can picture a classification notation that has small notations standing for subparts of the whole topic strung together to create a complete classification notation. This concept was named first by S. R. Ranganathan in explanation of his Colon Classification (CC). CC provides lists of designations for single concepts, with rules for combining them for complex concepts; the lists are not hierarchical.

Ranganathan posed five basic facets: personality (i.e., the focal or most specific subject); material; energy (i.e., an activity, operation, or process); space (i.e., place); and time. Using the first letters of the five words, he called this the "PMEST" formula. For example, "the design of wooden furniture in 18th century America" has all five facets. Furniture is the focal subject, or personality; wood is the material facet; design is an activity and so constitutes the energy facet; the space is America; and the time is the eighteenth century. If each facet has a specific notation (e.g., let's say P28 for furniture, M16 for wood, etc.), then these notations can be strung together according to the rules of the system.

Both CC and UDC use punctuation marks and symbols between the notations as "facet indicators." These help to identify the relationships among the facets. CC uses the "colon" in significant positions; thus the name of the scheme. The long notations created in faceted schemes are not easy to use for arranging physical information packages on shelves. However, in catalogs they are quite helpful, as each facet can be searched independently.

LCC has limited faceting capabilities. There are tables of geographic areas in some schedules, for example, that can be used to build notations that show place. Many of the table numbers, however, are literally mathematically added to a number in the schedule; the resulting notation does not show the geographic area as a facet. Only the geographic area notations that are "cutter numbers," consisting of the first letter of the geographic area name and one or more numerical digits, are recognizable as facets. (See discussion of cutter numbers in chapter 9.)

DDC has many faceting capabilities and gains more with each new edition. There are seven tables that can be used at various places in the schedules. The notations from tables are attached to the end of the notation from the schedule so that the facet is intact. In some cases, the end of the schedule notation and the beginning of the table notation are not demarcated; but most of the time the table notation is preceded by digit "0" or "1." As new editions create new faceting arrangements, they are using "0" and "1" to indicate the beginning of a facet.

CLASSIFICATION SCHEMES

Traugott Koch has pointed out that there are broadly four varieties of classification schemes:

- Universal schemes - examples include the Dewey Decimal Classification (DDC), the Universal Decimal Classification (UDC), and the Library of Congress Classification (LCC);

- National general schemes - universal in subject coverage but usually designed for use in a single country. Examples include the Nederlandse Basisclassificatie (BC) and the Sveriges Allmama Biblioteksforening (SAB);

- Subject specific schemes - designed for use by a particular subject community. Examples include Iconclass for art resources, the National Library of Medicine (NLM) scheme for medicine, and Engineering Information (Ei) for engineering subjects;

- Home-grown schemes - schemes devised for use in a particular service. An example from the Internet is the 'ontology' developed for the *Yahoo!* search service.[3]

At Koch's web site there is a good description of each of the schemes he mentions. The reader is referred there for more information. In addition there are a number of home-grown schemes in print form that are interesting and useful in particular contexts. One example is *A Classification System for Libraries of Judaica*, now in its third edition.[4] It is kept up-to-date by people who make use of it. For example, since the publication of the third edition, a synagogue librarian has created a Holocaust Expansion that is posted with the home page of the authors of the third edition.[5]

There are many more classification schemes not mentioned here. More could be said about each of the classification schemes mentioned and not mentioned in this section. At the end of the chapter are suggestions for places to read about these schemes and, in some cases, manuals for use in applying them.

CLASSIFICATION CONCEPTS

A number of classification concepts and issues affect the use of classification schemes. Some of these apply to the application of a scheme regardless of how the classification is going to be used (e.g., as a way of arranging physical information packages; as a way of identifying subject content in metadata; as a way of organizing and/or presenting virtual information packages; etc.). Others are issues particularly in the use of classification as a device for arranging physical information packages. The following sections are arranged from general to specific.

Broad vs. Close Classification

Broad classification is classification that uses only the main classes and divisions of a scheme and perhaps only one or two levels of subdivisions. *Close classification* is classification that uses all the minute subdivisions that are available for very specific subjects. This is somewhat like the "specific vs. general" issue in controlled vocabularies. It is necessary to decide when beginning to use a classification scheme whether one is only going to use the top levels of the scheme or whether one is going to use the scheme at the deepest level possible.

One issue here is that if the intent of using the scheme is to collocate topics, then broad vs. close may depend upon the size of the collection that is being classified. If the collection is very large, then using only the top levels of the scheme mean that very large numbers of information packages will be collocated at the same notation. On the other hand, if the collection is very small, then using close classification may mean that most notations are assigned to only one or two information packages, with the result that collocation is minimal (unless one is using a scheme like DDC where one can drop digits off the end of the notation to get to the next broader level of the concept being sought).

It might be observed that what is considered close classification for a small collection may be broad classification for a large collection. That is, for a small collection, DDC's 612.1, meaning the concept of "blood and circulation" in medicine, is a very specific level; but in a medical collection there may be a thousand or more information packages on blood and circulation, and for that collection, close classification would mean going to 612.112, meaning "white corpuscles."

Another issue has to do with the globalization of organization of information. Even if a collection in a particular place is small, its metadata may be being combined with that of many collections, producing a mega-collection. If some of the metadata has been created using close classification, and some has been created using broad classification, the combined effect will be confusing and less helpful. It may be necessary in today's world to use the closest classification available in the scheme being used. This is problematic in some institutions where the classification is used for arranging physical items.

Close classification often produces very long notations, which sometimes have to be placed on very small items. Gorman has suggested that this problem be solved by using shorter notations for *call numbers* but using close classification for the purposes of intellectual retrieval.[6] (See discussion of call numbers in chapter 9.) This, of course, is objected to in many quarters because of the extra cost of providing two notations; but there is a cost to the user who is trying to retrieve information when classification is not usable for collocating topics.

Classification of Knowledge vs. Classification of a Particular Collection

Classification of knowledge is the concept that a classification system can be created that will encompass all knowledge that exists. DDC started as classification of knowledge (at least Western knowledge as understood by Melvil Dewey). Classification of a particular collection is the concept that a classification system should only be devised for the information packages that are being added to collections, using the concept of *literary warrant*. Literary warrant is the name applied to the concept that new notations are created for a classification scheme and new terms are added to a controlled vocabulary only when information packages actually exist that are about a new concept. (See previous comments on literary warrant in chapter 7.) LCC started as classification of a particular collection.

Even though DDC began as a classification of knowledge, it has been forced to use literary warrant for updates and revisions. Some areas of knowledge that have developed in the twentieth century need significantly more space in the scheme than originally given, if indeed they existed and were given any at all. Dewey devoted a whole division to the artificial waterways called "canals," but the concept has been moved to allow expansion of other areas such as engineering, canals no longer being given the attention they were given in Dewey's day. And this is one value of the approach taken by LCC. The alphabet has twenty-six letters. In most places in LCC letters are doubled, and in the last revisions letters have been tripled, giving the potential for up to 1,352 divisions versus the 100 available to DDC. LCC has not come close to using the potential amount of space.

It can be seen that if a scheme has been devised using literary warrant, it can be more flexible than one devised on the basis of classification of knowledge. This issue may come down to preference as to the logical approach of a classification of knowledge versus the practical approach of a classification of what is being studied, created, or written about at the present time.

Integrity of Numbers vs. Keeping Pace with Knowledge

Integrity of numbers is the concept that in the creation and maintenance of a classification scheme, a notation, once assigned, should always retain the same meaning and should never be used with another meaning. *Keeping pace with knowledge* is the concept that in the creation and maintenance of a classification scheme, it is recognized that knowledge changes, and therefore it is necessary to be able to move concepts, insert new concepts, and to change meanings of numbers.

Melvil Dewey was a strong advocate of the concept of integrity of numbers. He did not want the users of his system ever to have to change a number because its meaning had been changed in the system. He wanted new concepts to be assigned to new numbers. As the twentieth century went forward, however, it became impossible to keep pace with new knowledge without sometimes changing the older notations. For example, in the field of mathematics the understanding of the field changed with new research. So it became necessary to change Dewey's arrangement of the basic sections of mathematics, with the following result:

DDC 1st edition	DDC 21st edition
510 Mathematics	510 Mathematics
511 Arithmetic	511 General principles of mathematics
512 Algebra	512 Algebra, number theory
513 Geometry	513 Arithmetic
514 Trigonometry	514 Topology
515 Conic sections	515 Analysis
516 Analytical geometry	516 Geometry
517 Calculus	517 [Unassigned]
518 Quaternions	518 [Unassigned]
519 Probabilities	519 Probabilities and applied math

Such changing of meanings of numbers always involves soul-searching on the part of classifiers. As cost is an ever-present issue, there is a desire not to have to change notations, because this can be expensive. On the other hand, if changes are not made, the system exists with, for example, 513 meaning both *geometry* and *arithmetic*. Collocation is compromised. Searches on classification notations produce confusing results. On the other hand it has been argued that leaving the older materials in the older numbers accurately reflects their contents, while newer materials reflect the new thinking that prompted the change in the scheme. This only works if the different schemes are kept separate both in arranging and in searching.

At the level of the classification scheme itself, its keepers must update it periodically or it will not continue to serve its purpose. If the scheme is flexible enough, updates can be accomplished by inserting new notations. LCC, for example, accomplishes most of its updating in this fashion. If the scheme is less flexible, as with DDC, some inserting can be done, but sometimes meanings of numbers must also be changed.

It was mentioned earlier that some classification issues are general, but others mainly are issues for the use of classification for arranging physical items. Integrity of numbers versus keeping pace with knowledge is an issue that has both general and physical implications and gives us a transition into the issues regarding physical entities. In this case reclassification of physical items when meanings of numbers have been changed is an expensive process. In most collections complete reclassification is not done. Instead there often is some kind of process set up to reclassify items as they are used. Items needing reclassification are taken care of as they are returned after the first use after a change in a number's meaning. Or sometimes a whole collection affected by a change of numbers in a whole section of the scheme will be reclassified on a project basis. Changing only some of a collection, of course, ignores the use of classification as a search key in an online system. Searching a system where certain notations bring up surrogate records for information packages on different subjects is not satisfactory.

Fixed vs. Relative Location

The term *fixed location* signifies a set place where a physical information package will always be found or to which it will be returned after having been removed for use. A fixed location identifier can be an accession number; or a designation made up of room number, stack number, shelf number, position on shelf, etc.; or other such designations.

The term *relative location* is used to mean that an information package will be or might be in a different place each time it is reshelved; that is, it is reshelved relative to what else has been acquired, taken out, returned, etc., while it was out for use. The method for accomplishing this is usually a *call number* with the top line or two being a classification notation. (See discussion of call numbers in chapter 9.)

Fixed location is often used for the purpose of space saving. If fixed location is used, space does not have to be left at the end of each shelf for potential new acquisitions in a particular area of the classification. This is particularly useful for remote storage facilities where space must be saved. Relative location, however, is desirable in a situation where users have access to the stacks and can browse (see discussion of closed versus open stacks below).

It is often argued that the cost of fixed location is much less than that of relative location. If classification numbers do not have to be assigned, and if space can used to the fullest, then cost of fixed location is less to the agency involved. However, especially in libraries, the cost is passed on to the user who loses the collocation provided by classification and the serendipity of being able to browse in the stacks.

Closed vs. Open Stacks

Closed stacks is the name given to the situation where information package storage areas are accessible only to the staff of the library, archives, or other place that houses information packages. *Open stacks* is the name given to the opposite situation where patrons of the facility have the right to go into the storage areas themselves. In closed stack situations users must call for items at a desk and then wait for them to be retrieved and delivered. This eliminates any possibility of what is called *browsing*. Browsing is a process of looking, usually based on subject, at all the items in a particular area of the stacks in order to find, often by serendipity, the items that best suit the needs of the browser.

In most cases where remote storage is used for older and less-used materials, compact shelving is used. This means that in order to make the most efficient use of space, items are shelved using every inch of shelf space, usually with fixed location. In such situations the storage areas are closed. A number of large research libraries have for a long time had closed stacks. There are various reasons for this: tradition, vandalism, precedence of certain classes of users over others, etc. In such libraries a proposal to stop classifying resurfaces every so often. The question asked is "Why classify if readers cannot browse?" Such a proposal includes data about how costs will be lowered if classification is stopped. However, classification is a major form of subject access, and if browsing of the stacks is not allowed, browsing of the classification listing in the catalog may be allowed. Reference librarians often use classification to assist users in finding subject-related material.[7]

In archives the storage areas are almost always closed. This hardly matters as far as classification goes because classification has not been found to be particularly useful for archives in any case. A collection of records can have individual pieces that are on diverse subjects, and dividing and separating these out to classify would violate the principle of provenance. It is conceivable that whole collections could be classified, but usually, the classification in such a case would be so broad as to be nearly meaningless.

Location Device vs. Collocation Device

Another controversy surrounding classification is that of whether classification serves as a collocation device or whether it is simply a location device. A *location device* is a number or other designation on an item to tell where it is located physically. It can be an accession number, a physical location number, a call number, etc. A *collocation device* is a number or other designation on an item used to place it next to (i.e., collocate with) other items that are like it. It is usually a classification number.

Those responsible for the costs of organizing collections tend to take the location device view. They believe that any call number is all right as long as the notation placed on the physical item matches the notation on the surrogate record for the item. The argument is that if the notations on item and surrogate record match, the user will be able to find the item. However, this assumes that the subject headings are sufficient for finding subject-related material in a catalog. Thomas Mann, cited above, and others have shown that both subject headings and classification are required for the most effective retrieval of subject-related material.

It is not clear whether the same notation is adequate to serve both the collocation and the location functions. Gorman, as mentioned above, has suggested that a fully detailed classification be assigned for the purpose of collocation, while a shortened version of it be used for a location device.[8] (This would not really be helpful in the case of LCC, because most notations, even for complex subjects, are relatively short.) In most of the United States one classification notation has served for both collocation and location for many decades. In some other places, especially where classified catalogs are used, the functions of collocation and location have been served by different notations for decades.

A recent point for discussion has been classification of Internet resources. Cost managers often believe that classification is mainly for location, and because Internet resources have location devices in the form of URLs, no classification is needed. However, from the viewpoint of the user, classification can be an effective means of organizing Internet information packages for subject retrieval (see discussion below).

Classification of Serials vs. Alphabetic Order of Serials

Serials are sometimes called journals or magazines. A *serial* may be defined as a publication issued in successive parts (regularly or irregularly) that is intended to continue indefinitely. Classification of serials means that a classification notation is assigned to a serial, and this classification notation is placed on each bound volume and/or each issue of that serial. Alphabetic order of serials means that the serials are placed in order on shelves or in a listing according to the alphabetical order of the titles of the serials. The issues involved in the classification/alphabetic order dilemma apply to runs of printed serials. Serials now produced only on the Internet have issues and problems, but classification is not yet one of these.

With serials it is sometimes quite difficult to discern the intended title because of its placement (e.g., following a corporate body name that is in larger type than the title). In addition serials are apt to have title changes, sometimes several times. They also can merge or split, and can be absorbed by another serial, all of which result in title changes. This is one of the most persuasive arguments against alphabetic order of serials. What to do with runs of serials when there has been a title change is not a resolved issue. Some institutions move the whole run and place at the alphabetic position of the old title(s) a "dummy block" that gives the new title. It is argued in this situation that users will expect to find all of that serial together in spite of the title change. Other institutions divide the serial at the point of the new title. It is argued here that when a title changes, it does so because of a change of emphasis in the serial; therefore, the two runs are almost like two different serials.

Classification of serials provides a solution to the title change dilemma. The new title can be given the same classification as the old. It also has the advantage of allowing the serial to be placed with monographs on the same subject; this is beneficial for browsing purposes. However, classification requires two look-ups. That is, a user comes to the collection with a citation to an article in a journal. If the serial collection is classified, the user must look for the journal title in the catalog, note its call number, and then go to the stacks to find that call number. If serials are placed alphabetically, the user goes to the serials stacks with the citation and finds the journal title. Classification also requires more cataloging/indexing time and thus seems to cost more, although the maintenance of title changes in an alphabetically arranged situation may offset some of the cost that would be incurred by classifying.

One other consideration is the arrangement of serials in a "special library." Many such libraries are subject area specific. In some of these situations most of the serials are on the same or closely related subject, which could mean that their classification numbers would be very near each other, resulting in a semialphabetic order. Such libraries often choose alphabetic arrangement in the first place. The actual arrangement of serials in all libraries in the United States is about 50 percent alphabetic and 50 percent classified.

Classification of Monographic Series
(*Classified Separately* vs. *Classified As a Set*)

First, let us define monograph. A *monograph* is a complete biblio-graphic unit or information package. It is often a single work, but may also be one work or more than one work issued in successive parts; but, unlike serials, it is not intended to be continued indefinitely. A work intended to be complete in, let's say, twenty-eight volumes, is a monograph. A *monographic series* is a hybrid of monograph and serial. In a monographic series each work that is issued as a part of the series is a monograph but is identified as one work in the series. The series itself may or may not be intended to be continued indefinitely. For example, the *Library and Information Science Text Series* published by Libraries Unlimited, Inc., continues to have new works added to it as appropriate works are identified by the publisher.

The difficulty with classification of monographic series is whether to classify each work in the series separately with a specific class number repre-senting its particular subject matter, or to treat the series as if it were a multi-volume monograph and give all parts of the series the same (usually broad) classification notation representing the subject matter of the entire series. Clas-sification of the series as a set results in the loss of collocation of the specific sub-jects contained in each of the works.

On the other hand, especially in public libraries, classification of the series as a set may meet with resounding approval by the users. There are readers who wish to go through a series one by one and find it satisfactory to have them classified together. It is obviously the intention of some publishers that some series be shelved together, especially those series that are bound alike. In some cases the situation is handled by acquiring duplicates, and then classifying one with the set and the other in its specific subject area. The cost of doing this usually is not supported, however, and sometimes cost is the deciding factor for classifying a series as a set—it is cheaper to slap on an already-conceived classification nota-tion than to do the subject analysis necessary for specific classification.

CLASSIFICATION OF THE INTERNET

Although classification has an obvious role in organizing tangible (physical) information packages, the role that classification can play in organizing the Internet is less well understood. Research has shown that browsing is quite useful for information discovery in a variety of environments.[9] Classification gives the ability to browse and also to narrow and broaden searches, another activity valued by users. In a physical arrangement the relationship of classifi-cation to browsing is obvious to the user, but this need not be true with Internet resources. A hierarchical or faceted arrangement can be exploited without the user seeing any classification notations. In this environment the concept might be better understood if it were called categorization.

Categorization is apparent in *Yahoo!*,[10] where web sites are placed into categories which have been created by the catalogers at *Yahoo!*; the categories can be viewed in hierarchical fashion. However, the hierarchies are not true hierarchies in the sense that categories at the same hierarchical level are narrower concepts of the concept at the next level up, nor are the subcategories at an equivalent level with each other. For example:

Under *Recreation* one finds (as of 4/30/98):

> Automotive
> Aviation
> Bibliographies
> Chat
> Employment
> Events
> etc.

interfiled with references for:

> Amusement and Theme Parks (categorized under *Entertainment*)
> Animals, Insects, and Pets (categorized under *Science : Biology : Zoology*)
> Cooking (categorized under *Entertainment : Food and Eating*)
> Dance (categorized under *Arts : Performing Arts*)
> Dating (categorized under *Society and Culture : Relationships*)
> Drugs (categorized under *Health : Pharmacy*)
> etc.

In comparing the terms in the list, one can see that "Automotive" and "Aviation" might be seen as kinds of "Recreation," but "Bibliographies" and "Chat" are about recreation, and "Employment" identifies opportunities in recreation.

Under *Automotive* one finds:

> Alternative fuel vehicles
> Audio
> British cars
> Buyer's Guides
> Chat
> Classic Cars
> etc.

with references for:

> Auto-free Transportation (categorized under *Business and
> Economy : Transportation*)
> Car Art (categorized under *Arts : Visual Arts : Sculpture*)
> Classifieds (categorized under *Business and Economy : Companies :
> Automotive*)

It is not clear what "Audio" means at this level, but it is clearly not at the same level of specificity as "British cars" and "Classic Cars." The references for "Auto-free Transportation" and "Classifieds" appear to have strayed somewhat from the idea of "Recreation."

It is unfortunate that *Yahoo!* chose not to take advantage of an already-existing classification or at least use classification theory. The subcategories in each category of the "hierarchy" now are able to be viewed on one screen, but as more categories need to be added, and the lists take more and more screens, users will be more and more dependent upon the terminology chosen to represent the categories. All of the keyword issues found in the various search engines will need to be addressed. An already existing classification has several advantages: it provides consistent levels in a hierarchy; it is kept up-to-date through consultation with many users; and it also is well known to many users.

As already mentioned classification of sites on the Internet can give assistance with browsing and with narrowing or broadening of searches. It can also assist with context for searches of concepts that can appear in more than one field of knowledge. For example, the concept of "children" can be seen in relation to psychology, religion, education, language, medicine, art, and others. Classification can let one know which context applies. In addition, on the Internet, an information package can be placed into as many categories as are appropriate. If a work discusses "children" in relation to both education and art, notations from both categories can be assigned. What one has, then, is essentially a classified catalog in electronic form.

Classification is a useful way to divide large databases logically. It offers an alternative to alphabetical subdivision, which is quite useful for known-item searches but not so useful for subject searches (unless the letters of the alphabet take one to a thesaurus instead of to titles arranged alphabetically). And if a classification scheme is chosen by several database sites, it is possible to enable searching across databases.

Finally, classification can be used as a switching language among many languages. The notations of a classification are not language-specific, and therefore the meanings of the notations can be given in whatever language is appropriate for the setting. For DDC, for example, translations into a number of languages either already exist or are being worked on: e.g., Arabic, French, Greek, Hebrew, Italian, Persian, Russian, and Spanish. Another classification system that is multilingual is the Universal Decimal Classification (UDC). There are full editions in English, French, German, Japanese, Russian, and eight other languages. Abridged editions exist in seventeen languages and five alphabets. Unfortunately, LCC has not yet moved in a multilingual direction.

A criticism of using classification for the Internet is that humans often need to assign the notations, and the sheer number of information packages makes the task daunting. Research is being conducted on automatic classification. One such project being carried out at OCLC is called "Scorpion." This tool analyzes the text of a web site and then compares text words to words available in headings and notes found in the DDC. It then assigns DDC numbers based on the comparisons.[11]

Many subject search services on the Internet use a classification scheme for organization. An excellent list of sites that use classification schemes or subject headings is one created by McKiernan called *Beyond Bookmarks*.[12]

ARTIFICIAL NEURAL NETWORKS (ANNs)

An artificial neural network (ANN) is a computer system inspired by the architecture of the human biological nervous system. Artificial neural networks have been used in a variety of applications such as pattern and handwriting recognition. They have also been used for automatic categorization. Automatic categorization with ANNs has been used in some Information Retrieval (IR) applications.

One of the most widespread artificial neural network models used for categorization is a browsing tool called a self-organizing map (SOM) based on the work of Kohonen.[13] The SOMs can be compared to the IR methodology of clustering. Clustering brings related items together, which allows for browsing by subject area.

Researchers at the Neural Networks Research Centre of the Helsinki University of Technology have recently developed an exploratory full-text information retrieval method and browsing tool called the WEBSOM,[14] which uses ANNs to categorize automatically a variety of web documents. The result is a map that provides visual representation of a collection of documents. Not only are similar documents clustered together, but the map also displays subjects located near similar subjects. The size of an area in the map corresponds to the frequencies of word occurrence in the document set (see fig. 8.3).

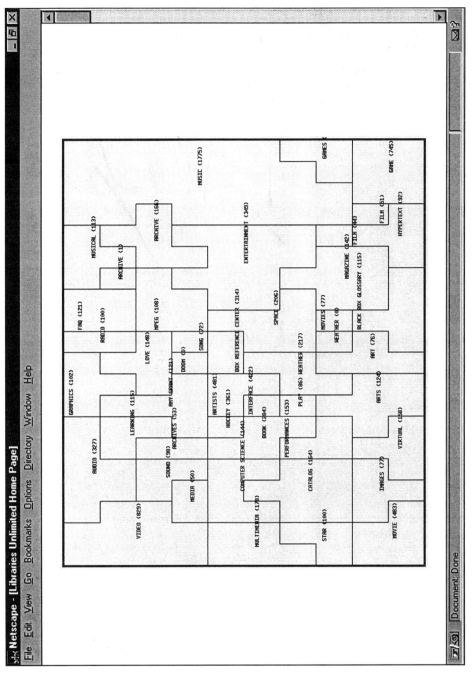

Fig. 8.3. Example of use of Artificial Neural Network principles to provide visual representation of the subject matter in a collection of documents. This SOM clusters words in an "entertainment" document set.

CONCLUSION

This chapter has addressed categorization and classification as a way to provide subject access to information packages. An understanding of classification theory has been shown to be helpful in understanding classification schemes in use today. Arrangement of classification schemes (i.e., hierarchical, enumerative, and faceted) is based in classification theory. Specific classifications are numerous and run from universal schemes to home-grown schemes. Regardless of which scheme is used, there are classification concepts and controversies that must be addressed in the application of any scheme. Some concepts apply to physical packages, while others apply both to physical and nontangible resources. Large numbers of sites of Internet resources are being organized with classification. The future holds the potential for the use of Artificial Neural Networks (ANN) for a kind of automatic categorization, especially the visualization of topics and relationships among those topics. One of the most important factors in information retrieval is to have information packages arranged or displayed in a logical fashion. Classification often plays a major role in such arrangement or display, which is the topic discussed in the next chapter.

NOTES

1.   George Lakoff, *Women, Fire, and Dangerous Things: What Categories Reveal About the Mind* (Chicago: University of Chicago Press, 1987), p. 6.

2.   Ibid., pp. 16–57.

3.   From "Executive Summary" in Traugott Koch, *The Role of Classification Schemes in Internet Resource Description and Discovery*, as captured February 9, 1998, available: http://www.ukoln.ac.uk/metadata/desire/classification/

4.   David H. Elazar and Daniel J. Elazar, *A Classification System for Libraries of Judaica*, 3rd ed., with the assistance of Rachel K. Glasser and Rita C. Frischer (Northvale, N.J.: Jason Aronson, 1997). Home page for this work is available at: http://www.geocities.com/Athens/Acropolis/6527/class.html, accessed October 1998.

5.   Carylyn Gwyn Moser, *Elazar Classification System Holocaust Expansion*, 1997, available: http://www.geocities.com/Athens/Acropolis/6527/holocaust.html, accessed October 1998.

6.   Michael Gorman, "The Longer the Number, the Smaller the Spine; or, Up and Down with Melvil and Elsie," *American Libraries* 12 (September 1981): 498–99.

7.   Thomas Mann, *Doing Research at the Library of Congress: A Guide to Subject Searching in a Closed Stacks Library* (Washington, D.C.: Library of Congress, Humanities and Social Sciences Division, 1994).

8.   Gorman, "The Longer the Number," pp. 498–99.

9.   Gary Marchionini, *Information Seeking in Electronic Environments* (Cambridge; New York: Cambridge University Press, 1995).

10.   *Yahoo!*, available: http://www.yahoo.com/, accessed October 1998.

11.   OCLC, *The Scorpion Project*, available: http://orc.rsch.oclc.org:6109, accessed October 1998.

12.   Gerry McKiernan, *Beyond Bookmarks: Schemes for Organizing the Web*, available: http://www.iastate.edu/~CYBERSTACKS/CTW.htm, accessed October 1998.

13.   Teuvo Kohonen, *Self-Organizing Maps*, 2nd ed. (New York: Springer, 1997).

14.   Timo Honkela, Samuel Kaski, Krista Lagus, and Teuvo Kohonen, *Self-Organizing Maps of Document Collections*, available: http://www.diemme.it/~luigi/websom.html, accessed October 1998.

SUGGESTED READINGS

Classification in General

Classification Research Group. "The Need for a Faceted Classification As the Basis of All Methods of Information Retrieval." In *Theory of Subject Analysis: A Sourcebook*, edited by Lois Mai Chan, Phyllis A. Richmond, and Elaine Svenonius, pp. 154–67. Littleton, Colo.: Libraries Unlimited, 1985.

Gorman, Michael. "The Longer the Number, the Smaller the Spine; or, Up and Down with Melvil and Elsie." *American Libraries* 12, no. 8 (September 1981): 498–99.

Lakoff, George. "The Importance of Categorization." Chap. 1 in *Women, Fire, and Dangerous Things: What Categories Reveal About the Mind*. Chicago: University of Chicago Press, 1987.

Langridge, D. W. *Classification: Its Kinds, Elements, Systems and Applications*. London: Bowker-Saur, 1992, pp. 1–23.

Mann, Thomas. *Doing Research at the Library of Congress: A Guide to Subject Searching in a Closed Stacks Library*. Washington, D.C.: Library of Congress, Humanities and Social Sciences Division, 1994.

———. "The Traditional Library Science Model, Part One: The Classification Scheme." Chap. 3 and "The Traditional Library Science Model, Part Three: Published Bibliographies and Indexes." Chap. 5 in *Library Research Models: A Guide to Classification, Cataloging, and Computers*. New York: Oxford University Press, 1993.

Wynar, Bohdan S. *Introduction to Cataloging and Classification*. 8th ed. by Arlene G. Taylor. "Classification of Library Materials." Chap. 16. Englewood, Colo.: Libraries Unlimited, 1992.

Specific Classification Schemes

Dewey Decimal Classification

Chan, Lois Mai, John P. Comaromi, Joan S. Mitchell, and Mohinder P. Satija. "Introduction to the Dewey Decimal Classification." Chap. 1 and "Structure and Organization of the Text of the Dewey Decimal Classification, Edition 21." Chap. 2 in *Dewey Decimal Classification: A Practical Guide*. 2nd ed. Albany, N.Y.: Forest Press, 1996.

Foskett, A. C. "The Dewey Decimal Classification." Chap. 17 in *The Subject Approach to Information*. 5th ed. London: Library Association Publishing, 1996.

Wynar, Bohdan S. *Introduction to Cataloging and Classification*. 8th ed. by Arlene G. Taylor. "Decimal Classification." Chap. 17, pp. 328–46. Englewood, Colo.: Libraries Unlimited, 1992.

LC Classification

Chan, Lois Mai. *Immroth's Guide to the Library of Congress Classification*. 4th ed. Englewood, Colo.: Libraries Unlimited, 1990.

Foskett, A. C. "The Library of Congress Classification." Chap. 22 in *The Subject Approach to Information*. 5th ed. London: Library Association Publishing, 1996.

Wynar, Bohdan S. *Introduction to Cataloging and Classification*. 8th ed. by Arlene G. Taylor. "Library of Congress Classification." Chap. 18. Englewood, Colo.: Libraries Unlimited, 1992.

Universal Decimal Classification

Foskett, A. C. "The Universal Decimal Classification." Chap. 18 in *The Subject Approach to Information*. 5th ed. London: Library Association Publishing, 1996.

Wynar, Bohdan S. *Introduction to Cataloging and Classification*. 8th ed. by Arlene G. Taylor. "Decimal Classification." Chap. 17, pp. 346–48. Englewood, Colo.: Libraries Unlimited, 1992.

Colon Classification

Foskett, A. C. "The Colon Classification." Chap. 21 in *The Subject Approach to Information*. 5th ed. London: Library Association Publishing, 1996.

Ranganathan, S. R. *Prolegomena to Library Classification*. 3rd ed. London: Asia Publishing House, 1967.

Other

Foskett, A. C. "The Bibliographic Classification." Chap. 19 and "The Broad System of Ordering." Chap. 20 in *The Subject Approach to Information*. 5th ed. London: Library Association Publishing, 1996.

Hearst, Marti A. "Interfaces for Searching the Web." *Scientific American* (March 1997): 68–72.

Wynar, Bohdan S. *Introduction to Cataloging and Classification*. 8th ed. by Arlene G. Taylor. "Other Classification Systems." Chap. 20. Englewood, Colo.: Libraries Unlimited, 1992.

Classification and the Internet

Koch, Traugott. *The Role of Classification Schemes in Internet Resource Description and Discovery*. Available: http://www.ukoln.ac.uk/metadata/desire/classification (See individual descriptions of several classification schemes.) (Accessed October 1998).

McKiernan, Gerry. *Beyond Bookmarks: Schemes for Organizing the Web*. Available: http://www.iastate.edu/~CYBERSTACKS/CTW.htm (Accessed October 1998).

Vizine-Goetz, Diane. *Online Classification: Implications for Classifying and Document[-like Object] Retrieval*. Available: http://orc.rsch.oclc.org:6109/dvgisko.htm (Accessed October 1998).

———. *Using Library Classification Schemes for Internet Resources*. Available: http://www.oclc.org/oclc/man/colloq/v-g.htm (Accessed October 1998).

Artificial Neural Networks (ANN)

Anderson, James A. *An Introduction to Neural Networks*. Cambridge, Mass.: MIT Press, 1995, pp. vii–xi, 1–15.

Doszkocs, Tamas, James Reggia, and Xia Lin. "Connectionist Models and Information Retrieval." In *Annual Review of Information Science and Technology*, vol. 25 (1990), edited by Martha E. Williams, pp. 212–14, 222–30. Amsterdam: Elsevier Science, 1990.

Honkela, Timo, Samuel Kaski, Krista Lagus, and Teuvo Kohonen. *Self-Organizing Maps of Document Collections*. Available: http://www.diemme.it/~luigi/websom. html (Accessed October 1998).

Kohonen, Teuvo. *Self-Organizing Maps*. 2nd ed. New York: Springer, 1997.

What Is an Artificial Neural Network? Available: http://www.nd.com/welcome/ whatisnn.htm (Accessed October 1998).

CHAPTER 9

ARRANGEMENT AND DISPLAY

$\mathcal{S}$*helving* and *filing* were the names traditionally given to the topics of this chapter. That is, books were shelved and cards were filed. In today's information environment there is still a great deal of shelving of physical information packages (their numbers have not diminished as predicted), and some filing of cards is still done. Some institutions still maintain card shelflists; and some smaller institutions still have no local online systems. Archives shelve collection boxes, but within the boxes archivists may file papers if the collection arrives with no discernible order.

In addition to shelving and filing, though, we have arrangement and display of nontangible resources and the order of displays on screens to be concerned about. This chapter addresses the following questions: How are information packages arranged? How are surrogate/metadata records arranged and displayed? How is categorization used in the arrangement of information packages and surrogate records? What is the significance of arrangement in the electronic environment?

ARRANGEMENT OF PHYSICAL INFORMATION PACKAGES

Libraries

Arrangement of physical information packages has been of concern to libraries for centuries. For the last couple of decades, there has been increasing concern about arrangement of electronic resources contained in physical packaging (e.g., CD-ROMs, videodiscs, music CDs, etc.). Now for the last few years there has been increasing concern about arrangement of intangible electronic resources.

Physical information packages in libraries are usually shelved by *call number*. A call number is a notation on an information package that matches the same notation in the surrogate/metadata record. It is the number used to "call" for an item in a closed stack library—thus, the source of the name *call number*. A call number usually consists of at least two lines on a label placed on the outside of the packaging. The top line is usually a classification notation. With long notations, the classification notation may continue onto a second line. The next line is usually a *cutter number*. Cutter numbers were devised by Charles A. Cutter a century ago for the purpose of alphabetizing all works that had exactly the same classification notation. Cutter devised a table in which letters of the alphabet were listed in one column and equivalent numerals were listed in an adjoining column.[1] For example:

Fonti	684
Fontr	685
Foo	686

A Cutter line for an author named Fontrain, for example, might be F685d. The small "d" is a *work mark* assigned to help keep the works of a particular author who writes on the same subject in alphabetical order. The work mark usually stands for the first word, not an article, of the title of the work; although for biographies, the work is usually "cuttered" for the name of the person the work is about, and the work mark stands for the last name of the author of the biography. This kind of Cutter number is most often used with DDC notations. LCC also uses cutter numbers (with a small "c"). LC borrowed Charles Cutter's idea, but created its own table that takes only a few lines.[2] A third line for a call number is often the date. Examples of call numbers are:

DDC	LCC
378.4	QE22.D25
F685d	S65
1998	1997

There are also alphabetical arrangements, accession order arrangements, and fixed location arrangements for physical information packages. In public libraries, in particular, fiction is often grouped together, subarranged in alphabetical order by author. Another use for alphabetical order is biographies, which may be arranged in alphabetical order by the last name of the person the biography is about. And, as discussed in chapter 8, serials are often arranged in alphabetical order by title. Accession order arrangements are used for materials waiting to be cataloged, and sometimes for more "permanent" backlogs. They are also used for fixed location settings, such as remote storage.

In most libraries there is more than one sequence of A-Z (if using LCC) or 000-999 (if using DDC) arrangement. There is usually a reference collection, for example, that has information packages from all classes. These are kept separately from the regular circulating collection. In academic libraries there is often a collection of reserve items for use for certain courses. In many libraries some kinds of information packages are separated by format. Microforms, CD-ROMs, sound recordings, videocassettes, etc., are arranged in their own groups with their own sequences. This is often for housing and preservation purposes. Some media centers have tried to interfile all formats in classification order, but the idea has never really caught on.

Archives

Archives seldom use classification. As mentioned in chapter 1 the principles for arrangement are *provenance* and *original order*. That is, to the extent possible, archival collections are arranged by their source, and within each source group, by the order in which they were kept by the person or corporate body from whence they came to the archives. The principle is based on evidence that the original order made some sense to the creator, and that order is important in any research that may be conducted where an understanding of the person or corporate body is important.

When an archives receives a new collection, it is assessed and a processing plan is made. This includes such things as determining what descriptive products will be created (e.g., finding aid, catalog record, etc.); whether samples from the collection will be scanned so that they can be viewed electronically; what kind of appraisal the collection will receive; what preservation measures will be taken; and whether the inventory will be created at the box level, the file level, or the item level.

The person responsible for description also determines what *series* are present. The word *series* is used very differently in archives than in libraries. In archival collections a series is a logically grouped set of files, books, correspondence, or other such set. For example, in the personal papers of a university professor, one might find files grouped in such a way that files for each of the professor's courses are together; files relating to the person's research and writing are together; and files relating to administrative issues (e.g., student advisees, doctoral comprehensive examinations, etc.) are together. Each of these groupings would be a series.

If a collection arrives in no discernible order, then the person responsible for its description must impose an order upon it. Such a situation almost always involves personal papers. The describer tries to put papers that have to do with the person's life in one grouping, manuscripts in another, correspondence in another, etc.

The physical placing of the boxes is by fixed location in closed stacks. An entire collection does not necessarily have to have all its boxes shelved together. The shelflist record records the fixed locations of boxes, whether they are shelved together or not.

ARRANGEMENT OF INTANGIBLE INFORMATION PACKAGES

Internet resources are literally organized by protocol (e.g., http://), server address (e.g., www.pitt.edu/), path (e.g., ~agtaylor/ala/papers/), and file name (e.g., blfictio.html). Stringing these together creates the Uniform Resource Locator (URL) for the information package. This is not useful in collocating resources by any of the usual measures: creator, title, subject matter, form/genre. In fact, to do a known-item search, one has to have all the above pieces of the URL exactly right even to capitalization.

In the organization of Internet resources we have to, first, accept that the entire Internet will never be organized. And why should it be? Libraries, archives, and museums have always chosen what they will organize based upon collection development policies. Seldom did the collection include advertisements, ephemera, and the like. There has been an attempt to organize materials of lasting value. The same should be true of the Internet. An advantage we have with the Internet is that we do not have to duplicate each other's efforts. With a little effort, organization can be divided up by, perhaps, subject area, geographic area, or some other means.

Currently, much organization of the Internet is being accomplished by individual persons or organizations pulling together materials of lasting value, and usually on a particular subject or person or related in some other fashion. These resources are not literally pulled together, of course, but are hot linked to a gathering page. The arrangement may be in the form of a large bibliography, as, for example, the International Federation of Library Association's bibliography "Digital Libraries: Metadata Resources."[3] Other pages are arranged using classification/categorization (see discussion in chapter 8). With some of the latter the classification notation is explicit; with others the notation is not visible to the user, but browsing and the ability to narrow and broaden searches is much appreciated by users. A list of sites that use classification schemes or subject headings is one created by McKiernan called *Beyond Bookmarks: Schemes for Organizing the Web* which is, itself, an example of a site where organization is evident.[4]

ARRANGEMENT OF SURROGATES (METADATA)

For most of the twentieth century catalogs were in card, book, or COM formats. In card catalogs the arrangement of surrogate records was by a filing arrangement achieved by humans. Persons doing the filing had rules to follow that would lead to an arrangement that was deemed to be conducive to helping users find what they were looking for. In early book catalogs, the same was true because book catalogs often were made from cards or "slips" created by catalogers and placed in order by filers.

As computers entered the picture, book and then COM catalogs began to be created in electronic databases where the actual "filing" was done according to computer algorithms. Finally, Online Public Access Catalogs (OPACs) came into use. The records were stored sequentially or randomly within the computer, but in order to display the results of a search to a user, the subset of records retrieved had to be arranged and then displayed on the screen in some order. Early computer algorithms dictated an order of characters: sometimes numerals preceded letters, sometimes not; and there was (and still is) great difficulty in even displaying diacritical marks, let alone arranging them to display in some meaningful order.

OPACs and other electronic databases continue to be arranged on screen by computer algorithm. A few systems have been developed to make use of MARC tags and subfield codes to create more logical arrangements. And, whatever the algorithm, no computer can make up for a typographical error the way a filer can. In a card catalog an alert filer would see such a "typo" as *Salve rebellions* and file it properly as *Slave rebellions*. In a computer, which would see "salve" as a properly spelled word in any spelling checker, the title with the typo would be arranged before all other entries for the correctly spelled title. Intervening between *Salve* and *Slave* would be *Scarlet letter*, *Search for sanity*, *Silent world*, and many hundreds of other titles. Note also that retrieval of known items is not possible when a typo is involved.

Filing History

Charles A. Cutter included filing rules in his cataloging code.[5] There have been separate filing codes, not connected with cataloging rules, ever since Cutter. Earlier filing codes reflected the influence of the classified catalog. They presorted catalog entries into categories. For example, entries beginning with the word "orange" were sorted into: personal names (separating single surname entries from compound surname entries); geographic entities; corporate bodies; subject headings (separating the fruit from the color); and titles. Even though the rules were for *dictionary* catalogs, the categories were to be filed one after another instead of being interfiled alphabetically. The earlier codes also reflected the many variant local practices that existed. The 1942 *A.L.A. Rules for Filing Catalog Cards*[6] had many rules with two or three "correct" alternatives for a particular filing dilemma. One library could use rules 1.a. and 2.b., while another library could use rules 1.b. and 2.a. Both could claim to be following the American Library Association (ALA) filing rules. Users going from one library to another had to learn new filing rules for each catalog.

By the mid-1960s frustration was mounting. People in ALA decided to create a consistent code of filing rules derived from one basic principle. The resulting 1968 *ALA Rules for Filing Catalog Cards*[7] recommended straight alphabetical order, but there were exceptions. For example, personal surname entries (for single surnames only!) were to be arranged before other entries beginning with the same word. Also, a filer had to spell out numerals and abbreviations in the language of the item and then file the card in the place that the spelled-out form would go in the catalog.

In 1980 ALA again published a code of filing rules[8] and this time they were so different that they were not called a third edition. They called for straightforward filing according to principles, but, still, alphabetical order was not absolute. A brief review of these rules serves to highlight some of the problems that serve to keep people from finding what they want in computer displays, especially when a displayed set takes up more than one or two screens.

General Rules for Arrangement

Traditional arrangement in catalogs is word-by-word. This means that everything beginning with a particular word should precede other entries beginning with a word that has the same beginning letters as the first word (e.g., New York files before Newark). Not all information retrieval tools use this arrangement. Some encyclopedias and dictionaries, for example, use letter-by-letter arrangement. The difference is that in word-by-word arrangement, a space between words is treated according to the principle: "nothing files before something." That is, a space is "nothing," and it should be filed before a character, which is "something." According to the *ALA Filing Rules*, spaces, dashes, hyphens, diagonal slashes, and periods are all considered to be "nothing." Arrangements using the letter-by-letter approach ignore spaces and some of the punctuation marks just mentioned, and the entry files as if it is all run together into one word (e.g., New York is treated as Newyork and follows Newark). A longer example may serve to assist in clarifying the distinction:

Word-by-Word	Letter-by-Letter
A book about myself	A book about myself
Book bytes	Bookbinding
Book-making (Betting)	Book bytes
Book of bells	Booker T. Washington
Book reports	Booker, William, 1905-
Bookbinding	Bookfinder
Booker T. Washington	Bookkeeping made simple
Booker, William, 1905-	Book-making (Betting)
Bookfinder	Book of bells
Bookkeeping made simple	Book reports
Books that changed the world	Booksellers and bookselling
Booksellers and bookselling	Books that changed the world

Another principle of arrangement is that numerals precede letters. Formerly, numerals were filed as spoken and spelled out, e.g.,

Twenty-four dramatic cases ...

24 ways to ...

XXIVth Congress of ....

However, in the 1980 filing rules the difficulties of mentally spelling out something like "24" in French, German, Russian, etc., for both filers and users were recognized. Numerals were to go first, but in numerical order, and Roman numerals filed with Arabic numerals. Thus, $\frac{1}{2}$ (the fraction) was to file before 1 (the first integer). But computers have difficulty with this. The computer sees *one-slash-two*, not *one-half* in $\frac{1}{2}$. In the following example one can see that numerical order for a computer is based upon column by column matching and Roman numerals are seen as letters:

Manual Filing	Machine Arrangement
6 concerti grossi	10 times a poem
9 to 5	1984
10 times a poem	6 concerti grossi
XIXth century drawings	9 to 5
90 days to a better heart	90 days to a better heart
1984	XIXth century drawings

Among other principles of manual filing are: letters in the English alphabet precede letters of nonroman alphabets; ampersands (&) may be ignored, or optionally, may be spelled out in their language equivalents; and, punctuation, nonalphabetic signs, and symbols are ignored. Computers generally treat these the same way except that they cannot follow the option of spelling out ampersands in their language equivalents. Ampersands are problematic for retrieval because a user who has heard a title but has not seen it does not know whether "and" is spelled-out or represented by an ampersand, and usually does not know to try the other way if one way does not work. Recently, catalogers have often made additional title access points for the spelled-out form when ampersands or numerals have been used in titles.

Filing/Display Dilemmas

There are quite a few situations that cannot be resolved by human intellect as was done in the past. It seems impossible to program computers to handle all these situations so that the outcome is logical. For example, when titles are transcribed from chief sources of information in the process of creating metadata, the title is taken character by character as it appears. This results in some titles that begin with or contain the same words appearing to a computer to contain different words. Names beginning with prefixes, for example, are sometimes written with a space preceding the prefix (e.g., De Gaulle and DeGaulle). Another case arises from words that began as two words and are in the process of becoming one word (e.g., on line, on-line, and online). Here is another case where a user, having heard a title spoken, would not know which way to look for it.

Another spacing problem comes from punctuation marks. As mentioned above, the *ALA Filing Rules* says that spaces, dashes, hyphens, diagonal slashes, and periods are all considered to be "nothing." However, this is not true in all computer systems. Such marks might be replaced by a space, or they might not even be replaced by a space, resulting in words being run together inappropriately (e.g., "surrogate/metadata records" might become "surrogatemetadata records").

Computers also have difficulty with abbreviations. A human or a Natural Language Processing system can tell whether Co. means "County" or "Company"; whether St. means "Street" or "Saint"; whether Dr. means "Doctor" or "Doktor." Most systems cannot tell the difference, however, and arrangement is simply done by the letters that are there. A retrieval challenge here is that even if users know the titles they are searching for word-for-word, if they have only heard the titles and have not seen them, they do not know if certain words are abbreviated or spelled out.

Dates in subject headings present yet another challenge. In traditional manual practice, dates are to be arranged in chronological order. With *Library of Congress Subject Headings* (*LCSH*), however, some dates are preceded by a verbal phrase identifying a name for the particular period of time. These headings can be placed in chronological order by a human, but a computer can't see "1775-1783" until it has arranged "Revolution" preceding or following all other numerals. For example:

Dates (Manual Filing)	Dates (Machine Arrangement)
United States--History--Revolution, 1775-1783	United States--History--1800-
United States--History--1800-	United States--History--1801-1809
United States--History--1801-1809	United States--History--1900-
United States--History--War of 1812	United States--History--1945-
United States--History--Civil War, 1861-1865	United States--History--Civil War, 1861-1865
United States--History--1900-	United States--History--Revolution, 1775-1783
United States--History--1945-	United States--History--War of 1812

Some machine systems place numerals after letters, but, in any case, the letters would be all together and the numerals would be all together. How many users know that in a long list of time periods for the history of a country, the named periods come last or the dates alone all come last? For that matter, how many know the names of time periods?

Initials and acronyms present yet another arrangement and retrieval challenge. If they are written with periods or spaces between them, they are filed as if each letter is a word (e.g., A B C files as if the first word is "A," the second is "B," and the third is "C"; while ABC files as a single word). For example:

> A.A.
> A.A.U.W.
> A apple pie
> A B C programs
> AAA
> Aabel, Marie
> Abacus calculating
> ABCs of collecting

Users are at a loss to know whether periods or spaces have been used. This kind of situation requires the assistance of someone to see that access points are provided both with and without spaces.

A final arrangement problem that we will discuss is the one surrounding such things as articles and elisions. Articles ("a, an, the" and their equivalents in other languages) that come at the beginning of a heading are supposed to be ignored in filing. This can only happen in all languages if the system is using an encoding scheme like MARC wherein a human can give in an indicator the number of characters that the computer should ignore before beginning the arrangement order. Even in the MARC format there is not provision for indicating articles for every possible title access point. In USMARC, for example, Uniform titles and titles in subfield "t" of several access point fields do not have indicators for articles. In addition, if a system is programmed to give access to subtitles, those beginning with articles will be arranged under the articles.

A system cannot just have a stoplist of all articles in all languages. First, some articles are ordinary words in other languages (e.g., the German *die*). Second, if the article is part of a proper name, it should be arranged under the article. For example:

> Los angeles custodios *[title in A]*
> Los Angeles in fiction *[title in L]*
> Los Angeles Bar Association *[corporate body in L]*
>
> L'enfant abandonee *[title in E]*
> L'Enfant, Edouard *[person in L]*

The main concern in the issues discussed above is that in online systems when searchers retrieve responses that take more than two screens to display, they have to understand the arrangement. If they think that responses are in alphabetical order, and if they expect, for example, an acronym to be at the beginning of the listing, they might not even go to the screen that actually has the entry. Although arrangement is done by the computer system, some profiling can be done by humans to enable displays to be more predictable.

CONCLUSION

Arrangement and display have evolved in the online world from shelving and filing in the paper world. Physical information packages continue to need to be shelved in fashions that allow them to be found again. The methods for doing this are well worked-out. We also face the need to arrange virtual information packages in ways that allow them to be found easily. This is a task that requires imaginative approaches and experimentation, just as organizing physical information packages once did.

Arrangement of surrogate/metadata records is also evolving. The first online catalogs were automated card catalogs, but without the sophisticated filing arrangements that could be accomplished in card catalogs. Display of search results has had many improvements, but problems still abound. An appropriate display is highly dependent upon system design, the topic of the next chapter.

NOTES

1. The various editions of the Cutter tables (including the Cutter-Sanborn tables) are available from Libraries Unlimited, Inc., P.O. Box 6633, Englewood, CO 80155-6633; 1-800-237-6124.

2. For more explanation of call numbers, see Bohdan S. Wynar, *Introduction to Cataloging and Classification,* 8th ed. by Arlene G. Taylor, "Creation of Complete Call Numbers," Chap. 19 (Englewood, Colo.: Libraries Unlimited, 1992).

3. International Federation of Library Associations, *Digital Libraries: Metadata Resources,* available: http://www.nlc-bnc.ca/ifla/II/metadata.htm, accessed October 1998.

4. McKiernan, Gerry, *Beyond Bookmarks: Schemes for Organizing the Web,* available: http://www.iastate.edu/~CYBERSTACKS/CTW.htm, accessed October 1998.

5. Charles A. Cutter, *Rules for a Dictionary Catalog,* 4th ed. (Washington, D.C.: Government Printing Office, 1904; reprint, London: The Library Association, 1962), p. 12.

6. *A.L.A. Rules for Filing Catalog Cards* (Chicago: American Library Association, 1942).

7. *ALA Rules for Filing Catalog Cards,* 2nd ed. (Chicago: American Library Association, 1968).

8. *ALA Filing Rules* (Chicago: American Library Association, 1980).

SUGGESTED READINGS

Arrangement of Information-Bearing Entities

Libraries

Wynar, Bohdan S. *Introduction to Cataloging and Classification.* 8th ed. by Arlene G. Taylor. "Creation of Complete Call Numbers." Chap. 19. Englewood, Colo.: Libraries Unlimited, 1992.

Archives

Miller, Frederic M. Chap. 7, pp. 77–78, and "Introduction." Chap. 1 in *Arranging and Describing Archives and Manuscripts*. Chicago: Society of American Archivists, 1990.

Internet

McKiernan, Gerry. *Beyond Bookmarks: Schemes for Organizing the Web*. Available: http://www.iastate.edu/~CYBERSTACKS/CTW.htm (Accessed October 1998).

Arrangement of Bibliographic/Surrogate Records

Buckland, Michael K., Barbara A. Norgard, and Christian Plaunt. "Filing, Filtering and the First Few Found." *Information Technology and Libraries* 12, no. 3 (September 1993): 311–19.

Wynar, Bohdan S. *Introduction to Cataloging and Classification*. 8th ed. by Arlene G. Taylor. "Filing." Chap. 28. Englewood, Colo.: Libraries Unlimited, 1992.

CHAPTER 10

SYSTEM DESIGN

The structure described in this book in chapters 4 through 9 requires an adequate system design that will enable one to find particular desired instances of metadata. In order to ensure this findability, the system must be designed to retrieve and display metadata in a useful and logical fashion. This chapter discusses the following questions: How does system design relate to the organization of information? How can existing systems be used and interpreted effectively? What suggestions for improving current systems and what new systems have been proposed for the organization of information?

HOW DOES SYSTEM DESIGN RELATE TO THE ORGANIZATION OF INFORMATION?

System design is the glue that holds together the separate metadata records that are surrogates for the information packages that exist in a particular domain. System design brought all the retrieval tools that now exist. In the print world system design was not separated from the process of creating surrogate records. Panizzi's rules included both principles for what information to include in a surrogate record and standards for placing those records into a cohesive catalog. Cutter's rules included record-creation rules that emphasized collocation (i.e., placing those records in logical juxtaposition with each other), and also included a section of filing rules (i.e., Cutter's design for the card catalog). Each edition of rules that has come through the American Library Association has assumed the system design of a card catalog. Standards for the creation of bibliographies and indexes have been for print in book form.

Of course, the term *system design* was not used for the process of deciding how print tools would be arranged and laid out. The same people who created the surrogate records also controlled the display of those records. They did not think of themselves as system designers. Yet, some print tools were and are quite sophisticated finding and collocation systems. They could be sophisticated because the designers knew the contents of the surrogate records so very intimately. As the tools became automated, though, the task of design was taken on by people who understood computers intimately, but often had little or no knowledge of the contents of the records that would make up the system being designed.

System design is a necessity for the retrieval of organized information whether it is or is not done by the same people who create surrogate records. It can be a design that simply displays, in no particular order, every record that contains a certain keyword. Or, it can be a design that displays records in a sophisticated way to show relationships among records and works as well as responding to requested words.

HOW CAN EXISTING SYSTEMS BE USED AND INTERPRETED EFFECTIVELY?

Existing online systems are an outgrowth of the early combination of print sources with computers. Users are often at a loss when faced with the differing approaches to retrieval that these systems take. The first online systems did no more than imitate print retrieval tools, and did not do the imitation very well. Some systems were programmed to respond to commands in which a "code" (e.g., "a" for author, "t" for title, etc.) was to be followed by an exact string of characters that would be matched against the system's internal index. In many early systems display of "matches" was by "last in-first out" (i.e., the order was the reverse order in which the records had been input to the system). Later, systems displayed responses to specific searches, such as those for author or title, in alphabetical (according to that system) order by a certain field. In catalogs and indexes, for example, main entry (or "author") was usually chosen as the one by which responses would be arranged. However, results of less specific searches, such as keyword, were often displayed in reverse chronological order, using date of publication or production.

As systems have become more sophisticated, more control of display has been given the user. Sometimes the user can choose which fields are to be displayed, and often users are able to specify a field to be used for the order of the displayed responses. However, system designs are all different from each other, and users are often confused when moving from one system to another (e.g., searching a local catalog, then doing an ERIC search on CD, then doing a real-time DIALOG search, then searching catalogs in distant locations that have different search commands).

In order to use today's online retrieval tools effectively a user must study each new system that is used. Some of the questions that must be answered are:

- How does the system accept queries? commands? forms to fill in? menus to be navigated? If commands are used, how are they constructed?

    Each method has advantages and drawbacks. Commands are faster than either filling in forms or navigating menus. However, they usually require that one know a set of abbreviations for the action wanted (e.g., fin[d], bro[wse], sca[n], etc.) and the label for the fields to be searched (e.g., au[thor], ti[tle], su[bject], etc.). These must be followed by search terms in the correct form (e.g., personal names may have to be entered in inverted order). Menus allow one to navigate by making choices, not by giving commands; but it is often a very slow process. Filling in forms has an intermediate speed; but one has to remember to make all the correct choices from the pull-down menus.

- In what ways can one search? by author? by title? by subject? by form/genre? by combinations of these? by keyword? If keyword searching is available, which fields are searched? Are searches for author, title, or subject treated as exact word-for-word searches or as keyword searches of the field(s) being tapped?

    It seems that users quite often do not know the differences among searching by author, title, and subject. This was discovered when card catalogs were divided into two or three catalogs (as discussed in chapter 2). Users were especially confused by looking for persons as authors in an "author catalog" versus looking for works about those same persons in a "subject catalog." The problem was alleviated in some card catalogs by placing all works by and about persons in a "name" catalog. Very few online systems have allowed this solution, however. Users have had to know that in order to find works *about* a person, one has to do a subject search; but to find works *by* a person, one has to do an author search.

Form/genre searching is relatively new, and it is hoped that users will find this concept easy to understand. Few systems, so far, allow searching by form/genre, but as more metadata incorporates the concept, the need for addition of this search to system design will increase.

The results of keyword searching are affected by which fields are searched in the system. Some systems have generic keyword searches that search almost every field of a record. In others choices have to be made. For example, some "word" searches may search only subject heading and title fields, while others may search only subject heading fields. Notes fields are often ignored by system designers as potential sources of subject-laden terminology.

- Are Boolean searches allowed? If so, in what order are operators executed? If default Boolean is used, is the default AND or OR?

  Allowance of Boolean searching is far from consistent among systems. Most allow more than one word per command or search, but the way in which multiple terms are treated in a search can vary considerably. Most online catalogs, for example, treat such a search as if the operator AND has been inserted between terms. That is, all terms in the search must be present in a record for that record to be retrieved. Many search engines, though, treat such a search as if OR has been inserted between terms. That is, each record retrieved contains at least one of the terms, but not necessarily all the terms.

  When operators are expressly inserted, a user must know the order in which operations are carried out. For example, in a search for "catalogs OR indexes AND libraries" most online catalogs execute the operators from left to right (i.e., records with either the term "catalogs" or the term "indexes" combined with the word "libraries"). But many online retrieval systems use algebraic sequence (i.e., either records with the term "catalogs," OR records containing both "indexes" and "libraries").

- How are results of a search displayed? In what order? Chapter 9 of this text includes a discussion of some of the challenges of machine filing and of the difficulties that are possible in the display of search results.

- Are "guides" presented before actual listings of records? If so, how do they divide up responses? If not, what method is to be used for finding a particular record or records in a multiscreen response?

  Related to the display issue is whether the whole list of headings for the retrieved records is displayed before the records are displayed. Some systems, in a response to a search for an author with the surname "Benson," will display all the Bensons in the system, grouped by given name initials. One can browse through this list and find the appropriate heading before having lists of works to sift through. Other systems include lists of works related to each Benson without one knowing first how many Bensons there are. One is required to page through the list of both authors and titles instead of being able to "browse" the list of names first. One current catalog system, with a web version of the catalog, displays, in its default mode, the responses in what appears to be random order—not by title, not by any author, not by publication date. If one chooses to have results sorted by author, then main entry is displayed, not necessarily the author being searched (e.g., not the Benson who is a second or later author listed).

  Many systems have a "guide screen" as the first display. The guide may be divided logically, or it may simply divide the responses by the number of lines available on one screen and then display the heading of the first response in each of the evenly divided groupings. Web displays of metadata notably do not have guide screens but display the first ten, twenty, or so, hits, even if the number of responses is in the hundreds or thousands; it is often impossible to determine an order in such displays.

- What kinds of information are included in records in the database?

  The information contained in *catalog* records is standardized by long-standing rules. However, in local situations many records may be either longer (e.g., addition of contents notes, reviews, etc.) or shorter (e.g., minimal level records) than the common standard. Information contained in *index* records is quite variable. Each commercial index has its own standard for inclusion of information in records. Differences include length of citation, abbreviations, inclusion of abstracts, and precoordinate or postcoordinate controlled vocabulary (or none).

In the case of metadata encoded with a MARC format, much of the data that the cataloger placed in a record is virtually never displayed to the public. There are elements that give information in coded form. In a good system design these could be programmed to display a meaningful translation of the code, or programmed to be searched in meaningful ways. Neither of these is available in any system of the author's knowledge. Indexes use their own encoding schemes, perhaps MARC-based, or local schemes, and display records in a variety of ways. Other kinds of metadata are so new that they have no "typical" ways of being displayed. The metadata formats so far seem to contain only information that is intended to be displayed.

- Is a record displayed in full, briefly, or in some intermediate fullness? What information is omitted at each level?
  There are often three levels of display of records: a one- or two-line version, a brief display, and a full display (although "full" seldom means that all information in an encoded record is displayed). The amount and kind of information omitted from a full record to make a brief display is different from system to system. For example, all notes are usually omitted in a brief display, but sometimes the first note is kept (unless it is a bibliography note). Another example is that statements of responsibility are sometimes omitted. In addition all access points other than the primary one may be omitted, or only subject headings may be omitted. In other words, one cannot approach a new system expecting that metadata information presented in the display will be the same as in the last system used.

- Do records contain subject data in the form of controlled vocabulary?

  Keyword searching is often touted as being sufficient instead of having to have controlled vocabulary. However, research has shown that keyword searching often results in many false drops (i.e., irrelevant retrievals because the word retrieved has a different meaning from the intended meaning) and in loss of retrievals because synonyms or near-synonyms were not retrieved with the word sought. Users need to know, when searching, whether or not there is controlled vocabulary, because if there is none, they will have to think of all synonyms themselves.

- Does the system support controlled vocabulary by displaying relationships (e.g., broader terms, narrower terms)?

  Similar to needing to know whether there is controlled vocabulary, users need to know whether subject relationships are available to help them browse in a subject area: to broaden or narrow searches and to look at related areas.

- How are author searches interpreted by the system—exact match, near match, keyword?

  For efficient searching a user must know that if a search for, let's say, "Smith, William" is input, will the system search for that word string exactly, no more and no less; or will it search for any entry beginning with that exact word string; or will it search for any author field that contains both the word "William" and "Smith" (e.g., "Barney, William Smith" or "William, Jonathan Smith")? If a user wishes to see records for a particular William Smith, whose middle names and/or dates of birth/death are not remembered, then an exact match or a keyword match will not be satisfactory. The user will need to know how to place a truncation symbol at the end of the search if the system returns only exact matches and will need to know how to find only surname "Smith" and first forename "William" if the system returns keyword matches.

- Which keys on keyboards have special functions in the system (e.g., function keys, control key used with another key)?

  In many existing systems it is necessary to use function keys, the control key, or the "alt" key in order to move around in the system. For example, pressing the control key and "c" key at the same time is often required to clear a screen or to exit a system. Knowing the difference is crucial. As web interfaces to retrieval systems become more common, "point and click" will replace reliance on special keys.

- How are hyphens, other punctuation, and symbols treated in the system?

  Removing punctuation from a string of text in order to provide better potential for matches between search strings and field information in records is called "normalization." Normalization is intended to allow better matching, because users are not always precise in placement of such marks as diacritics and commas. However, depending upon the algorithm used for normalization, results may be different from system to system. For example, hyphens may be treated as spaces, or they may be stripped out to make a single word (e.g., "on-line" may become "on line" or "online"). If the user types "on-line," the retrieved set may include responses with "on line" or "online" but not both.

- Does the system "remember" where a user is in a search, and can one get back to the first response to a search, or is the system "stateless" (i.e., unable to keep track of the searches done by a user, and unable to combine search "sets")?

  Many of the systems that searchers use are capable of allowing a user to return to previous results or to combine results from several searches. Current web interface catalogs and indexes must be particularly frustrating to users who have used sophisticated systems, considering that today's web servers are "stateless," that is, consider each response to a query to be a completed transaction. The browser's "back" button may take a searcher back to a previous response, but there can be no combination of previous search results. Work is being done to overcome this setback (e.g., registration of a user so that the system can be programmed to remember a user's previous search). One may hope to see results of this work in the near future.

Many users do not know to ask such questions as those above. Even if they do, there are numerous surprises that often lie in wait for the uninitiated. Among these are:

- too few error messages to help users understand mistakes

- no hits or too many hits; user does not know how to increase or reduce results

- long displays that are hard to scan

- misspelled search words that are not identified as such, and a user is left to guess whether the system does not contain the word or an error has been made

- help screens and messages that are not clear

- stopwords that differ from system to system; also variations as to whether stopwords apply only at the beginning of a string of words, such as a title, or apply anywhere in any searchable field

- no references at lower levels of a hierarchy (e.g., no reference from IRS Audit Division to United States. Internal Revenue Service. Audit Division, because there is a reference from IRS to United States. Internal Revenue Service)

These and many other issues related specifically to online catalogs are discussed thoroughly by Yee and Layne.[1] Their book contains excellent examples, to which the reader is referred.

WHAT SUGGESTIONS FOR IMPROVING CURRENT SYSTEMS AND WHAT NEW SYSTEMS HAVE BEEN PROPOSED FOR THE ORGANIZATION OF INFORMATION?

Over the years since the introduction of online retrieval systems, there have been researchers and practitioners who have made suggestions for improvement of those systems. Creators of the systems have not seemed to pay attention to many of the suggestions, however. A clear example of this is apparent in two articles by Christine Borgman. In 1986 she wrote an article titled, "Why Are Online Catalogs Hard to Use?"[2] A decade later she wrote another article titled,

"Why Are Online Catalogs *Still* Hard to Use?"[3] Borgman says that they are still hard to use because their design still does not reflect an understanding of user searching behavior on the part of system designers. She suggests that a long-term goal should be to design intuitive systems that require a minimum of instruction. Instruction has often been touted as the way around inadequate system design, but in this day of having access to retrieval tools from home computers, where instruction may not be available, one has to say with Borgman: "Good training is not a substitute for good system design."[4]

Standard Interfaces and Z39.50

Let us look at some of the other suggestions that have been made for the improvement of online systems. In the library cataloging community there have been recent calls for standard interfaces for library catalogs. The lack of standardization is reminiscent of a century ago when card catalogs contained cards of variant sizes (e.g., "2 x 5", "2 x 10", "3 x 5", etc.), and information placed on cards lacked a standard order. Standardization came when Melvil Dewey's 7.5 cm x 12.5 cm catalog cabinets won over other sizes and the Library of Congress began selling its cataloging on "3 x 5" cards.[5] Standard interfaces today would ensure that a user could enter any library and use the catalog without having to learn new commands or a new GUI interface screen containing buttons with different words and abbreviations on them.

A step toward solving the dilemma of users facing different catalogs has been the development of the Z39.50 protocol. This protocol is a national standard developed by the National Information Standards Organization (NISO), a group that acts to adopt standards that can be used by all in the information industry. Z39.50 (the number assigned to the first version of this standard) defines a protocol by which one computer can query another computer and transfer search results from one to the other. In simplistic terms, the Z39.50 protocol installed on one system translates the commands of that system into a set of universal commands that are then sent to another computer. The second system's Z39.50 translates the universal commands into equivalent commands for the second system. The results are returned to the first computer in the same fashion. If two institutions both have Z39.50 installed, OPAC users in one institution can search the catalog of the other institution using the commands of the local system; the result display looks like the display used in the local system. At this point the implementation of Z39.50 limits the searching of various catalogs to the "lowest common denominator." That is, if very sophisticated searching is available in one catalog but not the other, then the searching that can be done from the more sophisticated catalog can only be in terms of the searching allowable in the other catalog. The sophisticated programming of one system cannot be passed through Z39.50 to the other system.

Labels and Brief Displays

Another suggestion for making systems less confusing is to revisit the idea that labels are needed for each field of a display. Labels can be confusing and do not necessarily cover everything in a field. For example, in the MARC format, the field usually labeled "title" also contains the statement of responsibility (i.e., persons or corporate bodies responsible for the intellectual contents of an information package). If, instead of labeling every field, displays were to make use of *ISBD* format, confusing labels would be eliminated. In addition the *ISBD* format would allow more information about an information package to be displayed on one screen. All new metadata formats are calling for labels. These have the same problems as do labels of MARC formatted records and of records displayed in various commercial indexes.

The increase in use of labels triggered an increase in the use of brief displays. Research has shown that when *ISBD* format is used, only 30 percent of records need a second screen to display the entire record. With labels, 84 percent of records need a second screen to display the entire record.[6] David Thomas, in his dissertation on interface design, found that users spent no more time reading screens or performing tasks when the records were not labeled than when the records were labeled.[7] One could assume, then, that using non-labeled displays would cause few or no problems for users, and the need for brief records could be eliminated for four-fifths of records. However, labels and brief displays persist.

One difficulty with brief displays is that what is included in them from system to system is inconsistent. Some delete all notes, which can be confusing. Notes are designed to give information that clarifies data given in earlier areas of the description. Without the notes, users may be misled by the information that is given. Some brief displays show no added entries. If a user has done a title search, such a brief display may be sufficient, unless the title is only *part* of the information package represented by the record displayed. In such a case the title searched may be in an added entry, having been described in a note, and may not appear at all in the brief record. Likewise, if a user has searched for an author or other contributor, the brief display may not include mention of that person or corporate body, especially when the statement of responsibility is not included in the title area. This requires a user to understand the concept that "author" is only the first-named responsible person or body. Main entry continues to be used in order to provide a means for logical display, but if system design is correctly done, the user should never have to understand the concept of main entry. In addition a subject searcher may wish to see all subjects assigned to a record, but many systems do not include subject headings in the brief display.

Exploitation of MARC

There have been suggestions that making more use of MARC coding could improve system design. For example, the fixed field of a MARC record has coded information that could be used in searching to limit searches to a particular kind of information package. Type-of-record codes (e.g., indicating sound recording, serial, visual material, etc.) are already used in a number of systems. In addition the fixed field gives such information as whether the information package being represented contains an index or bibliographical information, whether it is fiction or a biography, what the predominant language is, in which country it was published, and its date of publication. For example, a searcher might wish to find everything written by a prolific author that was not fiction. Good system design should be able to accommodate such a search. In addition to the fixed field, use of certain subfield codes could enhance a system. For example, subfield codes in subject fields could be used to make indexes of geographic areas or form/genre terms.

Browsing

Browsing capability has been suggested as a preferable alternative to getting a result set of several hundred records in some order that has to be ferreted out by the user. For example, if a user searches for a personal surname and forename initial, a browsing option will put the searcher into an index listing of all personal names that begin with that surname and initial. The index listing should contain, in addition to the name, the entire authoritative heading for the name, including dates, and the number of records that are associated with the name. Likewise, a subject search would place the searcher first into a list of subjects that surround the subject word that was input as the search. A few systems now include this feature. Again, the listing would include the number of records associated with each term. If there is a subject heading with many subdivisions, an appropriate screen might list the heading, but then ask if the user would like to see the heading further delineated by topic, geographic area, form/genre, or chronological subdivision.

Spelling Correction

Yet another recommendation for improved system design is that spelling correction programs be incorporated into the search process. Many systems now include what is called "normalization" of search strings, which usually means that punctuation and other such marks are taken out of the search string and also out of the record strings with which the search string is to be compared. This eliminates the need for users to input diacritical markings, etc. However, research has shown that users make spelling errors often. Other industries, such as the airline industry, have systems that use sound-based codes so that names that sound alike but are spelled differently can be found easily. It has been suggested that such codes be incorporated into retrieval system design. In addition dictionaries of alternative (e.g., American/British) spellings might be incorporated into system design.

Controlled Vocabulary and Classification

In the area of subject searching there have been suggestions that keyword searches be matched against both free text terms and controlled vocabulary, and that system additions be made to assist users in taking advantage of the power of controlled vocabulary. For example, the development of ways to show subject relationships in such indexes as MEDLINE could be incorporated into other retrieval tools. Tree structures, in which broader and narrower terms are shown in a hierarchical relationship, with broader terms "branching" into narrower terms, which themselves branch again and again, have been shown to be quite useful and effective.

Another improvement to subject access would be to enhance subject terminology with classification terminology. Experimental systems have shown the viability of this approach. A notable one is the Cheshire II system created by Ray Larson and others.[8] In this system words from the classification schedule that match the classification notation on the surrogate record are brought together with subject heading words and with subject-bearing words from titles and other parts of a surrogate record to make subject clusters. Searching a cluster allows more accurate system responses than does searching each heading one by one.

The suggestions given here are not meant to be exhaustive, but only illustrative of the many ways in which system design might be improved for the benefit of users of retrieval tools. Borgman has suggested that systems should be made that will answer questions rather than just match queries.[9] As more work is done with natural language processing, ontologies, and artificial neural networks, Borgman's suggestion may become reality. In the meantime much can be done to improve even the query-matching process.

CONCLUSION

In this chapter we have discussed system design as it relates to the organization of information. In order for users to get the most benefit, organizers and system designers must work together closely. In the days of paper indexes and catalogs, organizers were also the designers of the systems. Perhaps a goal today would be for organizers and system designers to become so conversant in each other's languages and knowledge that each could step into the other's position with ease. Sophisticated design is wasted if the metadata that the system presents is inadequate, and sophisticated metadata is wasted if the system design is lacking.

NOTES

1. Martha M. Yee and Sara Shatford Layne, *Improving Online Public Access Catalogs* (Chicago: American Library Association, 1998).

2. Christine L. Borgman, "Why Are Catalogs Hard to Use? Lessons Learned from Information Retrieval Studies," *Journal of the American Society for Information Science* 37, no. 6 (June 1986): 387–400.

3. Christine L. Borgman, "Why Are Online Catalogs *Still* Hard to Use?" *Journal of the American Society for Information Science* 47, no. 7 (July 1996): 493–503.

4. Ibid., p. 501.

5. The size of the Library of Congress cards actually was and continued to be 7.5 cm x 12.5 cm, but the United States did not change to the metric system as Dewey believed was imminent. The size was just under 3 in. x 5 in., and the cards came to be called "3 x 5" cards.

6. Walt Crawford, Lennie Stovel, and Kathleen Bales, *Bibliographic Displays in the Online Catalog* (White Plains, N.Y.: Knowledge Industry Publications, 1986).

7. David H. Thomas, "The Effect of Interface Design on Item Selection in an Online Catalog." (Ph.D. diss., University of Pittsburgh, 1997), pp. 86–88.

8. Ray R. Larson, Jerome McDonough, Paul O'Leary, and Lucy Kuntz, "Cheshire II: Designing a Next-Generation Online Catalog," *Journal of the American Society for Information Science* 47, no. 7 (July 1996): 555–67.

9. Borgman, "Why Are Online Catalogs *Still* Hard to Use?" p. 501.

SUGGESTED READINGS

Aluri, Rao, D. Alasdair Kemp, and John J. Boll. "User-System Interaction." Chap. 10 and "Evaluation of Subject Retrieval in Online Catalogs." Chap. 11 in *Subject Analysis in Online Catalogs*. Englewood, Colo.: Libraries Unlimited, 1991.

Bates, Marcia J. "The Design of Browsing and Berrypicking Techniques for the Online Search Interface." *Online Review* 13, no. 5 (October 1989): 407–24.

———. "Subject Access in Online Catalogs: A Design Model." *Journal of the American Society for Information Science* 37, no. 6 (November 1986): 357–76.

Beheshti, Jamshid. "The Evolving OPAC." *Cataloging & Classification Quarterly* 24, nos. 1/2 (1997): 163–85.

Borgman, Christine L. "Why Are Online Catalogs *Still* Hard to Use?" *Journal of the American Society for Information Science* 47, no. 7 (July 1996): 493–503.

Dixson, Larry E. "Z39.50 and Its Use in Library Systems (Part One)," in *ALCTS Newsletter* 5, no. 6 (1994), and "Z39.50 and Its Use in Library Systems (Part Two)," in *ALCTS Newsletter* 6, no. 1 (1995).

Drabenstott, Karen M., with the research assistance of Celeste M. Burman and Marjorie S. Weller. *Enhancing a New Design for Subject Access to Online Catalogs*. Ann Arbor, Mich.: School of Information and Library Studies, University of Michigan, 1994.

Drabenstott, Karen M., and Marjorie S. Weller. "Failure Analysis of Subject Searches in a Test of a New Design for Subject Access to Online Catalogs." *Journal of the American Society for Information Science* 47, no. 7 (July 1996): 519–37.

Fidel, Raya, and Michael Crandall. "The AACR2 as a Design Schema for Bibliographic Databases." *Library Quarterly* 58, no. 2 (April 1988): 123–42.

Heaney, Michael. "Object-Oriented Cataloging." *Information Technology and Libraries* 14, no. 3 (September 1995): 135–53.

Hearst, Marti A. "Interfaces for Searching the Web." *Scientific American* (March 1997): 68–72.

Hildreth, Charles R. "The Use and Understanding of Keyword Searching in a University Online Catalog." *Information Technology and Libraries* 16, no. 2 (June 1997): 52–62.

Larson, Ray R. "Classification Clustering, Probabilistic Information Retrieval, and the Online Catalog." *Library Quarterly* 6, no. 2 (April 1991): 133–73.

Larson, Ray R., Jerome McDonough, Paul O'Leary, and Lucy Kuntz. "Cheshire II: Designing a Next-Generation Online Catalog." *Journal of the American Society for Information Science* 47, no. 7 (July 1996): 555–67.

Library of Congress's Z39.50 Gateway. Available: http://lcweb.loc.gov/z3950/gateway.html (Accessed October 1998).

Wool, Gregory J. "Bibliographical Metadata; or, We Need a Client-Server Cataloging Code!" In *Finding Common Ground: Creating the Library of the Future Without Diminishing the Library of the Past*, edited by Cheryl LaGuardia and Barbara S. Mitchell, pp. 398–401. New York: Neal-Schuman, 1998.

Yee, Martha M. "System Design and Cataloging Meet the User: User Interfaces to Online Public Access Catalogs." *Journal of the American Society for Information Science* 42, no. 2 (March 1991): 78–98.

Yee, Martha M., and Sara Shatford Layne. *Improving Online Public Access Catalogs*. Chicago: American Library Association, 1998.

CONCLUSION

In the preceding chapters we have discussed the past and present of organization of information. Organizing has been going on, I suspect, since the first appearance of humans, because it seems to be such an innate need. Even some nonhuman animals, birds, and insects are organizers (e.g., ants have highly organized societies with certain responsibilities assigned to various individuals). The organization of information among humans began as soon as language developed sufficiently for information to be passed from person to person. In oral traditions information was organized in people's minds, and, in recorded information traditions, ways of identifying information packages were developed at least as early as clay tablets.

Current retrieval tools, including bibliographies, catalogs, indexes, finding aids, and museum registers, represent the highest state of progress in organizing information that humans have achieved so far. These tools are far from perfect, though, and there is much room for organizers to improve metadata and for system designers to provide more helpful retrievals and more logical displays. Development of seamless interfaces among these tools is also a possibility.

Arrival at this current state of organization has taken centuries. Progress in the western world was given impetus by printing with moveable type, but even then, movement toward bibliographic control was slow as printing moved through the stage of imitating manuscript production to the stage of creating new type fonts just for printing. We are experiencing a similar stage now as we use computers to imitate our previous print culture. Alan Kay, the first person to conceive of the laptop computer, has said that the computer revolution has not yet begun:

> The printing press was invented in the middle of the 15th century, yet it took 100 years before a book was considered dangerous enough to be banned, 150 years before science was invented, almost 200 years before a new kind of political essay was invented, and more than 300 years before a country with an invented political system (the US) could be argued into existence via the press and a citizenry that could understand the arguments. Schooling and general literacy were also fruits of the press, and also took many

centuries to become established. The commercial computer is now about 50 years old and is still imitating the paper culture that came before it, just as the printing press did with the manuscript culture it gradually replaced. No media revolution can be said to have happened without a general establishment of "literacy": fluent "reading" and "writing" at the highest level of ideas that the medium can represent. With computers we are so far from that fluent literacy—or even understanding what that literacy should resemble—that we could claim that the computer revolution hasn't even started.[1]

Therefore, we cannot know what organized information will look like in another fifty years or even twenty-five years. I believe, however, that the principles of organization that have developed over the last several hundred centuries will not be thrown out but will continue to evolve into the organizing principles of the future.

NOTES

1. Alan Kay, "The Computer Revolution Hasn't Happened Yet" (lecture in the SCS Distinguished Lecture Series, presented at Carnegie Mellon University, April 29, 1998).

APPENDIX
SUBJECT ANALYSIS APPLICATION

A way to use the subject analysis concepts presented in chapter 7 is to follow an outline of the subconcepts to be identified. Such an outline might be:

A. Identify concepts, and determine what the purpose of the information package is (e.g., who the intended users are):
   1. Examine title and subtitle.
   2. Examine table of contents or equivalent.
   3. Examine preface and/or introduction, etc.
   4. Examine illustrations and their captions.
   5. Identify names used as subject concepts.
   6. Identify role(s) of any geographic name(s) present.
   7. Identify chronological elements.
   8. Identify form of the item in hand.
   9. Construct a sentence giving analysis of what this information package is about.
B. Identify index terms from sentence in A.8 to be searched in the controlled vocabulary.
C. Translate the terms into specific headings from the controlled vocabulary list.
D. Convert the sentence in A.9 into a classification number.

Here is an illustration of use of this outline:

Example:

The summarization-level analysis of the web site *Japanese Garden Database*[1] (see fig. A.1), created and maintained by Robert Cheetham, might proceed as follows:

A. Identify concepts

   1. Examine title and subtitle.

       Note that the title contains the word "Database." It will be necessary to determine if this web site fits the LCSH definition of "database."

   2. Examine table of contents or equivalent.

       Note use of several terms that seem not necessarily to be related to the concept of "Japanese Garden": e.g., "Administrative."

   3. Examine preface and/or introduction.

       Note that the Introduction states that the site was originally intended for professionals in the field of landscape architecture and garden history, but has been broadened to be made available to the general public through the Internet.

   4. Examine illustrations and their captions.

       Note that illustrations are of various gardens, some at varying times of year, and that there are also topographical and location maps. However, these do not constitute a large proportion of the work.

   5. Identify names used as subject concepts.

       The personal names involved are names of designers of gardens. There are too many to index separately at the summarization level. A few corporate names are given in lists such as bibliographies or lists of related sites; the work is not about these corporate bodies, however.

   6. Identify role(s) of any geographic name(s) present.

       The geographic area Japan provides the context for the topic of this work. The work is not about Japan, but the gardens discussed are of a type originally designed in Japan, and at this particular site, all the individual gardens discussed actually are in Japan.

   7. Identify chronological elements.

       The time periods involved here are from several centuries B.C.E. to the present, much too long a time to be meaningful in a subject heading string.

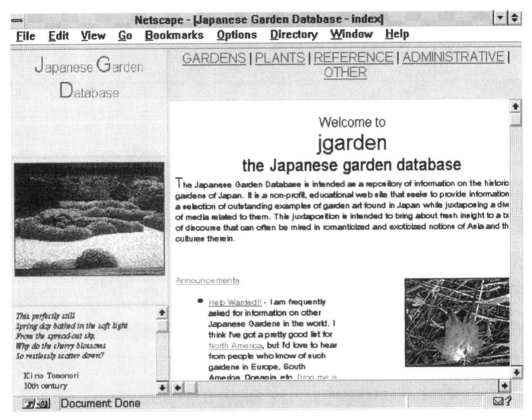

Fig. A.1. View of first screen of Robert Cheetham's *Japanese Garden Database*, found at http://pobox.upenn.edu/~cheetham/jgarden/index.html (accessed October 17, 1998).

8. Identify form of the item in hand.

   This item consists of many different kinds of form: text, pictures, maps, bibliographies, etc. Note that "database" is included in the title, but the work does not fit the usual definition of a database.

9. Construct a sentence giving analysis of what this electronic resource is about.

   This resource is about the history and design of Japanese gardens as a concept and also the history and design of major Japanese gardens in the country of Japan.

B.   Identify index terms to be searched in the controlled vocabulary.

Japan, Japanese

Gardens

History, Historic

Design

C.   Translate the terms into specific headings from the controlled vocabulary list.

LCSH:

Gardens, Japanese--Japan--History

Gardens--Japan--Design

Historic gardens--Japan

D.   Convert the sentence in A.9 into a classification number.

LC Classification: SB466.J3

Dewey Decimal Classification: 712.0952

NOTES

1.   Available: http://pobox.upenn.edu/~cheetham/jgarden/index.html

GLOSSARY

AAAF (Anglo-American Authority File). File implemented at the British Library using the USNAF (U.S. Name Authority File) and the BLNAL (British Library Name Authority List).

AACR2 (*Anglo-American Cataloguing Rules*, **2nd ed.**). A set of rules, published in 1978, for producing the descriptive and name-and-title access points part of a surrogate record for an information package; the creation of these rules was the result of collaboration among representatives from Canada, Great Britain, and the United States.

AACR2r (*Anglo-American Cataloguing Rules, Second Edition, 1988 revision*). A revision of *AACR2*; rules are monitored by the Joint Steering Committee (JSC) for *AACR*, which is made up of representatives from Australia, Canada, Great Britain, and the United States.

AAT (*Art & Architecture Thesaurus*). A thesaurus of terms in hierarchical order that cover content and materials in the disciplines of art and architecture.

Access control. (1) The results of the process of doing authority work, but without the necessity of choosing one form of name or title and one subject term to be the "authorized" selection. In access control every variant name, title, or term is given equal status, with one form chosen for default display; however, a searcher may use any of the forms to gain access to information packages related to the name, title, or subject (*see also* **Authority work**). (2) In the technical world of computers access control refers to an operating system feature that controls the access that certain categories of users have to files and to functions.

Access point. Any word or phrase used to obtain information from a retrieval tool or other organized system; in cataloging "access points" are specific names, titles, and subjects chosen by the cataloger, when creating a surrogate/metadata record, to allow for the retrieval of the record. *See also* **Primary access point** and **Added entry**.

Accession number. A notation assigned to an information package that is unique to the package; the notations are often based upon the order in which information packages are acquired.

Added entry. Any access point in a metadata record other than the primary access point.

Alphabetical catalog. Catalog in which the surrogate records are arranged or displayed in the order of the alphabet that is used in the institution that houses the catalog.

Alphabetico-classed catalog. Catalog in which subject categories are used for arrangement of surrogate records; broad categories are subdivided by narrower categories that are placed alphabetically within each broad category.

Analytical entry. An entry made for each of the works in a volume, as opposed to making only one entry for the entire volume.

ANN (Artificial Neural Network). *See* **Artificial neural network**.

Annotation. A brief note indicating the subject matter or commenting on the usefulness of information in a particular information package.

ANSI (American National Standards Institute). A body that takes responsibility for establishing voluntary industry standards; works closely with NISO (*q.v.*).

APPM (Archives, Personal Papers, and Manuscripts). A standard based on *AACR2r* for the description of archival materials that has been accepted by most of the archival community.

Archival description. The process of establishing intellectual control over the holdings of an archive through the preparation of finding aids.

Archival series. A logical group of files, books, correspondence, or other such set.

Archives. Organizations that preserve enduring value records that document activities of organizations or persons and are accumulated in the course of daily activities.

Artificial neural network (ANN). A computer system inspired by the architecture of the human biological nervous system.

ASCII (American Standard Code for Information Interchange). A standard code that assigns specific bit patterns to letters, numbers, and symbols; used for exchange of textual data in instances where programs are incompatible, because ASCII can be read almost universally by any computing machine.

Asynchronous responsibility. The situation in which the persons or corporate bodies involved in the creation of an information package have made different kinds of contributions to the creation of the work (e.g., author and illustrator; performer, conductor, choreographer, and producer; etc.).

Author. A person who is responsible for all or some of the intellectual content of a text. *See also* **Creator.**

Author entry. The place in a retrieval tool where a surrogate record beginning with the name of the creator of an information package may be found.

Authority control. The results of the process of doing authority work, which means that headings in surrogate records are consistent with the character strings for those headings established in the authority file.

Authority file. A collection of authority records.

Authority record. A means for recording all the decisions made in the process of authority work. Such records may be called "access control records" as the organizing world moves from authority control to access control.

Authority work. The process of determining and maintaining an "authorized" form of a name or title and/or determining and maintaining an "authorized" term or phrase to stand for a subject concept. The process includes identifying all relationships of variant names and titles to the authorized forms of names and titles. In the verbal subject area, the process includes identifying and maintaining relationships among terms—relationships such as synonyms, broader terms, narrower terms and related terms. *See also* **Access control.**

Bibliographic control. The process of describing items in the bibliographic universe and then providing name, title, and subject access to the descriptions, resulting in records that serve as surrogates for the actual items of recorded information. Bibliographic control further requires that surrogate records be placed into retrieval systems where they act as pointers to the actual information packages.

Bibliographic data. Information gathered in the process of creating bibliographic records.

Bibliographic database. A collection of bibliographic records held in a huge database; the database is available for a price.

Bibliographic record. Description of a tangible information package (e.g., book, sound recording); later terms used for descriptions of information packages are "surrogate record" and "metadata record."

Bibliographic universe. A concept that encompasses all instances of recorded information.

Bibliographic utility. A corporate entity that has as its main resource a bibliographic database; access to the database is available for a price, and members of the utility can contribute new records and download existing ones.

Bibliography. A list of information packages; bibliographies bring together lists of sources based on subject matter, on authors, by time periods, and the like.

Book catalog. Catalog in which surrogate records are printed on pages that are bound into book form.

Broad classification. Classification that uses only the main classes and divisions of a scheme and perhaps only one or two levels of subdivisions. *See also* **Close classification**.

Broader term (BT). A term one level up from the term being examined in a listing where terms for subject concepts have been conceived in relationships that are hierarchical.

Browsing. A process of looking, usually based on subject, at all the items in a particular area of the stacks in order to find, often by serendipity, the items that best suit the needs of the browser; in online systems browsing is the process of looking at all the surrogate records that fall under a certain subject or at a particular classification.

Call number. A notation on an information package that matches the same notation in the surrogate/metadata record; it is the number used to "call" for an item in a closed stack library—thus, the source of the name *call number*.

Card catalog. Catalog in which surrogate records are written, typed, or printed on cards (usually measuring 3 inches by 5 inches) that are placed in file drawers in a particular order (usually alphabetical or classified order).

Catalog. Retrieval tool that provides access to individual items within collections of information packages (e.g., physical entities such as books, videos, and CDs in a library; artists' works in an art museum; web pages on the Internet; etc.).

Catalog record. *See* **Surrogate record**.

Cataloger. Person in an archive, a library, or other such organization who creates surrogate records for the information packages collected by the organization and who works to maintain the system through which those surrogate records are made available to users; the person may also be an independent contractor. *See also* **Indexer**.

Cataloging. The acts of creating surrogate records for information packages, choosing appropriate access points, and maintaining the system through which the records are made available. Such work done in not-for-profit agencies is usually called *cataloging*, while such work done for commercial enterprises is usually called *indexing*.

CD-ROM (Compact Disk - Read Only Memory). A computer storage medium that is "read" with a laser beam and can store 680 megabytes of data on a single disk.

Character-by-character filing. *See* **Letter-by-letter filing**.

Chief source of information. The location from which much of the information is to be taken that is used to create the descriptive part of a surrogate record (e.g., title page of a book, title screen of a motion picture, label on a sound recording tape or disc).

CIP (Cataloging-in-Publication). A program in which cataloging is provided by an authorized agency to the publisher or producer of an information package so that the cataloging can be issued with the information package; ordinarily the phrase is applied in the case of cataloging provided by the Library of Congress to the publishers of books.

Classical theory of categorization. Theory based on Aristotle's theory that categories contain items based on what they have in common and that categories are like abstract containers with things either in or out of the container.

Classification. The placing of subjects into categories; in organization of information, classification is the process of determining where an information package fits into a given hierarchy and then assigning the notation associated with the appropriate level of the hierarchy to the information package and to its surrogate.

Classification notation. A set of numbers, letters, symbols, or a combination of these that is assigned to a certain level of hierarchy in a classification scheme.

Classification schedule. A listing of the hierarchy of a classification scheme along with the notation for each level.

Classification scheme. A specification of a systematic organization of knowledge.

Classification table. Supplementary part of a classification scheme in which notations are assigned for concepts that can be applied in conjunction with many different topical subjects. Tables commonly exist for geographic locations, time periods; standard subdivisions (e.g., dictionaries, theory, serial publications, historical treatment, etc.); racial, ethnic, and national groups; etc.

Classified catalog. Catalog in which surrogate records are arranged or displayed in the order of the classification scheme used in the institution that houses the catalog.

Close classification. Classification that uses all the minute subdivisions that are available in a particular classification for very specific subjects. *See also* **Broad classification**.

Closed stacks. The name given to the situation where information package storage areas are accessible only to the staff of the library, archives, or other place that houses information packages. *See also* **Open stacks**.

Code (as a noun). (1) A set of rules. (2) A specific designation in an encoding standard that defines and limits the kinds of data that can be stored at that point.

Code (as a verb). The process of assigning the appropriate specified designations of an encoding standard.

Codification. The process of creating sets of rules to govern such things as the making of surrogate records.

Coextensive subject entry. A subject heading that covers all, but no more than, the concepts or topics covered in the information package.

Collocation. The bringing together of records and/or information packages that are related in some way (e.g., same author, same work [different titles or different editions], same subject, etc.).

Collocation device. A number or other designation on an item used to place it next to (i.e., collocate with) other items that are like it.

Colon Classification. Classification scheme devised by S. R. Ranganathan in the early 1930s; it was the first fully faceted classification scheme.

Colophon. A set of data at the end of a "document" that gives varying kinds of bibliographic data. It might give information usually found on a title page, and, in items after the invention of printing with moveable type, it gives such information as date of printing, printer, typeface used, etc.

COM (Computer Output Microform) catalog. Catalog in which surrogate records are produced on either microfiche or microfilm and require a microform reader in order to be able to use them.

Contract cataloging. An institution's use of a contractual relationship with a person or agency to provide surrogate records that represent the institution's acquisitions for its collection.

Controlled vocabulary. A list or database of subject terms in which each concept has a preferred term or phrase that will be used to represent it in a retrieval tool; the terms not to be used have references from them to the chosen term or phrase, and relationships (e.g., broader terms, narrower terms, related terms, etc.) among used terms are identified. There may also be scope notes for the terms and hierarchical listings.

Core Record. Standard set by the Program for Cooperative Cataloging (PCC) that presents the minimum requirements for elements to be included in a nationally acceptable *AACR2* record.

Corporate body. A group of persons who have a group name and who act as an entity.

Creator. Person who is responsible for the intellectual content of an information package.

Cross reference. *See* **Reference**.

Crosswalks. Visual instruments for showing equivalent values in two or more schemes; for example, a crosswalk could be used to show which value in one metadata standard matches a particular value in another standard, or it could be used to show which classification notation in, say, DDC is equivalent to a notation in LCC.

CSDGM (FGDC Content Standards for Digital Geospacial Metadata). A specification that provides a common set of terminology and definitions for metadata about digital geospatial data. *See also* **FGDC (Federal Geographic Data Committee) metadata standard**.

Cutter number. A designation that has the purpose of alphabetizing all works that have exactly the same classification notation; named for Charles Cutter.

Cyberspace. The intangible place in which some electronic documents, such as web pages or e-mail messages, exist.

Data administration. The terminology applied to the control of the explosion of electronic information in offices and other administrative settings.

Data modeling. The process of designing a system for managing office and administrative records; the process involves developing a conceptual model of an activity in a particular setting, followed by a logical model that includes much more detail, which is then translated into a physical data model that can be implemented as a database management system.

Database. A set of records that are all constructed in the same way and are often connected by relationship links; the structure underlying retrieval tools.

DDC (Dewey Decimal Classification). *See* **Dewey Decimal Classification**.

Depth indexing. Indexing that extracts all the main concepts dealt with in an information resource, recognizing many subtopics and subthemes. *See also* **Exhaustivity**; **Summarization**.

Description. *See* **Descriptive data**.

Descriptive cataloging. The process of providing the descriptive data and access points (other than subject) for surrogate records that are to be part of a catalog.

Descriptive data. Data that describes an information package, such as its title, its associated names, its edition, its date of publication, its extent, and notes identifying pertinent features.

Descriptor. Subject concept term, representing a single concept, usually found in thesauri and used in indexes. *See also* **Subject heading**.

Dewey Decimal Classification (DDC). Classification devised by Melvil Dewey in 1876; it divides the world of knowledge hierarchically into ten divisions, which are in turn divided into ten sections, and so on, using the ten digits of the Arabic numeral system. DDC is enumerative but with many faceting capabilities, especially in its later editions.

Diacritics. Modifying marks over, under, or through characters to indicate that pronunciation is different from that of the characters without the diacritics.

Dictionary catalog. Catalog in which surrogate records are arranged in alphabetical order by access point, intermixing name, title, and subject access points.

Divided catalog. Catalog in which surrogate records are arranged or displayed in separate files or displays, separated by name access points, title access points, and subject access points.

Document. An information package; often associated in people's minds with text and illustrations having been produced on paper, but increasingly associated with a video, a CD music disk, a computer file, or other such manifestation.

Document retrieval vs. Information retrieval. A dichotomy that is created by the level of exhaustivity used in subject indexing; summarization allows for retrieval of a document which can, itself, then be searched for relevant information, while depth indexing allows for retrieval at a much more specific level than the whole document.

DTD (Document Type Definition). An SGML application; defines the structure of a particular type of document.

Dublin Core (shortened form of Dublin Metadata Core Element Set). An internationally agreed-upon set of elements that can be "filled in" by the creator of an electronic document in order to create a metadata record for the document.

EAD (Encoded Archival Description). An SGML DTD created specifically to encode finding aids.

EAD header. Descriptive data about the metadata in the rest of the EAD record. It is based heavily on the TEI Header, and the content is based on the rules in the *APPM*.

Edition. Specific version of the intellectual content (work) found in an information package.

Encoding. The setting off of each part of a record so that the part can be displayed in certain positions according to the wishes of those creating a display mechanism, and so that certain parts of a record can be searchable.

Entity. A term used in the field of organization of information to indicate an item; both "entity" and "item" are used in order to avoid using "book" or other such specific designation.

Entry. The place in a print retrieval tool where a surrogate record is found.

Entry word. The first word of a *heading*.

Enumerative classification. A subject concept arrangement that attempts to assign a designation for every subject concept (both single and composite) needed in the system.

ERIC thesaurus. A commonly used term for the *Thesaurus of ERIC Descriptors*, a thesaurus for indexing and searching documents indexed by the Educational Resources Information Center.

Exhaustivity. The number of concepts that will be considered in the process of providing subject analysis; two basic degrees of exhaustivity are *depth indexing* and *summarization*.

Faceted classification. A subject concept arrangement that has small notations standing for subparts of the whole topic, which, when strung together, create a complete classification notation for a multipart concept.

FGDC (Federal Geographic Data Committee) metadata standard. Provides a common set of terminology and definitions for metadata about geospatial data (e.g., maps) that are in digital form. *See also* **CSDGM**.

Field. A separately designated part of an encoded record; it may contain one or more subfields.

Filing. The process of placing paper records (e.g., catalog cards, acquisition forms, etc.) in order, usually in drawers.

Finding aid. A long, inventory-like description of an archival collection; it describes a whole collection rather than individual pieces of the collection. A catalog record may be made for the finding aid.

Fixed field. A field of an encoded record that is always the same length from record to record.

Fixed location. A set place where a physical information package will always be found or to which it will be returned after having been removed for use.

Full entry. *See* **Main entry (record)**.

Fuzzy set theory of categorization. A theory that holds that some categories are not well defined and sometimes depend upon the observer, rather than upon a definition.

GILS (Government Information Locator Service) record. Metadata describing the information holdings of a U.S. federal agency.

GMD (General Material Designation). In an *AACR2* record, the GMD indicates the class of item being described (e.g., art original, electronic resource, motion picture, text, etc.).

GUI (Graphical User Interface). A computer interface that uses icons and other such graphics to make a screen more intuitive for users.

Heading. (1) An access point printed at the top of a copy of a surrogate record or at the top of a listing of related works in an online resource. (2) The exact string of characters of the authorized form of the access point as it appears in the authority record.

Hierarchical classification. A subject concept arrangement that follows the classical theory of categorization, creating categories from general to specific.

HTML (HyperText Markup Language). A scheme for encoding text, pictures, etc., so that they can be displayed using various programs because the coding is all made up of ASCII text.

HTTP (HyperText Transfer Protocol). The part of a URL that lets the browser know that a web page is being sought.

Hyperlink. An electronic connection between two separate pieces of information: it may be between two web pages, between two parts of an electronic information package, between text and an image, etc.

Imprint. The information in a textual publication that tells where it was published, who published it, and when it was published.

Index. A bibliographic tool that provides access to the analyzed contents of information packages (e.g., articles in a journal, short stories in a collection, papers in a conference proceeding, etc.). Back-of-the-book indexes provide access to the analyzed contents of one work.

Indexer. A person who determines access points (usually subject terms, but may be authors or titles) that are needed in order to make surrogate records available to searchers; an indexer also may create surrogate records. *See also* **Cataloger**.

Indexing. The process of creating surrogate records, especially the access points for information packages; such work done in commercial enterprises is often called *indexing*, while similar work done in not-for-profit agencies is usually called *cataloging*.

Indexing vocabulary. *See* **Controlled vocabulary**.

Indicators. In the MARC encoding standards, indicators for a field contain coded information that is needed for interpreting or supplementing data in the field.

Information package. An instance of recorded information (e.g., book, article, video, Internet document or set of "pages," sound recording, electronic journal, etc.).

Information retrieval vs. Document retrieval. *See* **Document retrieval vs. Information retrieval**.

Internet. The series of interconnected networks that provides services such as electronic mail, remote login, and file transfer services; the networks all use TCP/IP (Transmission Control Protocol/Internet Protocol).

Inventory. A tool whose purpose is to provide a record of what is owned.

ISBD (International Standard Bibliographic Description). A standard that was designed in the early 1970s to facilitate the international exchange of cataloging records by standardizing the elements to be used in the description, assigning an order to these elements, and specifying a system of symbols to be used in punctuating the elements.

ISBN (International Standard Book Number). A number that is accepted as an international standard for a unique number for a monographic item.

ISM/LIS (Information Systems Management / Library Information Services). A bibliographic utility that serves Canada and a few customers in the northeastern United States.

ISSN (International Standard Serial Number). A number that is accepted as an international standard for a unique number for a serial.

Item (as opposed to "work"). A manifestation of a work, focusing on the packaging of an information package rather than its contents.

Keyword. A term that is chosen, either from actual text or from a searcher's head, that is considered to be a "key" to finding certain information.

Keyword searching. The use of one or more keywords as the intellectual content of a search command.

Letter-by-letter filing. An arrangement of entries in a retrieval tool in which spaces and some punctuation marks are ignored so that the entry files as if it is all run together into one word (e.g., New York is treated as Newyork and follows Newark). *See also* **Word-by-word filing**.

Library of Congress Classification (LCC). Classification scheme created by the Library of Congress beginning in the late 1890s; it divides the world of knowledge hierarchically into categories using letters of the English alphabet and then using Arabic numerals for further subdivisions. LCC is basically an enumerative scheme, allowing only a limited amount of faceting.

Library of Congress Subject Headings (LCSH). A list of terms to be used as controlled vocabulary for subject headings created by the Library of Congress and used by any agency that wishes to provide controlled subject access to surrogate records.

Literary warrant. The concept that new notations are created for a classification scheme and new terms are added to a controlled vocabulary only when information packages actually exist about new concepts.

Location device. A number or other designation on an item to tell where it is physically located.

Main entry (access point). The access point that is chosen as the main or primary one.

Main entry (record). A copy of the surrogate record that contains a complete set of all elements of the record as provided by the cataloger.

Manuscripts. Papers created by an individual (not organizational papers); original handwritten or typed documents that usually exist in single copies (unless they have been copied).

MARC (Machine Readable Cataloging). A standard that prescribes a method for encoding surrogate records so that they can be read by machine.

Medical Subject Headings (*MeSH*). A list of terms to be used as controlled vocabulary for subject headings created by the National Library of Medicine and used by any agency that wishes to provide controlled subject access to surrogate records in the field of medicine.

Metadata. An encoded description of an information package (e.g., an *AACR2* record encoded with MARC, a Dublin Core record, a GILS record, etc.); the purpose of metadata is to provide an intermediate level at which choices can be made as to which information packages one wishes to view or search, without having to search massive amounts of irrelevant full text.

Monographic (as opposed to "serial") work. A complete bibliographic unit or information package. It is often a single work, but may also be one work or more than one work issued in successive parts; but, unlike serials, it is not intended to be continued indefinitely.

Museum accession record. A record used as a surrogate for an object acquired by a museum; it contains many kinds of information about the object such as its provenance, financial history, location in the museum, historical significance, etc.

Museum registration. *See* **Registration.**

Narrower term (NT). A term one level down from the term being considered in a listing where terms for subject concepts have been conceived in relationships that are hierarchical.

National Union Catalog (*NUC*). A publication of the Library of Congress that cumulated cataloging records from many libraries and indicated by "NUC symbol" those libraries that owned a particular item.

Natural language. The language used by a person when expressing a concept about which information is desired.

Natural language processing (NLP). Computer analysis of written or spoken language in order to interpret meaning in a way that can allow the computer to "understand" and "respond."

Neural network. *See* **Artificial neural network.**

NISO (National Information Standards Organization). A corporate body that oversees the creation and approval of standards to be used in information processing.

NLP (Natural language processing). *See* **Natural language processing**.

Nonbook materials. Terminology used for any information-bearing entity that is not text in book form.

Notation. A representation of a system, such as a classification system, with a set of marks, usually consisting of letters, numbers, and/or symbols.

OCLC (Online Computer Library Center). A bibliographic utility that is the largest and most comprehensive utility in the world.

Online catalog. Catalog in which surrogate records are encoded for computer display and are stored in computer memory or on CD-ROM disks; arrangement within the memory or on disk is irrelevant to the user, as arrangement is created in response to a query.

On-the-fly record. A record created electronically for an information package between the request by a searcher and the display of responses.

Ontology. In the field of artificial intelligence, a formal representation of what, to a human, is common sense; in NLP, a formal representation of language, including realities of such things as grammar, semantics, and syntax.

OPAC (Online Public Access Catalog). *See* **Online catalog**.

Open stacks. The name given to the situation where patrons of the facility have the right to go into the storage areas themselves. *See also* **Closed stacks**.

Original order. The order in which records in a collection were originally kept when they were in active use.

Outsourcing. A management technique whereby some activities, formerly conducted in house, are contracted out for completion by a contracting agency; technical services operations are sometimes outsourced.

Paris Principles. The conventional name of the Statement of Principles agreed upon by attendees at the International Conference on Cataloging Principles in Paris, October 9–18, 1961.

PCC (Program for Cooperative Cataloging). An international cooperative program coordinated jointly by the Library of Congress and participants around the world; effort is aimed at expanding access to collections through useful, timely, cost-effective cataloging that meets internationally accepted standards.

Postcoordinate indexing. Assigning subject concepts to surrogate records in a fashion that requires the searcher of the system to coordinate the terms through such techniques as Boolean searching.

Precoordinate indexing. Assigning subject concepts to surrogate records in such a way that some concepts, subconcepts, place names, time periods, and form concepts are put together in subject strings.

Primary access point. Access point that is chosen as the main or primary one; usually referred to as "main entry" in the library and archival worlds.

Protocol. A standard set of rules that determines how computers communicate with each other across networks (e.g., HTTP and Z39.50 are protocols); it describes the format that a message must take and the way in which computers must exchange a message.

Prototype theory of categorization. The theory that categories have prototypes (i.e., best examples, e.g., most people think a robin is a better example of a bird than is an ostrich) and that some categories are dependent upon the view of the person doing the categorizing.

Provenance. The origin of an archival document or collection, or of a museum object. In the case of an archival collection the origin may be an organization, office, or person that created, received, or accumulated and used the item or the records in the collection. In the case of a museum object, the origin may be a person, family, etc., that once owned the object, or it may be an archaeological expedition, or it may be the location where a natural history specimen was found.

Publisher. The person or corporate body responsible for issuing information packages to make them available for public use.

RDF (Resource Description Framework). An infrastructure that enables the encoding, exchange, and reuse of structured metadata; it uses XML as the means for exchanging and processing the metadata.

Record. *See* **Bibliographic record**.

Reference (cross reference). An instruction in a retrieval tool that directs a user to another place in the tool.

Register (accession log). Primary control tool for a museum; it functions like a catalog with a number of additional kinds of access points (e.g., donor, style, provenance, etc.).

Registration. The process of creating a surrogate record that uniquely identifies an object belonging to a museum; the records form the register for the museum.

Related term (RT). A term at the same level of specificity or bearing a nonhierarchical relationship to another term in a listing where terms for subject concepts have been conceived in relationships that are hierarchical.

Relational database. A database in which records are structured in such a way that information is not all stored in the same file; files for different kinds of information are created (e.g., a bibliographic file, a personal name file, a corporate name file, a subject file, a classification file, etc.); records in the bibliographic file contain pointers to records in the other files and vice versa. A relational database structure conserves storage space, allows for faster searching, and allows for easier modification of records. Pointers establish "relationships" among records.

Relative location. The situation in which an information package will be or might be in a different place each time it is reshelved.

Reprint. A new printing of an item either by photographic methods or by resetting unchanged text.

Retrieval tools. Devices such as catalogs, indexes, search engines, etc., created for use as information retrieval systems.

Retrospective conversion. The process of changing information in eye-readable surrogate records into machine-readable form.

RLIN (Research Libraries Information Network). A bibliographic utility that is particularly aimed at academic/research libraries and is especially important for special collections.

Scope note. A statement delimiting the meaning and associative relations of a subject heading, index term, or classification notation.

Search engine. A retrieval tool on the World Wide Web that, in general, matches keywords input by a user to words found at web sites; the more sophisticated search engines may allow other than keyword searching.

Sears List of Subject Headings (Sears). A controlled vocabulary of terms and phrases that is used mostly in small libraries to provide subject access to information packages available from that library.

Serial (as opposed to "monographic") work. A publication issued in successive parts (regularly or irregularly) that is intended to continue indefinitely.

Series. A group of separate works that are related in subject or form and are published by the same entity.

Series (archives). A logically grouped set of files, books, correspondence, or other such set.

SGML (Standard Generalized Markup Language). An international standard for document markup.

Shelflist. Originally, a list of physical information packages owned by an institution in the order in which they appeared on the shelves of the institution in which they were housed; in time the meaning has developed to indicate classification order of surrogate records for information packages, which now allows for intangible as well as physical information packages.

Shelving. The process of placing physical information packages on shelves in the order of the arrangement of their call numbers or other notations that indicate their appropriate locations.

Subfield. A separately designated segment of a field in an encoded record.

Subject analysis. The part of indexing or cataloging that deals with the conceptual analysis of an information package, the translation of that conceptual analysis into a framework for a particular classification, subject heading, or indexing system, and then using the framework to assign specific notations or terminology to the information package and its surrogate record.

Subject authority file. A record of choices made in the development of a controlled vocabulary. The authority file contains such things as justification for the choice of one synonym over another; references from unused synonyms or near-synonyms; references for broader terms, narrower terms, and related terms; scope notes; citations for references used; etc. *See also* **Subject heading list.**

Subject cataloging. The process of providing subject analysis, including subject headings and classification notations, when creating catalog records for archives, libraries, museums, etc.

Subject entry. The place in a retrieval tool where a surrogate record containing a particular controlled vocabulary term is found.

Subject heading. Subject concept term or phrase found in a subject heading list and used in catalog records; sometimes used in indexes. *See also* **Descriptor**.

Subject heading list. A list of authorized controlled vocabulary terms or phrases together with any references, scope notes, and subdivisions associated with each term or phrase. *See also* **Subject authority file**; **Thesaurus**.

Subject subdivision. A method of precoordinating subject headings by using terms or phrases following main concepts to show special treatment of a subject.

Summarization. Indexing that identifies only a dominant, overall subject of an information package, recognizing only concepts embodied in the main theme. *See also* **Depth indexing**; **Exhaustivity**.

Surrogate record. A presentation of the characteristics (e.g., title, creator, physical description if appropriate, date of creation, subject(s), etc.) of an information package.

Switching language. A mediation language used to establish equivalencies between or among different subject indexing languages or classification schemes.

Synchronous responsibility. The situation in which all persons or corporate bodies involved in the creation of an information package have made the same kind of contribution to the creation of the work (e.g., joint authors, etc.).

Syndetic structure. The system of controlled vocabulary with all its references as used in a catalog or other retrieval tool.

Synonym. A term with the same meaning as another term; often, in controlled vocabularies, used for a term that has nearly the same meaning as well as for a term that has the same meaning.

Tag. A number, set of letters, certain set of punctuation marks, etc., that designates the kind of field in an encoding standard.

Technical services. The group of activities in an institution that involves acquiring, organizing, housing, maintaining, and conserving collections and automating these activities. In some places circulating collections is also considered to be a technical service.

TEI (Text Encoding Initiative). Refers to both the corporate organization with that name and to the encoding standard created by that group. The encoding standard was originally intended for the encoding of literary texts, although it has expanded to be used for other types of texts.

TEI Header. A set of encoded metadata at the beginning of a TEI document that describes the document, its contents, and its origins.

Thesaurus. A list of authorized controlled vocabulary terms representing single concepts together with any references, scope notes, and subdivisions associated with each term. *See also* **Subject heading list**.

Title entry. The place in a retrieval tool where a surrogate record containing the name of an information package may be found.

Tracing. On printed surrogate records (e.g., catalog cards, records in book catalogs), the set of name, title, and subject access points, other than the main entry, that appear at the bottom of the record and are used to "trace" the additional copies of the surrogate record.

UBC (Universal Bibliographic Control). *See* **Universal Bibliographic Control**.

UDC (Universal Decimal Classification). *See* **Universal Decimal Classification**.

Uniform title. A title chosen for a work so that all manifestations will be displayed together under the same main entry and also will be displayed together among all the entries for that main entry.

UNIMARC (UNIversal MARC). Originally conceived as a conversion format, in which capacity it requires that each national agency create a translator to change records from UNIMARC to the particular national format and vice versa; a number of countries have now adopted it as their national format.

Union catalog. A catalog that represents the holdings of more than one institution or collection.

Universal Bibliographic Control. The concept that it will someday be possible to have access to surrogate records for all the world's important information packages.

Universal Decimal Classification (UDC). A classification devised by Otlet and LaFontaine in the late 1890s. It was originally based on DDC, but has evolved into a much more faceted scheme than DDC.

URL (Uniform Resource Locator). The address of an information package on the WWW; made up of the protocol name, server address, directory path, and file name.

USMARC (United States MARC). A system for encoding data—usually the data that comprises a bibliographic record; the version of MARC used in the United States.

USNAF (United States Name Authority File). A file housed at the Library of Congress (LC), containing not only the authority records created by LC and its cooperating United States contributors, but also records contributed from Australia, Canada, Great Britain, and others.

Variable field. A field of an encoded record that can be as long or as short as the data to be placed into that field.

Vocabulary control. The process of creating and using a controlled vocabulary.

VRA (Visual Resources Association) Core Categories. A set of guidelines for describing visual documents depicting works of art, architecture, and artifacts or structures from material, popular, and folk culture.

Warwick Framework. A container architecture for pulling together distinct packages of metadata that are related to the same information package, but that need to be separately controlled.

WLN (Western Library Network). A bibliographic utility that serves western North America, while its software is used in Australia, Canada, and other places.

Word-by-word filing. An arrangement of terms in a retrieval tool in such a way that spaces between words take precedence over any letter that may follow (e.g. "New York" appears before "Newark"). *See also* **Letter-by-letter filing**.

Work (as opposed to "item"). A designation for a specific expression of content or ideas, regardless of the physical packaging in which the content or ideas are expressed.

Work mark. A designation added to a cutter number that usually stands for the first word, not an article, of the title of the work, but may stand for other entities depending upon the circumstances.

WWW (World Wide Web). A nonlinear, multimedia, flexible system to provide information resources on the Internet and to gain access to such resources; based on hypertext and HTTP.

XML (Extensible Markup Language). A subset of SGML; omits some features of SGML and includes a few additional features (e.g., a method for reading non-ASCII text).

Yahoo! A "search engine" on the World Wide Web that attempts to describe and categorize the web pages that it indexes, rather than just indexing web sites by words used in them.

Z39. The standards section of ANSI/NISO that is devoted to libraries, information science, and publishing.

Z39.50. A national standard that provides for the exchange of information, such as surrogate records or full text, between otherwise noncompatible computer systems.

Z39.50 protocol. A standard applications level tool that allows one computer to query another computer and transfer search results without the user having to know the search commands of the remote computer.

shelflist function, 22
standardization and, 22–23, 24–25
subject analysis, 6
subject search, 21
system design and records, 215–16
union catalogs, 7, 22, 31
and Z39.50 protocol, 22–23, 24, 25
Categorization, 190–91. *See also* Classification
CC (Colon Classification), 48, 177, 180
Cheshire II system, 223
Chronological elements for subject analysis, 141
Church libraries, 39–40
CIMI (Consortium for the Interchange of Museum Information), 89
Citation and main entries, 107–8, 109–12fig
Classification, 173–98. *See also* Cataloging; Dewey Decimal Classification (DDC); Library of Congress Classification (LCC); Universal Decimal Classification (UDC)
ad hoc categories, 176
alphabetic order of serials, 187–88
for archives, 186
Aristotle's theory of categories, 174
artificial neural networks (ANNs), 192–93, 193fig
automatic, 192
basic-level categories, 175
broad classification, 182
for browsing, 186, 189, 191
call numbers, 182–83, 185
cataloging part of, 6–7, 12
or categorization, 190–91
classical theory of categories, 174–75
close classification, 182, 183
closed stacks, 186
of collections, 183
collocation and, 182, 184, 187
Colon Classification (CC), 48, 177, 180
concepts, 181–89
Cutter numbers, 6, 180
for databases, logical division of, 191

development of information organization, 47–48
enumerative classifications, 177, 179fig
Expansive Classification, 47–48, 177
faceted classifications, 177, 180
faculties, divided into, 177
family resemblances, 174
fixed location, 185–86
fuzzy set theory, 174, 176
globalization of information organization and, 182
hierarchical classifications, 176–77, 178–79fig
home-grown schemes, 181
integrity of numbers and, 184–85
of Internet, 187, 188, 189–92
keeping pace with knowledge and, 184–85
of knowledge, 183
literary warrant principle, 183
location device, 187
of monographic series, 189
of monographs, 189
national general schemes, 181
Online Computer Library Center (OCLC), 22, 192
open stacks, 186
personality, material, energy, space, time (PMEST) formula, 180
Pinakes (Callimachus), 176
prototype theory, 176
provenance (originator), 186
reclassification and, 185
relative location, 185–86
schemes, 181
Scorpion tool, 192
for searches, broadening or narrowing, 189, 191
self-organizing map (SOM) clusters, 192, 193fig
of serials, 187–88
subject specific schemes, 181
for switching language, 191–92
system design and, 223–24
theory of, 174–76